China's New Strategies For Governing the Country

Feng Jun
Chief Editor

Published by
ACA Publishing Ltd.
University House
11-13 Lower Grosvenor Place
London SW1W 0EX, UK
Tel: +44 (0)20 7834 7676 Fax: +44 (0)20 7973 0076
E-mail: info@alaincharlesasia.com

Web: www.alaincharlesasia.com
Beijing Office
Tel: +86(0)10 8472 1250 Fax: +86(0)10 5885 0639
Written by Feng Jun
Edited by Graham Prophet
Translated by Cai Junmei
© People's Publishing House, 2015
This translation is published by ACA Publishing Ltd in association with People's Publishing House

ALL RIGHTS RESERVED. NO PART OF THIS
PUBLICATION MAY BE REPRODUCED IN MATERIAL FORM,
BY ANY MEANS, WHETHER GRAPHIC,
ELECTRONIC, MECHANICAL OR OTHER, INCLUDING
PHOTOCOPYING OR INFORMATION STORAGE, IN
WHOLE OR IN PART, AND MAY NOT BE USED TO PREPARE
OTHER PUBLICATIONS WITHOUT WRITTEN
PERMISSION FROM THE PUBLISHER.

The greatest care has been taken to ensure accuracy but the publisher can accept no responsibility for errors or omissions, or for any liability occasioned by relying on its content.
ISBN 978-1-910760-20-8
China's New Strategies for Governing the Country is available from the National Bibliographic Service of the British Library.

Preface

What is the state system of China? How has the Communist Party of China (CPC) managed to exercize long-term governance and to lead the Chinese people from one victory to another? What are the 'secrets' of the CPC's governance? What is China's development road? What significant strategies have been adopted in China? What is the next step in China's development? Why has China been able to achieve such rapid economic development? These are just some of the many questions frequently asked by the international community, especially foreign political parties and statesmen on their visits to China. For the purpose of providing answers to these questions and enabling readers to be informed about the real China and the CPC, we arranged for the *Understanding Modern China* Series (hereinafter referred to as the Series) to be written, to serve as elementary documents introducing the CPC, as well as China's development road, development theories and development experience.

The Series is inspired by the new philosophies, new ideas and new strategies for the country's governance put forward by General Secretary Xi Jinping since the 18th National Congress of the CPC, aimed at the following aspects: strenuously reflecting the development vision of 'the Chinese Dream' and the development prospects of the 'Two Centenary' goals; strenuously reflecting the coordinated promotion of the overall situation of a 'five-pronged approach to building socialism with Chinese characteristics to build up socialist economy, socialist democracy, socialist advanced culture, socialist harmonious society and socialist ecological civilisation; and the strategic arrangements for the 'Four-Pronged Comprehensive Strategy' comprehensively completing the building of a moderately prosperous society in all respects, comprehensively deepening reform in all respects, comprehensively advancing the rule of law, and comprehensively exercising strict discipline for the party; strenuously reflecting the 'new normal' facilitating and leading China's economic development and the implementation of the 'five major development concepts' to promote innovative, coordinated, green, open and shared development; strenuously reflecting the three major economic development strategies of the 'Belt and Road', the coordinated development of Beijing, Tianjin and Hebei province, and the Yangtze river economic belt. On the basis of a great number of fresh cases and experiences, the Series tells China's story, transmits China's voice, analyzes China's problems, and offers China solutions.

The Series has been written on the basis of telling China's story and transmitting China's voice, oriented around the following four aspects: the first is to illustrate the new measures taken to deepen reform since the 18th National Congress of the CPC, the new ideas on economic development and the new philosophy on foreign affairs, on the basis of an all-round introduction to the achievements since the reform and opening up; the second is to analyze the reason for the achievements, the underlying operating law, and the process of evolution, while presenting the development achievements of China's economy and society; the third is to keep to problem orientation and demand orientation, rather than attempt to be all-embracing and systematic, so as to clear up targeted doubts and confusion on the basis of the demands of foreign readers; the fourth is to introduce China not only in terms of 'where it is coming from', but also in terms of 'where it is going', for the purpose of enabling readers to know about China's historical development process on the one hand, and on the other hand, exemplifying and clarifying how China assures the organic unification of its past, present and future, the organic combination of legacy and innovation, and how China is planning its future development.

Under the guidance of the International Department of the CPC Central Committee, the writing of the Series has been organized by China Executive Leadership Academy Pudong (CELAP).

The International Department of the CPC Central Committee is the functional department of the CPC in charge of foreign affairs. So far, the CPC has established connections of various types with more than 600 political parties and organizations in over 160 countries and regions, which include left-wing and right-wing parties; both ruling parties and opposition parties. Foreign affairs work is of paramount importance to the CPC, and an indispensable component of national diplomacy as a whole, whose target is to promote state-to-state and people-to-people communication and understanding.

Preface

CELAP is a national leadership institution in China, and as a platform on which international cooperative training and exchange are carried out, CELAP has held fast to its characteristics of internationality and openness since March 2005 when it was founded. CELAP spares no effort in implementing international cooperative training, with target participants being foreign political parties and statesmen, high-ranking business executives and senior professionals. By the end of 2015, CELAP had offered training programs to more than 6,000 participants from over 130 countries, and thus has won wide recognition and received a favorable reception from the countries, regions and participants that are involved.

To cater for the needs of foreign participants, CELAP initiated the writing of the Series at the beginning of 2012, and after four years of modifications and improvements, the finalized manuscripts were completed at the end of 2015. The first batch of 10 books to be published in this Series are: *China's New Strategies for Governing the Country*; *The Communist Party of China: the Past, Present and Future of Party Building*; *China's Reform, Opening Up and Construction of Development Zones*; *The Framework of the Chinese Government and Public Services*; *A New Analysis of Urbanization in China*; *China's Agriculture and Rural Development in the Post-Reform Era*; *The Evolution of China's Diplomacy in the Modern Era*; *Leadership Selection and Appointment in China*; *Leadership Education and Training in China*; and *Shanghai – the 'Pacesetter' of China's Reform and Opening Up*.

The authors of the Series are mainly professionals in CELAP, and functionaries and specialists in the Development Research Center of the Shanghai Municipal People's Government, Shanghai Institute for International Studies and Hangzhou Research Center for Urban Studies.

The Series is published in Chinese and English, with the English translation done mainly by senior professors at Shanghai International Studies University, to whom thanks are due. Gratitude also goes to the People's Publishing House for its great support and positive suggestions in the process of writing and translating.

Writing such a series of textbooks for mature foreign students is a first in China. Constructive criticism is welcome, for the Series as a new endeavor can hardly be free from mistakes.

Editorial Committee of the *Understanding Modern China* Series
January 2016

The Editorial Committee of the Understanding Modern China Series

Directors: Guo Yezhou Feng Jun

Vice Directors: Zhou Zhongfei   An Yuejun

Members: (Listed alphabetically)

An Yuejun	Chen Zhong	Feng Jun
Guo Yezhou	He Lisheng	Jiang Haishan
Li Man	Li Yanhui	Liu Genfa
Liu Jingbei	Wang Guoping	Wang Jinding
Yang Jiemian	Zhao Shiming	Zheng Jinzhou
Zhou Zhenhua	Zhou Zhongfei	

Editor-in-Chief: Feng Jun

Alain Charles Asia (ACA) Publishing Ltd is delighted to be associated with the People's Publishing House to bring this series of 10 *Understanding Modern China* books to an English-speaking readership.

ACA, formerly known as ACP (Alain Charles Publishing) Ltd Beijing, was founded in October 1989 and was the first foreign-owned publishing company to be allowed to open an office in China.

In 2007, ACP Beijing was renamed ACA Publishing Ltd to better reflect its focus on China and the Asia-Pacific region. The company specialises in publishing books about China for international readers and has offices in Beijing and London.

ACA Publishing Ltd,

April 2016

Contents

Introduction XI
    I. Building a Moderately Prosperous Society in All Respects XII
    II. The Chinese Dream XIV
    III. The Five-pronged Approach to Building Socialism with
        Chinese Characteristics XV
    IV. The Four-pronged Comprehensive Strategy XV
    V. The Five Major Development Concepts XVII

1. Lead China's New Normal 1
    I. The New Normal of Economic Growth: Upgrading
       China's Economy 1
    II. Rational Coordination of the 'Invisible Hand' and the
        'Visible Hand' 12
    III. Structural Adjustment of the Economic New Normal 20
    IV. Effective Implementation of the Innovation-driven Strategy 31

2. Advance All-round and Deeper-level Reform 43
    I. Decisive Role of Reform and Opening Up in Determining the
       Destiny of Contemporary China 43
    II. The Targets and Tasks of Reform 49
    III. Fundamental Issues and Drastic Mistakes 53
    IV. Methodology Adopted for Reform and Opening up 57
    V. The Principal Position of the People to Advance Reform 61

3. Develop a Law-based Country 65
    I. The Rule of Law: the Basic Way of Governance 66
    II. The Organic Integration of the Leadership of the Party
        and the Law-based Governance 73
    III. The Synergy between the Rule of Law and the Rule of Virtue 76
    IV. The Legal Mentality and the Basic-standard Mentality
        in Governance 79

4. Promote Deliberative Democracy 86
   I. Deliberation and Democracy 87
   II. Down-to-earth Democracy 95
   III. Negations of 'Imported' Deliberative Democracy 105
   IV. 'Multi-Party Cooperation' instead of 'Multi-Party System' in Contemporary China 111

5. Shape the Chinese Spirit 117
   I. Ideological Progress: One of the Party's Top Priorities 118
   II. Standing Firm in the Global Mingling and Clashing of Cultures 121
   III. Building the Core Socialist Values: a Significant Aspect of a Nation's Governing System and Capacity 126
   IV. Saying 'No' to De-Sinicization 130

6. Improve People's Livelihood 134
   I. Outlook on People's Livelihood 135
   II. The Bottom Line of People's Livelihood 139
   III. Promotion of Equity and Justice and Improvement of People's Living Standards 144
   IV. Participation of Citizens and Social Organizations in Social Governance 150

7. Pursue Ecological Progress 154
   I. Ecological Progress Boosts National Civilization 154
   II. Clean Waters and Green Mountains Are Golden and Silver Mountains 158
   III. The Ecological Red Line 162
   IV. 'A Major Political Issue: the Eco-environmental Protection' ... 165

8. Exercise Strict Self-Governance In Every Respect by the Party 169
   I. The Party's Great Emphasis on Exercising Strict Self-Governance 169
   II. The Party's Strictness in Exercising Self-Governance in Every Respect 175

III. The Party Members and Officials' Exemplary Role in Observing
　　　　Rules and Disciplines 190
　　IV. Understandings on 'Make Party Building Our Biggest
　　　　Achievement' 194

Chapter Follow-up Questions and References 199

Introduction

At the 18th National Congress of the Communist Party of China (CPC) in November 2012, the CPC elected and established a new Party Central Committee with Comrade Xi Jinping as its core and at the same time set new goals for China's development and new strategies for the governance of China, thereby ushering in a new era in the history of China.

At the 18th CPC National Congress, the CPC as a governing party put forward the 'Two Centenary Goals' for China's future development. As is widely known, around 2020 the CPC - founded in 1921 - will mark its centenary, and around 2050, the PRC established in 1949 will celebrate its centennial. The CPC led the whole nation in completing the New Democratic Revolution, establishing a New China, realizing national independence and liberating the whole of the Chinese people. The CPC has become the governing party and chosen to take the path of socialism. Since 1978 when China initiated its policy of reform and opening up, the country has embarked on the path of socialism with Chinese characteristics. More than 30 years' implementation of the policy has led to the country's prosperity and strength as well as to the people's wellbeing. A continuous high growth rate over 30 years has enabled China to develop into the world's second largest economy. How should China continue to develop in the future? Undoubtedly, China will continue to follow the path of socialism with Chinese characteristics. "As long as we remain true to our ideal, are firm in our conviction, never vacillate in or relax our efforts or act recklessly, and forge ahead with tenacity and resolve, we will surely complete the building of a moderately prosperous society in all respects when the CPC celebrates its centenary, and turns China into a modern socialist country that is prosperous, strong, democratic, culturally advanced and harmonious when the PRC marks its centennial. The whole

Party should have every confidence in our path, in our theories and in our system."[1]

I. Building a Moderately Prosperous Society in All Respects

'To Complete the Building of a Moderately Prosperous Society in All Respects' is the first 'Centenary Goal'. The concept of 'a moderately prosperous society', formerly known and translated as 'a well-off society', was introduced by Mr. Deng Xiaoping in his meeting with Japanese Prime Minister Masayoshi Ōhira on December 6, 1979. Deng, for the first time, expounded his views on "a well-off life" and his conception of "a well-off society" that was expected to be put in place by the end of the 20th century. This very concept was officially approved and adopted in the report to the 12th CPC National Congress in 1982, and set forth as the strategic goal to be accomplished by the end of the 20th century. In 1997, Comrade Jiang Zemin officially established 'Building a Well-off Society' as a new historic mission in the report to the 15th CPC National Congress. In 2002, the 16th CPC National Congress set the goal for *Completing Building a Well-off Society in an All-Round Way* by 2020. In 2007, the report to the 17th CPC National Congress noted clearly that every effort must be made to ensure the attainment of the goal for 'Building a Moderately Prosperous Society in all Respects' by 2020, and set new requirements for promoting economic, political, cultural, social and ecological progress. The report to the 18th CPC National Congress required endeavours to be made to ensure completing the Building of a Moderately Prosperous Society in all Respects by 2020.

In traditional Chinese culture, 'moderate prosperity' is a relative concept that denotes 'affluence and being a person of substance', but to develop 'a moderately prosperous society' has definite and specific quantitative indices. Let us take economic index as an example. The 16th CPC National Congress stated that efforts should be made to quadruple China's 2000 GDP by 2020. The 17th CPC National Congress continued to use that index but with more emphasis on balanced development to ensure sound and rapid economic growth. The 18th CPC National Congress put forward the 'Two Doubles' for its economic objectives: one is to double China's 2010 GDP and the other is to double the same year's per-capita income for both urban

---

[1] *Hu Jintao's Report to the Eighteenth National Congress of the CPC*: Firmly March on the Path of Socialism with Chinese Characteristics and Strive to Complete the Building of a Moderately Prosperous Society in all Respects

and rural residents. Besides economic indices, there are other development requirements for socialist democracy, ethics, culture, social undertakings and environmental protection.

The essence of 'Building a Moderately Prosperous Society in All Respects' by 2020 set out at the 18th CPC National Congress lies in 'All Respects'. 'All Respects' means that the goal of a moderately prosperous society is to benefit all the Chinese people without any exception or without leaving anyone behind, and regardless of regional differences, covering the whole population of over 1.3 billion. 'All Respects' also means that the goal, involving all areas of endeavour, is an overall plan for the promotion of economy, politics, society, culture and ecological progress. The moderately prosperous society requires 'upright officials, clean government and clear politics'. It attempts to 'secure the greatest achievements in response to all the wishes and needs of the people'. It will 'break down the dichotomized structure of urban and rural areas and help farmers live a pleasant life in their sweet homes'. It aims to 'strengthen our national material and spiritual power, and improve the physical and mental life of the Chinese people of all ethnic groups'. It will 'bring back to life our unpolluted homeland so that we can bear in our mind sweet reminiscences about our homes with green mountains and clear waters'. To complete the 'Building of a Moderately Prosperous Society in All Respects' is a strategic goal of paramount importance.

There are only five years to go before completing the building of a moderately prosperous society in all respects. This is our goal in the near future, but how will China continue to develop around 2050, 30 years from now? China will undoubtedly continue to follow the path of socialism with Chinese characteristics. By doing so, we must, 'under the leadership of the CPC, based on the essential realities of the state, around the core of economic advancement, sticking to Four Cardinal Principles, and to the policy of reform and opening up, liberate and develop our productive force, to foster a socialist market economy, socialist democracy, socialist advanced culture, a socialist harmonious society and socialist ecological progress so as to promote the well-rounded development of the individual, and gradually achieve the common prosperity of all the people to build a prosperous, strong, democratic, culturally advanced, and harmonious modern socialist country'.[1] 'To build a prosperous, strong, democratic, culturally advanced,

---

[1] **Hu Jintao's Report to the Eighteenth National Congress of the CPC**: *Firmly March on the Path of Socialism with Chinese Characteristics and Strive to Complete the Building of a Moderately Prosperous Society in All Respects*

and harmonious modern socialist country' includes the requirements to promote the well-rounded development of the individual and to achieve prosperity for all the people. This is exactly the second 'Centenary Goal' to be achieved around 2050: 'the Chinese Dream' of 'the Rejuvenation of the Chinese nation'.

II. The Chinese Dream

To fulfill the goals and tasks requires a core concept to cover all aspects, together with a spiritual banner to boost the morale of the people and to stimulate the positive forces of the whole society. General Secretary Xi Jinping established the concept of 'the Chinese Dream' in his improvised speech to the press when he and other Party and state leaders visited the exhibition entitled 'The Road to Rejuvenation' on November 29, 2012. He developed the connotations of 'the Chinese Dream' on several subsequent occasions. 'The Chinese Dream' connotes 'the greatness and prosperity of China, the rejuvenation of the Chinese nation, the happiness of the Chinese people'. To realize the rejuvenation of the Chinese nation has been the greatest dream of China in modern times. 'The Chinese Dream' is the dream of the people, of the nation, of every Chinese family and even every individual, enabling every Chinese citizen to share equal opportunities, enjoy the excellence of life and make their dreams come true. It is the response to the calls and expectations of the people. The people's aspiration for a better life is our goal to strive for. To realize 'the Chinese Dream', we must keep to our socialist path, carry forward our Chinese spirit and pool our own strength. Meanwhile, 'the Chinese Dream' has much in common with the dream of people in other countries all over the world. To complete the 'Building of a Moderately Prosperous Society in All Respects' is a momentous milestone in the process of realizing the rejuvenation of the Chinese nation. "China has entered a decisive historic stage to completing the Building of a Moderately Prosperous Society in All Respects. To accomplish this goal is a key step in realizing 'the Chinese Dream' of the Rejuvenation of the Chinese nation." The proposal of 'the Chinese Dream' is vivid and inspiring. It is the 'greatest common denominator' of the strength from all sectors of the society, and has become the theme of the times for which the CPC has been leading and striving together with the Chinese people of all ethnic groups. The Chinese Dream has become an important guiding principle and governing concept put forward by Comrade Xi Jinping since the 18th CPC National Congress.

III. The Five-pronged Approach to Building Socialism with Chinese Characteristics

The report to the 18th CPC National Congress set forth an overall plan for seeking economic, political, cultural, social, and ecological progress as a five-pronged approach to building socialism with Chinese characteristics. In other words, to develop socialism with Chinese characteristics, we should make concerted efforts to promote economic, political, cultural, social and ecological progress in all areas of endeavour. To be more specific, we are going to 'build up socialist economy, socialist democracy, socialist advanced culture, socialist harmonious society, and socialist ecological civilization'. The focus of economic advancement is laid on 'accelerating the improvement of the socialist market economy and the change of the growth model'. The political advancement stresses 'keeping to the socialist path of making political advance with Chinese characteristics and promoting reform of the political structure'. The cultural advancement highlights the mission of 'building a culturally strong socialist country and strengthening the core socialist value system'. Social advancement accentuates 'improving people's living standard and innovating social management'. Ecological progress emphasizes the following tasks as 'conserving resources, protecting the environment and striving for green, sustainable and low-carbon development so as to make China a beautiful country'. All these five respects are indispensable to building socialism with Chinese characteristics, which is an overall strategic plan. The Party's leadership lies at the core of the grand undertaking of completing socialism with Chinese characteristics and guarantees its foundation and development. Accordingly, the overall plan for seeking economic, political, cultural, social, and ecological progress should incorporate one more respect, that is, Party building.

IV. The Four-pronged Comprehensive Strategy

In November 2012, the report to the 18th National Congress of the CPC put forward the goal of 'completing the Building of a Moderately Prosperous Society in All Respects'. Since then, the CPC Central Committee with Comrade Xi Jinping at its core has successively initiated the 'Two Centenary Goals' and the goal of 'Realizing the Chinese Dream of the Rejuvenation of the Chinese Nation'. In November 2013, the Third Plenary Session of the 18th CPC Central Committee called forth 'intensifying reform in all respects', and fixed its general goal as 'improving and developing socialism with Chinese characteristics and promoting the modernization drive of the national governance system and capacity'. The Fourth Plenary Session of the 18th CPC Central Committee held in October 2014, brought forward the goal of 'comprehensively advancing the rule of law' and defined its overall target as 'building the legal system of socialism with Chinese characteristics and developing socialist country built on the rule of law'. Later, 'to exercise strict self-governance by the Party in every respect' was proposed by Xi Jinping during an tour of inspection in Jiangsu Province on December 13 and 14 of 2014, and thus together with other three strategies, it was integrated into the 'Four-pronged Comprehensive Strategy' which was illustrated and established as a holistic development arrangement. The 'Four-pronged Comprehensive Strategy', just as the term indicates, has four principal strands, pinning down strategies to help continue and develop the path, the theories and the system of socialism with Chinese characteristics.

The 'Four-pronged Comprehensive Strategy' was brought forth as a response to our ever-changing national development conditions and as an answer to the earnest expectations of the people to tackle pronounced conflicts and problems confronting us. In respect of governing the whole country, this strategy captures the key target for a stable reform and development, covers a general development plan of China, and specifies the work of the Party and the country under new circumstances regarding strategic development direction, key areas and major targets. Adhering to the question-oriented approach and a scientific outlook, laying the base on Chinese realities and drawing on Chinese experience, General Secretary Xi Jinping has proposed the Four-pronged Comprehensive Strategy for tackling Chinese problems, from a comprehensive perspective of a modern Chinese communist member with a strategic vision and firm confidence in China. These four strategies are interconnected in facilitating, promoting and complementing each other. They include one target and three measures. In other words, they contain a general plan as well as specific key points, with each strategy directed at a matter of paramount strategic significance. Among them, 'to complete the Building of a Moderately Prosperous Society in All Respects' is the general strategic target, while the other three are specific measures. Among them, 'intensifying reform in all respects' and 'governing the country thoroughly based on law' are parallel strategies, as in, 'both wings of a bird and two wheels of a cart'. A further strategy, 'exercising strict self-governance in every respect' is a political safeguard for forging a more solid core leadership for our cause. These four strategies are not simply paralleled but organically integrated and interrelated in their top-level design, sketching a promising blueprint of socialist China where one can find a moderately prosperous society aglow with revolutionary spirit, the people sharing a solid view of law-based governance, and a ruling party strictly and completely self-governed.

V. The Five Major Development Concepts

The Fifth Plenary Session of the 18th CPC Central Committee, held in Beijing from October 26 to 29, 2015, mainly deliberated on the economic and social development of China in the following five years (2016 – 2020), and approved the document *Central Committee of the CPC: Recommendations for the 13th Five-Year Plan for Economic and Social Development.* The period of the '13th Five-Year Plan' is the decisive stage in finishing building a moderately prosperous society in all respects, while the most noteworthy contribution highlighted by the Fifth Plenary Session of the 18th CPC Central Committee is the proposal to promote innovative, coordinated, green, open, and shared development. These 'Five Major Development Concepts set out methods, direction and focus of national development during the 13th Five-Year Plan period, or even longer. They fully embody our experience of development over the past three decades of reform and opening up, and reflect our Party's new understandings on our internal laws of development.'[1] They enrich and elaborate the Party's theories on development. They demonstrate a breakthrough in, and new development of, the Scientific Outlook on Development; they summarize and conclude new ideas, new thoughts and new strategies concerning governance of the country under the guidance of the Party Central Committee with Comrade Xi Jinping at its core.

Firstly, among the five concepts, innovation is prioritized to an unprecedented extent. In pursuing innovative development, 'Innovation should be placed at the heart of China's development and promoted in every field, from theory to institutions, in science, technology, and culture. Innovation should permeate all work of the party and the country and become an inherent part of the society.'[2] Since the 16th CPC National Congress, our party has been governing the state involving all parts of work in accordance with the principle of reform and innovation and in an effort

---

[1] Xi Jinping. *Explanatory Notes for the Central Committee of the CPC: Recommendations for the 13th Five-Year Plan for Economic and Social Development.*
[2] *Central Committee of the CPC: Recommendations for the 13th Five-Year Plan for Economic and Social Development* (Adopted at the Fifth Plenary Session of the 18th Central Committee of the CPC on October 29, 2015)

to improve our self-initiated innovation capability and develop our country into an innovative state. The 18th CPC National Congress put forward the innovation-driven development strategy, and required us to conduct reform in every area and at all levels in economic and social development, and to promote innovative development through reform. At the Fifth Plenary Session of the 18th CPC Central Committee, innovation was cited as 'the primary driving force for development', and was put in 'a central place in China's development strategy'. This is a significant development of concepts and approaches, functioning as a response to requirements of the times. Accordingly, this concept involves 'innovation in our theories, institutions, science and technology, and culture' - rather than scientific and technological innovation alone. The first and foremost aspect of innovation is theoretical innovation. The Four-pronged Comprehensive Strategy is a kind of theoretical innovation; so too are the 'Five Development Concepts'. Theory is the precursor, the soul and the master switch. With the guidance of new theories, the direction of development and the path to be followed are clear. Institutional innovation is next in terms of importance. Modernization of the national governance system and its capacity is the overall goal of a comprehensive reform agenda, as well as being the greatest institutional innovation that guarantees other kinds of innovation. The key matter of scientific and technological innovation is the most dynamic innovation. That is why we should promote public entrepreneurship and innovation, and drive the emergence of new technology, new formats and new industries. Cultural innovation in a broad sense refers not only to the innovation in various areas of arts, cultural undertakings and industries but also to that of socialist core values, spiritual, political and ethical culture. 'Innovation should permeate all work of the party and the country, and become an inherent part of society.' This is a remarkable breakthrough in the Scientific Outlook on Development.

Secondly, the Five Major Development Concepts lay greater stress on coordinated development. In pursuing coordinated development, "While keeping firmly in mind the overall strategy of socialism with Chinese characteristics, we should properly handle relationships between major areas of development, focusing on promoting balanced development between urban and rural areas as well as between different regions; promoting coordinated economic and social development; and promoting the synchronized development of a new type of industrialization, information technology, urbanization, and agricultural modernization. While increasing China's hard power, we should also work to enhance its soft power, striving constantly to make development more comprehensive."[1] Besides the notions of 'promoting balanced development between urban and rural areas as well as between different regions' and 'promoting the synchronized development of a new type of industrialization, information technology, urbanization, and agricultural modernization', two more notions are proposed. These are; 'coordinating material progress and cultural and ethical progress' and 'integrating the development of the economy and national defense'. In this context, coordinated development is extended to cover a wider and larger scale, and will substantially realize 'a comprehensive, balanced and sustainable development' rather than economic coordination alone. For the first time, cultural and ethical progress is included in coordinated development, demonstrating determination to promote both material progress and cultural and ethical progress without favouring either at the expense of the other. Their coordinated development is a prerequisite to upholding and developing socialism with Chinese characteristics and a fundamental task in building a moderately prosperous society in all respects.

Third, the Five Major Development Concepts accentuate a harmonious green development between the people and nature. In pursuing green development, "We should adhere to the fundamental state policy of conserving resources and protecting the environment so as to promote sustainable development, and pursue a civilized development path that ensures increased levels of production, better living standards, and a sound ecology. We should move faster to build a resource-conserving, environmentally friendly society and bring about a model for modernization in which mankind develops in harmony with nature. We should move forward with building a Beautiful China and make new contributions toward ensuring global ecological security."[2] We should make green development a mode of production, a way of life, even a fashion of the society. 'Green development' corresponds to 'sustainable development' in the Scientific Outlook on Development, but it enriches the latter concept. Besides 'promoting low-carbon and sustainable development, conserving resources wherever possible and putting them to efficient use, stepping up environmental governance efforts and building ecological security shields', "We should take a green approach to developing a prosperous China and ensuring the wellbeing of its people. We should provide more quality green products for the people, encourage green forms of development and green lifestyles, and ensure that all work is in concert

---

[1] Ibid
[2] Ibid

to help the people become prosperous, make our country strong, and build a Beautiful China." Compared with the past, this principle highlights the concept of harmony between human and nature, stresses the notion of functional zones, and adds the goal of building a Beautiful China.

Fourth, the Five Major Development Concepts highlight open development. In pursuing open development, "In adapting to China's ever-deepening integration into the global economy, we should pursue a mutually beneficial strategy of opening up. We should develop a new level of openness within our economy, participate actively in global economic governance and the global supply of public goods, seek to have a greater say in the institutions for global economic governance, and look to build communities of common interests with more international partners."[1] Over 30 years have elapsed since the implementation of reform and opening up. At the start of this century, we proposed the integration of two approaches of 'bringing in' and 'going global' as our opening-up strategy. Since the 18th CPC National Congress, the situation concerning opening up has changed tremendously. In the past, we made more efforts to introduce the outside world to China, follow the world political and economic order and integrate ourselves into their institutions, and use others' platforms to display ourselves and promote our work. However, today we are increasing our efforts to go to the outside world, build up our own platforms for international collaboration, and set up new political and economic institutions as in the practices of the 'Belt and Road' Initiative, the Asian Infrastructure Investment Bank, the Silk Road Fund and Free Trade Zone. In changing circumstances, we should adapt to China's ever-deepening integration into the global economy, put into perspective the international and domestic conditions, and develop an open economy at a higher level. We should upgrade our opening-up strategy to establish a new framework. In addition, we should construct a new layout of complete openness for synchronized development of both land and marine economies, together with opening up to both east and the west regions. We should also leverage international and domestic markets and resources. We should participate actively in global economic governance in an effort to have a greater say in its institutions, and look to build communities of common interests with more international partners. China has become the world's second largest economy. To demonstrate our trustworthiness as a big country, we are going to assume more international responsibilities and obligations. The concept of open development reflects

---

[1] Ibid

our new perspectives on, and understanding of, opening-up policy under current world circumstances, and it is a renewal of the Scientific Outlook on Development.

Fifth, the Five Major Development Concepts underscore shared development. In pursuing shared development, "we should ensure that development is for the people, that it is reliant on the people, and that its fruits are shared by the people. We should improve our institutions to ensure that the people have a greater sense of benefit as they contribute to and share in development, thus strengthening the impetus for development, enhancing unity among the people, and helping them move steadily toward common prosperity."[1] Over the past 30 years of reform and opening up, we have shifted from a focus on development rate, efficiency and effectiveness, to place more emphasis on the people's standard of living, and have paid more and more attention to fairness and justice. Since the 16th CPC National Congress, we have proposed, 'the principle of all the people building and sharing a harmonious socialist society', and have created 'a lively situation in which everyone is duty-bound to work for, and benefit from, social harmony' The concept of shared development embodies the orientation of the party's work to the people and the principle of putting the people first, and requires us 'to ensure that living standards are improved through the involvement and dedication of all people and the shared enjoyment of benefits therein' and to take the fundamental interests of the people as our starting point and as the ultimate goal of our work, to enable the people's expectations to be met. The key features of shared development proposed at the Fifth Plenary Session of the 18th CPC Central Committee lie in their orientation to people's wellbeing and fairness. They are illustrated by the following aspects: bridging the income gap, ensuring that personal income grows in step with economic growth, and that remuneration for labour grows in step with rising productivity. In addition, to combat poverty, we should adopt targeted measures to alleviate and eliminate poverty in light of local conditions. To proactively respond to population aging, we should establish a multilevel elderly support system, providing more services and products for the elderly. To promote the building of a Healthy China, we should implement a food safety strategy. To promote balanced population development, we should implement the policy of allowing all couples to have two children. All of these points are shining examples, signalling innovative ideas and highlighting new development.

---

[1] Ibid

Development is the theme of the times and a common objective in all countries of the world. The 'Five Major Development Concepts' constitute a development theory that is completely in step with the times, and are evidence of a change in the mode and approach of thinking. It is a synthetic application of dialectical and systematic methodology with a consideration of the worst-case-scenarios.

The Party Central Committee with Comerade Xi Jinping at its core is leading the Chinese people in accomplishing the following missions: attaining the Two Centenary Goals; completing the Building of a Moderately Prosperous Society in All Respects; realizing the Chinese Dream of the Great Rejuvenation of the Chinese Nation; conducting the Five-pronged Approach to an overall plan for promoting all-round economic, political, cultural, social, and ecological progress towards socialism with Chinese characteristics; coordinating the progress of the Four-pronged Comprehensive Strategy; and putting into practice the 'Five Major Development Concepts'. All these key words epitomize the core contents of the new principles and strategies for the governance of China under the leadership of General Secretary Xi Jinping.

Feng Jun is the chief editor of the book. Each section and chapter of the book is written by different authors, and they are, respectively: Introduction is written by Feng Jun, Chapter One by He Lisheng, Chapter Two by Wang Youming, Chapter Three by Liu Zhexin, Chapter Four by Hu Hanjin, Chapter Five by Huang Lizhi, Chapter Six by Yu Hongsheng, Chapter Seven by Yan Nailing, and Chapter Eight is written by Liu Jingbei.

Chapter 1

China's New Normal

China is still in a significant period of strategic opportunity. We must boost our confidence, adapt to the 'new normal' condition based on the characteristics of China's economic growth in the current phase; and stay cool-minded. China should also attach great significance to preventing a range of risks for its economy and take timely countermeasures to reduce potential negative effects.

— Xi Jinping's Speech during an Inspection Tour in Henan Province in May 2014.[1]

I. The New Normal of Economic Growth: Upgrading China's Economy

Literally, 'new normal' contains two terms, in which the 'new' means a different economic growth model compared with the 'old' one, and the term 'normal' refers to a usual state. Making the distinction from an economy that is overly driven by input and investment and grows inefficiently at a high rate, the economy under the 'new normal' condition refers to a long-lasting growth model with a lower rate of growth, a more optimized structure, a progressive transition to innovation as its key driver, and a deeper reform of its system. Adapting to the 'new normal' of growth indicates that China envisages a new period of economic development moving towards structural upgrading and relying more on domestic market. "Under the 'new normal' condition", as pointed out by General Secretary Xi Jinping, "China's economic development has three major features: a lower growth rate, an

---

[1] When Inspecting in Henan Province, Xi Jinping Stressed that We Must Deepen the Reform, Capitalize on Advantages, Innovate Ideas, and Make Overall Plans and Take All Factors into Consideration to Ensure Stable and Sound Economic Development as well as a Harmonious and StableSociety. People's Daily, May 11, 2014(1).

optimized structure and a different motive force. Specifically, the economy will shift gear from the previous high speed to a medium-high speed growth; the focus of growth model will be shifted from scale and speed to quality and efficiency; the economic structure will be changed from the expansion of production volume and capacity, to the dual goal of adjusting stock and upgrading the quality of production, instead of continuing to rely on natural resources and low-cost labor, the leading engine of development will be innovation. Independent of man's will, all this must be carried out according to the current development phase of the China's economy."[1]

1. Shifting gear from the previous high speed to a medium-high speed growth is the basic characteristic of the 'new normal' economy.

China is changing gear from an annual growth rate of 10% to a lower rate of about 7%, which is a manifestation of the 'new normal'. Because of the increasing costs or prices of labor, resources, land and other factors, the peak growth rates of the past cannot be sustained or afforded. Contributing factors include the enormous stress caused by the limitations imposed by environmental factors, consumption of resources and market restrictions. Therefore, it is impossible for the model of economic development that is driven only by elements of input, expansion and investment-driven growth to go further. Although seeing a lower growth rate under the 'new normal' situation, China still "aims to double the 2010 GDP and per capita income of urban and rural residents by 2020 on the basis of making China's development much more balanced, inclusive and sustainable,"[2] and continues to be the most vigorous economy leading global growth.

China is striving to achieve the 'Two Centenary Goals' as a grand blueprint and to accomplish the building of a moderately prosperous society in all aspects by 2020. Economically, as long as China keeps its growth rate at 7% during the 10 years from 2010 to 2020, even if the GDP drops by 1% every 10 years thereafter, namely at 6% from 2020 to 2030, 5% from 2030 to 2040, and 4% from 2040 to 2050, it will be an economy with GDP growth rate equal to that of America in 2030, and its economy will exceed that of America by 1.34 times in 2050. As General Secretary Xi Jinping pointed out in the Boao Forum for Asia Annual Conference 2015, "When looking at

---

[1] Xi Jinping. Explanatory Notes for the *Central Committee of the CPC: Recommendations for the 13th Five-Year Plan for Economic and Social Development*. Xinhuanet. November 3, 2015.
[2] *Central Committee of the CPC: Recommendations for the 13th Five-Year Plan for Economic and Social Development*. Xinhuanet. November 3, 2015.

China's economy, one should not focus on growth rate only. As the economy continues to grow in size, around 7% growth would be quite impressive, and the momentum it generates would be larger than that of the double-digit growth in previous years."[1]

2. Economic growth under the 'new normal' situation is genuine and uninflated.

When assessing the economic growth rate in an objective manner, it is crucial to take into account economic size as well as the quality and efficiency of development. Since the introduction of the reform and opening-up policy, China has witnessed a high economic growth rate. However, during this period, some regions and fields have seen the problems of 'GDP only' and inappropriate pursuit of a high growth rate regardless of other factors, which is closely related to problems such as over exploitation of resources, severe environmental pollution, and unhealthy economic structure we are encountering. Therefore, General Secretary Xi Jinping has repeatedly emphasized that "we must fully realize the relationship between sustainable and healthy economic development and GDP growth", and that, "we must avoid simply measuring development by the GDP growth rate." Avoiding simply measuring development by the GDP growth rate is an essential requirement for China's economy under the 'new normal' situation.

Since China has become the second largest economy in the world after more than three decades of high-speed growth, it is no longer realistic to continue to grow at this pace and at double-digit-percentage rates on the higher base level of economic activity. In addition, limitations of resources and environmental pollution, rule out continuing to pursue those levels of growth rate. Besides, solving the deep-seated problems accumulated during the high-speed development requires us to shift the economy to an appropriate speed, sparing space for stable and sustainable economic development.

Since China's economic aggregate activity and the base figure of GDP have already increased greatly after over three decades of high-speed development, an increase in economy of 1% GDP growth is by no means a negligible figure. Statistics show that China's GDP reached Rmb63.6 trillion in 2014 (calculated at current price, with the same factor applied hereafter),

---

[1] A Keynote Speech at the Boao Forum for Asia Annual Conference 2015 Delivered by President Xi Jinping. Xinhuanet. March 29, 2015.

exceeding $10 trillion at the current exchange rate, representing 13.3% of the world economy. Its annual increase in GDP was equivalent to the aggregate economic output of a medium-size developed country; the per capita GDP totaled $7,594, which, according to the World Bank estimates, placed China at a mid level among the countries with medium-to-high income in the world. The per capita disposable income of urban and rural residents is respectively Rmb29,000 and Rmb11,000.

Compared with that of 2013, the economic output of 2014 increased $866.5 billion, which means that at present the increase that China achieves in one year exceeds its total economic output in 1996, by $5.7 billion. Measured against other economies, that increase is $27.5 billion more than the aggregate economic output in 2013 of Turkey, which is the 17th largest economy in the world. Contrasts are even greater if we compare the figures for 2014 with those of 2007. Although the GDP growth rate in 2014 fell to 7.4%, the lowest since the beginning of the 21st century, every percentage point of GDP growth brings about an increase of $117.1 billion, twice as much as that of 2007. If we take the adjustment of industrial structure into consideration, every percentage point of GDP growth of 2014 is estimated to create 1.8 million new jobs. And the target of growth rate in 2014 means an increase of over Rmb5 trillion, equivalent of the entire economic output in 1994.

Each year since 2013, the increase created by the tertiary industry (service sector) in China as a proportion of GDP has surpassed that of the secondary industry. However, the service sectors in some developed countries have already accounted for more than 80% of their GDPs. Thus, the proportion of this sector in China's economy will be increasing for a long time under the 'new normal' situation. During the period of a change in the pace of economic growth, China has to emerge from the phase of rapid growth and develop at a reasonable growth rate, ensuring that the economy operates within an appropriate range. It is both possible and necessary to maintain a medium-high growth rate and keep the economy developing towards a medium-high level.

What speed, therefore, is it appropriate for China to grow at? "To achieve the goal of doubling per capita income by 2020 from its 2010 level, China must maintain an average annual economic growth rate at 6.5% or above while seeing growth of both income and the economy during the 13th Five-Year Plan period. Medium-high economic growth will help improve the living standards and quality of life with people truly enjoying the fruits brought about during the building of a moderately prosperous society in all respects."[1]

An excessively low growth rate will bring about many problems associated with structure rebalancing, employment security, improvement of livelihood and social stability. If the growth drops too fast or even goes into a stall, government revenue will shrink. This would be followed by a decrease in public expenditure, a soaring unemployment rate and a sharp fall in income, which would go beyond acceptable limits of social endurance.

Therefore, avoiding simply measuring development by the GDP growth rate does not mean ignoring economic growth. Instead, great importance is attached to an efficient, high-quality and sustainable growth. When determining a certain growth rate, we must take into consideration the need to finish building a moderately prosperous society in all respects, the necessities of expanding economic output and upgrading structure, the principles of reality and economic development, the requirements of both stabilizing economic growth and rebalancing the economic structure, and the pursuit of full employment and stably increasing income.

In general, the 'new normal' growth involves a dynamic balance of industrial structure, real improvement of social welfare, coordinated development between regions, integration of quality and efficiency as well as energy conservation and environmental protection. In other words, the economic growth under the 'new normal' situation is genuine and uninflated.

Just as General Secretary Xi Jinping stressed in the Central Economic Work Conference in December 2013, "The growth rate we are pursuing is genuine and not inflated, and is the one that could improve people's wellbeing and help achieve full employment. At this kind of rate, the economy should develop both in higher quality and efficiency and with no after-effects, and at the same time the labor productivity will be raised, economic vitality increasingly injected, and economic structure effectively adjusted."[2] We strive for sustainable economic growth accompanied by a transformation of the growth model, optimization of economic structure, improvement in the ecological environment and growth of quality and efficiency.

---

[1] Xi Jinping. Explanatory Notes for the *Central Committee of the CPC: Recommendations for the 13th Five-Year Plan for Economic and Social Development*. Xinhuanet, November 3, 2015.
[2] *Central Committee of the CPC: Recommendations for the 13th Five-Year Plan for Economic and Social Development*. Xinhuanet. November 3, 2015.

3. Structural optimization is an inherent feature of the 'new normal'.

What we are supposed to see when the restructuring starts to be carried out is that "major economic indices will be balanced and coordinated; the space and layout of development will be optimized; efficiency of investment and performance of enterprises will be improved; industrialization and informatization will be further integrated to raise the level of development; the development of industries will be promoted toward the medium-high end; the development of advanced manufacturing industry will accelerate, new industries will keep growing, the services industry will account for a higher proportion of the national economy; economic growth will be increasingly driven by consumption; the population urbanization rate will be improved rapidly; and major progress in agricultural modernization will be made. Fulfilling these objectives will turn China into an innovative and talent-rich country."[1]

China has accomplished remarkable achievements in its economy since the policy of opening up and reform was implemented, and its model and path of economic development have been recognized globally. The rapid-economic-growth model did fit China as an emerging economy, and as a post-industrial country with comparative advantages as a developing country. During that period it supported China's uninterrupted growth at a high rate. However, this kind of growth model has led to some serious structural problems and conflicts, including inefficient economic growth, a deteriorating trade environment, and energy, resources and the environment under heavy pressure or even too weak to support the growth.

For example, China's development has been excessively reliant on high investment; in the global division of labor it has been excessively reliant on trade linked to processing and manufacturing. It has depended excessively on cost price to prevail in international competition. But at the same time, high-value-added elements such as R&D and design, marketing, brand management and supply chain management in both industrial and value chains, have been absent. That can be summarized as 'three excessives' and 'one deficiency'. Dynamic structural optimization requires a focus on economic growth to shift from merely increasing output and expanding the operating base, to stock adjustment and quality upgrading. To lead the 'new normal'

---

[1] An important speech at the Central Economic Work Conference delivered by Xi Jinping. Xinhuanet. December 11, 2014.

and complete the upgrading of its economy, China needs to address certain problem areas and drive its economy from extensive model to intensive one, It must move from a low-technology model to a high-end one and overcome further difficulties, among which structure rebalancing is highlighted as a rather tough one.

Just as Xi Jinping put it, "We must capitalize on the resilience and great potential of China's economy, which still has much leeway to grow, to persist in improving its quality and efficiency and upgrading through reform and restructuring. And what we are striving to achieve is lower-speed economic growth without losing momentum and a growing economy providing higher-quality production."[1] As we know, the economic structure is required to be dynamically optimized all the time due to the constant change of market, technology and demand. The balance of economic structure and dynamic optimization will become the 'new normal' of the economy, which is based on the integration of growth rate, restructuring and power transformation.

Concurrently, we will bring revisions and changes into China's economic structure in terms of industrial structure, market structure, regional structure, urban and rural structure, capital structure and distribution pattern. Then, we will achieve multidimensional and dynamic adjustment and rebalancing of the economic structure. In terms of the industrial structure, we should pursue a transformation from a large manufacturing country to a country with both powerful manufacturing and service industries; in terms of regional structure, we should pursue a pathway of regional coordinated development instead of a separate one. As for the financial structure, we will get rid of financial controls to facilitate development of the real economy; and with respect to quality and structure, China has experienced a time when quantity and scale mattered most. But now we strive for efficient growth of high quality. Economic restructuring based on demand requires optimization of the demand structure. To maintain long-term stable economic growth, we must realize the transformation from a supply-constrained economy during the period of the planned economy to a demand-driven economy characterized by the socialist market economy, that is, we must develop domestic demand to address the inadequacy of final consumption. At the same time we must increase demand for final consumption by urban and

---

[1] An important speech at the Central Economic Work Conference delivered by Xi Jinping. People.cn. December 11, 2014.

rural residents with the goal of maintaining long-term economic stability and development. When optimizing the economic structure from the perspective of demand, we must recognize that the advantage of low costs of production factors is lessening, the constraints of limited resources and environmental pollution are increasing, and the conflicts caused by overcapacity are growing. Only with a full understanding of these changes in the process of economic development can we choose the optimum path for industrial innovation and integration. Besides, economic restructuring requires improvement of the quality of economic growth, the promotion of environmental protection to a new level, a low-carbon approach, and the consistent enhancement of people's living standards with the growth of the economy. The main challenge China is facing is restructuring. Only through the restructuring and optimization of the economy, can the quality of economic growth be improved quantitatively and qualitatively in a mutually complementary fashion.

Since government transformation is a prerequisite for economic transformation, during the economic restructuring and dynamic optimization, we must deepen the reform of the government system. This specifically includes the transformation of government functions, reform and improvement of the institutions and mechanisms concerning investment, demand, industry, and distribution, and a clear understanding of the structures of investment, demand, and distribution. We should maintain the consistency and stability of macroeconomic policies and let the market play the decisive role in allocating resources. Practice has shown that it is the market that chooses the present industrial and demand structures in which businesses are the main body. In the market economy, compared with preferential policies granted to some industries by the government, a leveled playing field is more important. We must change the customary policies of regulation and support for some industries because some of these policies breed profiteering practices by businesses instead of encouraging a focus on effective competition in the market, or improving the industrial value chain and brand promotion. The government must fully perform its functions in protecting property right or rights and interests, improving market conditions, providing infrastructure upgrades and ensuring public services and security. We must limit governmental functions and focus efforts on addressing negative aspects. In other words, the government should concentrate on effectively managing all issues that fall within its purview, and appropriately delegating powers where that is appropriate. We must ensure that governments at all levels identify their powers and responsibilities, and encourage businesses through deregulation. We must build a sustained force to drive microeconomic development, and give vitality to market entities through delegating powers; we must fill gaps, ensuring that all things have been done well, and increasing the supply of public goods; we must boost the real economy, issue effective, necessary policies and lay a solid microeconomic foundation for economic growth.

4. Valuing the real economy is an inherent demand of the 'new normal'.

General Secretary Xi Jinping has repeatedly stressed that industrialization is significant for building a strong nation that relies on the real economy and under no circumstances tolerates economic 'bubbles'. In *Made in China 2025*, the State Council emphasized that "the manufacturing industry is the main body of the national economy, the foundation of the state, an important way to rejuvenate our country, and the base of building a stronger China. Since the industrial civilization was welcomed in the middle of the 18th century, the rise and fall of great powers in the world and China's history of struggle have proved again and again that a country would never be strong and prosperous if a powerful manufacturing industry is not achieved. Thus building an internationally competitive manufacturing industry is the only path we can take to enhance China's comprehensive strength, defend national security, and propel it to become one of the strongest countries around the world."[1]

Practice has proved that with greater maturity in the real economy, the stronger the economy becomes and the greater the risk tolerance is. This is a hard truth of modern economic development. Since China's economy is evolving into more sophisticated forms, more complicated division of labor, and more rational structures, a key part of China's economic transformation is to enhance the real economy. At present, the nub of some structural problems and conflicts such as the lack of balance, coordination and sustainability in economic development lies in the statement, 'the real economy has not been purely 'real' and the virtual economy is overly inflated'. The difficulty lies in finding a new way out of the negative situation of the real economy in which we are trapped: it is crucial to upgrade and transform the real economy. The real economy, or manufacturing, is the pillar of national competitiveness, so we must unwaveringly take positive steps

---

[1] Notice of the State Council on Issuing *Made in China 2025*. people.cn. May 19, 2015.

to develop a modern manufacturing industry. The service sector accounts for more than 70% of the national economy of the US, but nearly 60% of it goes to services driven by manufacturing industry. This indicates that manufacturing industry plays an important role in supporting and leading the service sector. For example, advanced communication equipment helps drive information services, which creates an annual increase of about Rmb1.4 trillion an advanced automobile industry will boost the automobile customer service industry with the market potential being several times higher than that of a car.

In order to strengthen the real economy from the perspective of consumption, only by accelerating the upgrading of manufacturing industries can China transform from a large manufacturing country to a powerful one. We aim to realize intelligent manufacturing and move towards an advanced manufacturing and commercial model, including elements such as personalized customization, flexible production and network sales. This will be required to meet the needs of growing personal and diversified consumption and to support the upgrading of consumption structure. Manufacturing industry is the main field for implementation of the development strategy driven by innovation. It is the main battlefield for research and development, and the most active and fruitful field, which will fundamentally determine the overall innovation capacity of China. For example, in respect of exports, manufactured products account for 95% of all the exported goods. It is a necessity for us to adjust and optimize the structure of industry and products so as to improve the competiveness of 'Made in China' products. From the perspective of investment, there exists a big gap in terms of economic capital stock and per capita stock between China and developed economies. For example, the gross capital stock of China is equivalent to 30% of that of the US, and per capita stock is equivalent to 8% and 17% of that of the US and of the Republic of Korea respectively. The proportions of those figures relating to water and electricity, and to investment in railway, education and health per capita to GDP are all lower than world average.

There is more room for investment in China. The country's high national saving rate, which now stands at over 40%, has led to high investment rate, high contribution of investment growth, consumption growth and net growth of goods and services to GDP growth. In recent years, investment opportunities have emerged in great numbers in the fields of industrial logistics, communication and other infrastructures, as well as new technologies, new products, new forms of business and new models. At the same time, intelligent manufacturing, intelligent logistics, high-end equipment, industrial robots, new energy vehicles and other investment fields are becoming new 'hot spots'. In terms of employment, the development of an emerging service industry and the optimization and upgrading of industrial structure are creating high-quality jobs, improving the entire employment structure.

Additionally, significant breakthroughs have been made in manned space flight, the lunar exploration program, high-speed rail transport, high performance computers and new generation mobile communications. The 'Internet of Things', intelligent robots and other innovative technologies have been widely used in a variety of industries, and innovation is becoming the main driving force of economic and social development. A new round of scientific, technological and industrial revolution is surging. The deep integration of industrial technology and information technology has become the new trend in industrial development. Only by accelerating integration and innovation in ICT and industrialization, and shifting the driving force of industrial development to innovation-driven development, can we shift China's industries from the low-end to the high-end on the global value chain, enabling the fundamental change from expansion of scale to a new model featuring better quality and higher efficiency.

The 18th National Congress of the CPC was held in Beijing from November 8 to 14 in 2012. (Xinhua News Agency)

II. Rational Coordination of the 'Invisible Hand' and the 'Visible Hand'

The relationship between the government and the market represents a core issue in our economic structural reform. Concerning their roles, we should appeal to both dialectical and dichotomous approaches so as to reasonably coordinate and make full use of the market, the 'invisible hand', and the government, the 'visible hand'. They should complement and coordinate with each other to form an integral and reciprocal force. Letting the market play the decisive role in allocating resources and letting the government better perform its functions are not contradictory. It does not mean that the market can replace the government's functions, nor vice versa.[1]

The Third Plenary Session of the 18th CPC Central Committee clearly put forward a scientific judgment of "letting the market play the decisive role in allocating resources and the government better perform its functions", the core of which is balancing the relationship between the market, the 'invisible hand', and the government, the 'visible hand', and allowing the market to play the decisive role in allocating resources.

The relationship between the market and the government is directly related to not only the direction of the reform of the economic system but also the orientation and result of all-round and deeper-level reform. "Only when in trials and tribulations, can one's courage be revealed; and it is the sincere practice that makes it precious." The government and the market are not contradictory, nor is one superior to the other; instead, they should take up their respective positions and complement each other's advantages. The government should define and protect property rights, guarantee the performance of contract and conduct market oversight by relying on monocracy. The government should also maintain fair and orderly competition, regulate behaviors of market entities, inspire the creativity and energy of market entities, and guide them through rational resource allocation to promote sustained and sound economic development. The important foundation of letting the market play a decisive role in allocating resources is the construction of an efficient government. In terms of allocation

---

[1] The "Invisible Hand" and the "Visible Hand" (May 26, 2014). *The Governance of China*, Eng.ed.Foreign Languages Press. Oct 2014. p. 128.
  Note: This is the speech delivered by General Secretary Xi Jinping at the 15th group study session of the Political Bureau of the 18th CPC Central Committee. The theme of the speech is to let the market play the decisive role in allocating resources, while allow the government to better perform its functions.

of resources, the market plays a decisive role in the relationship between the market and the government. From a strict economic perspective, the allocation of resources is mainly a microscopic problem, which means the market should be allowed to play the decisive role on a micro level. So what are the market and the government supposed to do? We need to understand the following points.

1. The government is the macro-manager, and the enterprise is the autonomous operator.

From a microscopic perspective, such issues as allocation of resources, manufacturer behaviors, the pricing of products and resource elements, industrial distribution, and the determination of industrial structures are mainly defined as market competition behaviors rather than being subject to prearrangement by government policies. For example, the government should reduce intervention in enterprise behaviors, which is rightfully an autonomy matter for enterprises. The government enacts market rules, and what the enterprises should do is to abide by the law, pay tax by law, operate legally, and act on the principle of maximum benefit in the market. There seems no difference in the understanding of autonomy of enterprise behavior. Industrial structure is a micro issue rather than a macro one. Industrial structure is determined by the hub effect that is developed amid competition among enterprises.

Why is excess production capacity such a serious problem? Is it caused by blind market competition, government plans or government industry regulation? For a long time, during the period of 'the Tenth Five-Year Plan', 'the Eleventh Five-Year Plan' and 'the Twelfth Five-Year Plan', the National Development and Reform Commission listed several leading industries and emerging strategic industries, which immediately attracted great attention across the whole nation. Local governments used low land prices and government credit as a guarantee, on the basis of which, banks engaged in loan activity; and development areas were set up before markets were ready, thus, repetition was not surprising. If the appointed plans are instructive without fostering policy, will the government streamline administration of industrial development and leave it to the market? The government should act on macroscopic rather than on microscopic levels. That is, the government should make efforts to perfect 'rules', and create an environment that is fair, open and transparent, and to implement unified market access and uniform market oversight. And on the basis of a negative list, all kinds of market entities may do business in sectors excluded from the negative list, equally and legally. We must strive to remove all hidden barriers of the non-public sectors in particular.

2. The government controls social aggregate supply, and the market regulates social needs.

The distribution of consumption and investment demand is rather about microscopic behaviors of the market. It depends upon the discretion of enterprises and consumers and is well beyond the capacity of the government, especially the local government. In terms of aggregate control as well as macroscopic management of supply and demand, the emphasis of governments at all levels should be on the supply side rather than on the demand side, which means keeping quality and safety standard of supplies under control. China has not operated in an era when supplies create demands. At the stage of capitalist liberalization, products would be consumed as long as they were produced. However, the goal of consumption would come to nothing if we failed to produce qualified goods in China. Therefore, during the current period of deepening transformation in systems, for the macroscopic supply management and demand management, the emphasis of the government is on supply management. The government should lay more stress on controlling the quality and safety standard of supplies rather than demands. The government should create larger development space for market entities.

In this respect, there is susbstantial scope for reform of what is and is not in the area of government power. To cut government power, that is, to streamline administration and delegate more powers to lower-level governments, will give more space to market for the development of enterprises. More responsibilities should be undertaken by the government; leaner management and a higher efficiency are in demand. For example, we should change the ratification system and approval system on foreign investment projects into a record system; change the paid-in capital registration system of business registration into a subscribed capital registration system; turn certification before licensing of enterprises into licensing before certification. We should replace annual inspection with an annual report, and implement transparency of information on enterprises information and anomalies in their operation. We should offer one-stop service for business registration procedures, take gradual steps to integrate the business license, the certificate of organization codes, and the certificate of taxation registration into one certificate, and change wholly foreign-invested advertising enterprise examination and approval for the record; and supervise the information sharing mechanism and comprehensive law enforcement system.

The government should "develop new ways of conducting and improving macro regulation. In response to the requirements of developing gross adjustment and adopting targeted steps simultaneously, it should take into consideration both the domestic and international situations and coordinate reform and development; the government should improve macro regulation, adopt a precise and well-timed regulation, timely and moderate pro-cyclical fine-tuning, pay more attention to expand employment, keep prices stable, make structural adjustments, improve the performance, guard against risks and protect the environment."[1] The function of the government is to maintain the stability of the macro-economy, strengthen and improve public services, safeguard fair competition, strengthen the oversight of the market, maintain market order, promote sustainable development and common prosperity, and intervene in situations where the market fails. This clarifies the responsibility of the government, better defines the function of the government and points out the direction to transform government functions. That is to say, the government should be the 'navigator' of national economy, the drafter of market rules, the 'judge' of the market operation, the provider of basic public services and the watchdog of fair play and justice. In supply management, the government does not interfere in any specific project and its production, but administers standards and orders, and seeks to refrain from providing private goods.

The government invests in public goods. In fact, China is suffering from a lack of public goods rather than an excess, as is evidenced by the so-called 'city diseases', like environmental pollution, market failures and traffic congestion, which are mostly caused by inadequate supply of public goods. Thus, the government investment should focus more on the provision of public goods, instead of on private products. Where the market can produce private goods, the government should not interfere. At present, there is a huge gap between the limited provision of public products and China's economic status and requirement of modernization. We can make up for the shortage of government funding in its open construction with the help of the market. We can strengthen the weaknesses in people's livelihood through

---

[1] *Central Committee of the CPC: Recommendations for the 13th Five-Year Plan for Economic and Social Development.* Xinhuanet. November 3, 2015.

multi-channel, which is the PPP model. We will improve the efficiency and quality of the development of public facilities, lower the entry barriers to infrastructure and public utilities for private capital, and deepen the reform of the system concerning matters subject to government examination and approval through market-based mechanisms. We will also improve the professional and scientific level of public utilities.

3. The government and market should take up their positions and perform their respective functions.

China's economy continues to enjoy a high-speed, robust and even balanced development. A vital reason is that the government plays an important role in investment, which is an advantage that cannot be denied. We should "further transform government's functions through deepening the reform of the administrative management system, so as to streamline administration and delegate power to the lower levels with the combination of surveillance, and optimize our services. We should improve the efficiency and capability of the government, so as to catalyze the dynamism of the market and the creativity of our society."[1]

The problem with government investment in China is not that it is higher than that in Western countries but rather, where it should be directed. The government should invest more in public goods and public infrastructure. However, the critical role that governments of all levels have played in guiding investments cannot be denied, since it served as one of China's strengths in counteracting the economic crisis. We should emphasize the balance of 'the troika' of investment, consumption and foreign trade in China's economic growth. We should not simply stress any specific one of the above three aspects during a certain period. Because of special consideration in different periods, we emphasized investment in the past, while we pay more attention to consumption at present. We should emphasize balanced development of these three factors. Thus, in investment and consumption, the government should lay emphasis on investment and have a clear set of goals and pathways. In the field of consumption, the market should play a dominant role.

In the socialist market economy, the government should use the 'visible hand' less, and should not compete with the market for the power of manipulation or take its place. We should implement structural reform

---

[1] *Central Committee of the CPC: Recommendations for the 13th Five-Year Plan for Economic and Social Development.* Xinhuanet. November 3, 2015.

of the government, cancel the requirement for verification or approval for professional qualifications, open the approval system and reduce approval items. What is the approval system? It is about powers, control, and interests. The role of the government should be more reflected in the allocation and reallocation. The issues in production are micro behaviors in the allocation of resources and should be delegated more to the market. The government may play an important role in allocation, and especially the reallocation, of national income. We can discuss the issues in the allocation of national income from macro-view, medium-view and micro-view levels, respectively. At the macro level, the national income is allocated to governments as fiscal revenue, to enterprises as capital surplus and to residents as income.

In fact, government revenue has grown fastest among these three factors in recent years. The percentage of residents' income as a proportion of GDP has been decreasing continually. According to the China's National Bureau of Statistics, residents' income has been dropping at an annual rate of 1% in recent years. This exposes the actual cause of long-term weak consumer demand in the recent decade -- the government and enterprises took the lion's share in money allocation. The Gini coefficient is 0.4. Such a big income gap will be inevitably detrimental to the propensity to consume. Problems at medium-level are problems of the economic structure. The big income gaps exposed among regions, industries and between the towns and the countryside require adjustments by using the transfer payment policy of national fiscal, tax policy and monetary policy. The income gaps are manifested at three levels: macro, medium and micro. These problems cannot be solved by the market, but can only be solved by the government. The government should pay more attention to the distribution field, and issues in the field of production should be, to a greater extent, left to the market to solve.

4. Enterprises are responsible for the internal competition mechanism of the market; the government is responsible for the competition mechanism outside of the market.

There are two internal competition mechanisms in the market: the entity order and the trading order. The former refers to the enterprise property right system, and the latter is about the pricing system. The former answers the question of who are the players in the competition, and the latter is the answer to the question of how they compete. The internal competition mechanism of the market is more about the enterprise, and the relationships between competitors. The competition mechanism outside of the market is composed of two aspects: one is the ethical order, and the other is legal order. It is difficult for any one of these two aspects alone to give rise to an effective mechanism if we rely solely on the market, and so we need to rely on the nation and government to a large extent. One of Montesquieu's famous quotes is that a nation does not lie in its laws and regulations, but in its spirit of rule of law. During an economic transitional period, the spirit of legality is often the scarcest. There are many laws in China, the quality of which may not be superior, but we have time to improve them. The most terrible thing is that some legislators and law enforcement officers take the lead to disobey the law. This is clearly not a matter that can be resolved by the market, and it is necessary to rely on the government's self-reform.

In the moral order, a modern market economy is an economy of honesty and trustworthiness. Debit and credit, buying and selling, currency and contracts are all credit relationships, depending on the ability of the players to take responsibility for the society. However, during the transitional period, the moral mansion, the core of which is integrity, begins to tremble. It implies the state of moral anarchy, to cite James M. Buchanan. In order to redress the anarchy, first of all, we need to rely on the government to strengthen the rule of law, making people pay for any fraud and antisocial behaviors to the full extent, rather than relying on the blind and discrete market forces. The reason is that the market failure cannot play the role of resolving the above issues. To this end, we should advocate and implement ideas of rule of law. That is, any behavior that is not forbidden by law is permitted; any behavior that is not authorized by law should be prohibited; any behavior that is required by law must be done, while all duties and functions assigned by law are performed by the government. The 'invisible hand' should be freed according to the law and the over-riding right of the allocation of resources should be given to market, so as to tap the creativity of market entities and give full play to all sources of social wealth. We should curb the 'visible hand' by law, standardize government behaviors, reduce market distortions led by excessive intervention, and minimize the leeway for possible abuse of power which harms public interests.

The key to striking a balance between the government, or the 'visible hand', and the market, or the 'invisible hand' is to have a good understanding of functions and limitations of the 'two hands'. The government should get involved in what it should regulate, and let the market do what it is supposed to do. If the 'visible hand', the government, has a preference for short-term races in economic expansion, it is hard to create a unified market and a leveled playing field; if the 'visible hand', or the government, undermines the pricing mechanism of resource products, then the basic signal or source information will be distorted, and an imbalanced industrial structure will also be inevitable. If the government cannot better perform its functions in the development of technology, and of the provision of talent resources, there will be little momentum for 'innovation', or the cost of innovation will be too high, which will become a bottleneck for China's innovation-driven development.

Therefore, the 'visible hand', the government, is an essential requirement to improve the modern market economy: First, to 'abolish' first and then to 'establish', which means that we should abolish market rules which are unfair and opaque, and then establish the negative list and the social credit system. Second, to 'delegate power' and 'strengthen regulation', which means that government should delegate powers in the pricing mechanism of resource products which should not be delegated or are poorly managed, and strengthen regulation where the market fails. Third, be 'clever' and 'flexible'. Being 'clever' means that we should have a clear understanding about the operating mechanism of the technology market and promote its development in a sound and rapid manner. Being 'flexible' means that we should do our best to pool all our resources of talent and let our people fully display their abilities. In the process of improving the market economy system, the transition to a 'strong' market economy requires the support of a 'strong' government, but the government should take advantage of its strength to master the timing of 'abolishing' and 'establishing' accurately, and take a resolute attitude towards 'delegating power' and 'strengthening regulation', and attach great importance to practical results of 'being clever and flexible'. If the 'visible hand' better performs its functions, it not only means that the 'invisible hand' can play a better role in the right direction, but the 'visible hand' can make greater progress in the transformation of government functions. We firmly believe that on the path of socialist market economy and with a sustainable and vigorous market and scientific and effective governance, we can certainly make China's transformation and upgrading of its economy a great success, and realize the brilliant Chinese dream.[1]

---

[1] Liu Wei. *Six Points of View on the Relationship between Government and Market*. China Times. June 5, 2014. Note: This article is out of the material collected by the China Times reporter, Shang Hao, derived from the speech by executive vice president of Peking University, professor Liu Wei, at the second session of the China Democratic National Construction "Urban Development Forum".

III. Structural Adjustment of the Economic New Normal

Carrying out economic restructuring and achieving the dynamic optimization of economic structure lays a foundation for a steadily growing economy and is essential to adapt to the 'new normal' of economic growth, while structural reform is extremely complex and critical. "**Making major headway in carrying out strategic adjustment of the economic structure is an irreversible and pressing task. International competition is always on time and speed. The country that acts fast can get a head start, gain advantage and initiative in terms of the competition; the country that acts slowly may lose chances and be left behind in the competition.**"[1] Just as Xi Jinping has stated, "The Chinese economy has entered a new stage of development. Its growth mode and structural readjustment are undergoing profound transformation. In this process, there will inevitably be one challenge after another. Efforts to meet these challenges will be accompanied by the throes of readjustments and other troubles in the development process, which will prove to be unavoidable. Rainbows mostly appear after wind and rain."[2] Thus we need to weigh the contents, the methods and subject of economic restructuring.

1. Adjusting economic structure will not be a smooth process, and there will inevitably be must be periods of turmoil. The practice of world economic development has proved that gross GDP in a country or a region is important, but what is more important, is the improvement of economic structure; the level of total factor productivity; and economic growth. Although it has achieved gross expansion, the Chinese economy has also accumulated obvious structural imbalances. It has moved into an accelerated period of structural adjustment, featuring a shift from imbalance of structure to improvement and rebalance of structure.

In terms of industrial structure, there is a degree of industrial overcapacity, mainly in processing and manufacturing industry, while service industry capacity is insufficient, manifested in inadequate medical services, school education and financing difficulty. This influences the improvement of living standards and enterprise operation. In terms of quality structure, the achievement assessment mechanism triggers competitive efforts to attract investments in different places, making the investment and export grow

---

[1] Xi Jinping Presided over a Forum on Economic Work in Guangdong Province. *People's Daily*, December 11, 2012.
[2] *Deepen Reform and Opening up and Work Together for a Better Asia Pacific*–President Xi Jinping's Speech at the APEC CEO Summit. Xinhuanet. October 8, 2013.

excessively, while the consumption ratio relatively declines. Considering regional structure, eastern coastal areas have grown rapidly, while some western areas lag behind. The 'urban maladies' in big cities, especially in megacities, are becoming more pronouced, while intrinsic character in middle-sized and small cities and small towns are relatively weak. Thus, in most cases improvement of economic structure is more important than overall economic activity.

On the issue of the economic development, we need to weigh the relationship between speed, gross economic activity and structure, and handle the relationship between quantity, quality and efficiency: all while applying dialectical scrutiny. Xi Jinping points out that: "The greatness in quantity is not equal to the strength in its quality; on the contrary, it may be an illusion of insubstantiality."[1] If we one-sidedly and simplistically regard increased production volume as the growth of our economy, or even "measure development solely by the GDP growth rate" and only pay attention to 'volume' and 'strength' of GDP rather than quality and efficiency, regardless of the cost in environmental resources, and violation of economic law and natural law, the result will not only be a 'bloated economy', but will also aggravate existing conflicts and bring about numerous risks.

For example, during the Opium War in 1840, the GDP of China was ahead of that of UK. But with an imbalanced economic structure, the products that made up China's GDP were mainly agricultural products and handicrafts. Cotton cloth was hand-loomed. Products for exports were tea, porcelain, silk, Tung oil and so on. Prior to 1840, the UK had been experiencing the Industrial Revolution for seventy years, since 1770, and had made progress in industrialization. Its GDP structure, with a high output of steel and iron and advanced equipment manufacturing technologies, moved in step with the development of science and technology. All the UK's cotton cloth was mechanically woven textile; this accounted for a proportion of the UK's export while other products for export were steam engine machinery. Their vehicles for transportation were steam ships and trains.

Although the GDP of China ranks the second in the world now, there still exist many problems in its economic structure. Compared with some developed countries, China's high technology products have accounted for a smaller proportion of GDP and have been on the low end of the value chain

---

[1] *A Series of Important Speeches by General Secretary Xi Jinping.* Beijing: Xuexi Publishing House. 2014.

globally. The industrial structure between secondary industry and service industry is irrational. Also, further adjustments are required in income distribution, and in the structure of urban, rural and regional development. In that respect, the priority and difficulty of our country's reform lie in structural adjustments.

As is known to all, every financial crisis brings a period of economic restructuring, and also a process for dynamic rebalancing, transforming and upgrading. Likewise, the economic transformation of any country will be accompanied by the disruptions of readjustment, and other troubles. Economic transformation cannot always run smoothly, for it is not an easy job to adjust structure and transform the growth model to realize an innovation-driven economy. To achieve all these, we still have a long arduous journey ahead during which it is inevitable we will experience 'throes' and 'twists and turns'.

At present, China's economic restructuring is based on the requirements of economic opening, technology development, and increase of total factor productivity, and is against the backdrop of an imbalanced economic structure. It is obvious that structural adjustment and optimization depend on investing in factor resources. In particular, the industrialization of capital accumulation is unsustainable in the long term, therefore sustainable and effective development can only be achieved by technology improvement, innovation in institutions and economic models and boosting the efficiency of institutions, technology and distribution of resources.

The strategy of sustainable development is not only to achieve the goals of technology-driven development, low resources consumption, less environmental pollution, and making full use of human resources, but also to realize the optimization of factor allocation efficiency. Such optimization, instead of simply shifting from a labor and capital factor-driven approach to one driven by innovation requires making full use of the market mechanism, especially to deepen the market system. Our government must transform to provide prerequisites for it, so as to provide institutional arrangements for realizing scientific and technological innovation-driven and intelligence-driven transformation, and massive entrepreneurship and innovation. Practice has proven that cultivation of a factor market is necessary in the factor driving model or it will certainly lead to factor price distortion.

No modernized country can realize industrialization without opening to the outside world. Resource factors should be allocated in a unified and open market, which indicates that economic opening-up is the basis of new industrialization. Opening can be a powerful tool to obtain new knowledge, conduct institutional innovations and improve technology. But it depends on various gaps in a country or enterprises within a certain business, especially the gap between demand and supply of skilled labor, technological absorptive capacity and payment of factors. It is imperative to specify the adjustment achieved by market prices or market mechanism: and that achieved by government institutional reform or exerting government functions, to overcome institutional inertia to restructuring.

For example, under a market economy, the market can address the problem of over-capacity, while the government must make efforts to promote energy saving and emission reduction to build a beautiful China. The problems of severe overcapacity, imbalance of enterprise competitiveness and industrial structure are the results of inadequate system and mechanism reform. The resolution to these complex problems depends on the innovation of efficiency-oriented marketing, and these problems can only be solved by pursuing efficiency-oriented innovation in the market institution and by shifting towards substantial market reform.

The problem of unbalanced income distribution cannot be addressed by relying solely on the market, for certain regulations and adjustments from the government are also necessary. The market's malfunction in these areas requires the government to exercise its fiscal policy, currency and tax policies to the fullest. In this process the government conducts the first distribution as the basis, the second distribution as a supplement and the arrangements of the other policies as improvements. The government, to better play its role in solving problems, should focus on coordinating government revenue, enterprises income and public income, including the problem of the high Gini coefficient among different strata and the widening gap between the rich and the poor, which will lead to social hierarchical system solidification.

2. The key to structural adjustment is to solve the problem of structural imbalance. Structural imbalance in China manifests itself mainly in two aspects, one of which is the imbalance among investment, consumption and exports structure. The economic structure of a country will be seriously unbalanced when the country overly relies on a certain driving force for its economic development. For example, China's economic development has long been over-reliant on exports and government investments, making it impossible for residents' consumption to play its part in the driving force to stimulate economic growth, which results in imbalanced industrial structure. The accumulated problems due to imbalanced structure have become increasingly difficult to solve as the economic scale enters middle income stage with returns to scale decreasing progressively. This also results in path dependence on increasing mechanism and interest distribution, that is, the coordinated development of structure is based on the original mechanism. Therefore the real problem of restructuring lies in how to find a growth mechanism derived from the imbalanced increase of structure to enable it in the context of a coordinated increase of structure. The criterion for this possibility is the motivation of prioritizing efficiency, and sustainable development. Through rectification of imbalanced structural mechanism, we can give full play to the fundamental role of consumption on growth, the important impetus function of investment on growth, and the supporting role of exports on growth. The other is the imbalance between the real economy and virtual economy. The imbalance in the current economic structure lies not only in industry but also in the spatial structure and even in the severe imbalance in development between the real economy and virtual economy, which means that 'the real economy has not been featured with purely 'real' and the virtual economy is overly inflated'. The problems of the real economy are mainly seen in three aspects. Firstly, instead of engaging in industry, many enterprises are attracted by the high profits of 'bubble territory'. Secondly, there is poor innovation ability in enterprises. Some so-called strategic emerging industries are actually carrying on traditional industry in the name of hi-tech industry. Thirdly, productivity and added value are low. Many entity enterprises are in loss as a result of being unable to absorb the pressure from increasing production factor costs.

The problems of an overly inflated virtual economy normally manifest themselves in four aspects. Firstly, real interest rates are high. The increasing interest rate and labor cost have made the real interest rates exceed the limitations of the real economy. It is a general issue that entity enterprises find it difficult and costly to obtain financing. Secondly, the exchange rate is high. The RMB exchange rate has continued to rise significantly and consequently, this has led export enterprises to suffer losses and even go bankrupt. Thirdly, the asset price is high. For a long time, asset prices, with real estate as the principal part, have increasingly pulled up the level of M2 and interest rate, curbing public consumption and restraining the strategy to expand domestic demand. Fourthly, the rate of debt is high. The debt of local governments and enterprises is in large scale and at high level. In terms of the structure, it mainly contains inverse yield curve public infrastructure projects and debt collateral which are mainly land assets with artificial high prices. The last challenge is to achieve the coordinated development of industrialization and urbanization.

Viewed from the perspective of economics, industrialization provides supply and urbanization influences mostly demands. Thus, they should develop in a coordinated way. The accelerated promotion of industrialization and urbanization drives high speed development of the Chinese economy. However, the advance of rapid industrialization and urbanization cannot be ignored in economic structural adjustment. The key to this problem is to take an efficient approach to industrialization or a new type of industrialization.

Also, in an economic catch-up period, urbanization can be the driving force as well as the major cause of structural imbalance. Urbanization is not only the growth mechanism derived from the 'unbalanced structural growth', but also a new route in the 'coordinated structural growth', with the prerequisite to adopt the efficient urbanization strategy.

Practice has constantly proved that the speed of dynamic balance of economy is dependent on that of structural adjustment. A fast structural adjustment means a rapid economic recovery. For example, the economy soon recovered after the 2008 financial crisis by a series of effective measures. They are; the debt reduction through the bankruptcy of the Lehman Corp; the reemergence of innovative enterprises represented by California; continuous innovative ability; and a sharp decline of exploitation cost of new shale gas in the traditional energy industry represented by Texas. The delayed structural adjustment in the EU made it hard to eliminate debt and, due to its slow structural adjustment, its economic recovery was slow. With its economy in a critical and difficult period, China takes enterprises as the principal part in its structural adjustment, and at the same time, makes the market play its decisive role and government better play its due role. Industrial structure is the result of the balance of market supply and demand. We should change the government's previous regulatory policy and the industrial support system of 'penalty kick' policy, since some unfair industrial support policies in most cases are the sources of enterprises' rent-seeking from the government.

A saying has it that, 'A watched flower never blooms, but an untended willow grows'. In practice, some industries, like photovoltaic, did not gain what they had expected, and it did not take long for them to turn from an emerging sector to an overcapacity one. By contrast some other industries, such as internet enterprises including Alibaba, Tencent, Baidu, and Jingdong, have made unexpected gains and rapid development.

3. The key of industrial structure is stock adjustment, increase of quantity and upgrade of quality. The impetus of traditional industry has been weak and emerging industries' impetus still lags behind, which resulted in a temporary shortage. The reason is largely related to the slowness of industrial structural adjustment. From the perspective of industrial structure, the capacity of traditional sectors has significantly surpassed demand and products prices have continued to decline. It is becoming tougher for some enterprises to operate. They are unwilling or even unable to invest. Consequently, it is imperative to solve the problem of overcapacity, merger and reorganization of enterprises.

Meanwhile, a new generation of information technology accelerates its integration with traditional industries. New technology, new products, new types of business, and new models emerged continuously. Features including intelligentization, digitization and servitization are becoming increasingly distinct. The route to structural adjustment is to expedite the transformation and upgrading of traditional industry and accelerate the development of emerging industry.

The new global industrial revolution provides a great opportunity for China's industrial transformation, technology promotion and upgrade of structure. In terms of scale, China's manufacturing has surpassed Japan, ranking the second in the world. However, from the perspective of economic structure, the proportion of advanced manufacturing, especially service-oriented manufacture, is still small. Trapped in the plight that our manufacturing is big in scale but not strong, we still have a long way to go before we achieve the dream of 'a great power of manufacture'.

In considering how to realize the structural adjustment, the main choices are: first, we will work to upgrade manufacturing, absorb overcapacity and encourage business acquisitions and reorganizations. With reference to the Belt and Road Initiative, we will intensify efforts to open even wider, and conduct industrial output. We will implement the 'Made in China 2025' plan and focus on ten critical fields, most of which are in strategic economic industry and advanced manufacturing industry. We should accelerate formulation of the '2025 Special Program' for each industry. Other basic sectors concerning national economy and the people's livelihood cannot be neglected, like steel and iron, petrochemical industry, nonferrous metal, building material, textile industry, light industry, food and so on, for these traditional industries need transforming and upgrading by advanced technology.

As is stated in the 'Made in China 2025' plan, intelligent manufacturing and research and development in digital design will increase to 84% by 2025. We will lift the efficiency and quality of R & D design by further promoting the information tools of analog simulation, 3D description, HD operation and big data. Efforts should be made to integrate electronic information technology into products and improve the quality, function and additional value of the product and to raise the quality and self sufficiency in particular of key components, components and parts, critical materials, so that OEM assembly will be transformed into self manufacturing. We should implement numerical control of manufacturing equipment and generalize high-grade CNC machine tool, intelligent industrial robot, 3D printing, production manufacturing and so on.

The second focus is to promote the development of service oriented manufacturing industry. Along with the deepening of the trends of information, network and intelligence, and the growing intensity of globalization, the division of labor in manufacturing has gradually been refined, cross-regional industrial convergence constantly been upgraded, and enterprises' integration of manufacture and service are on the rise. The general trend of global manufacturing is transforming from production-oriented to service-oriented manufacturing industry.

Service-oriented manufacturing industry, which is the key to breakthroughs in the low-end of the industrial chain stagnation as well as to securing competitive advantages, indicates the development direction of global manufacturing and new industrial revolution. At a macro level, it refers to the formation of service-oriented economy; at an intermediate level, it shows the transformation from manufacturing city to service-oriented city; at a micro level, it manifests the transformation from production-oriented enterprises into service-oriented enterprises. As is shown in *the Research Based on Global Service and Parts Management* from Deloitte, among the eighty manufacturing enterprises investigated, service income accounted for more than 25% of the average revenue; the service income of 19% manufacturing enterprises is more than 50% of their total revenue.

Also shown in *Research Based on Global Service and Parts Management* from Deloitte is that the level of service-oriented manufacturing industry in developed countries is clearly higher than that of countries in the process of industrialization. In the US, the number of manufacturing and service integrated enterprises accounts for 58% of the total manufacturing enterprises, with 51% in Finland, 40% in Netherlands, and 37% in Belgium; China's proportion of service-oriented manufacturing industry is relatively backward, and the number of enterprises that have realized service-oriented manufacturing accounts for only 2.2% of all the enterprises.

One method is to expand productive service industry by relying on manufacturing. For example, GE applies services to their daily operation management, and develops a modern service industry with high profits and with broad prospects including business finance, consumer finance, and information technology, by relying on manufacturing. GE Corp produces medical devices and at the same time provides services concerning finance and lease of medical device. Consequently, their business chain is extended and its competitiveness is improved accordingly. GE Corp has been the world's largest multi-service company and also the provider for high quality, hi-tech industry and consumer products.

Second, enterprises should become the providers of service and a set of solutions from the seller of manufactured goods. A typical example is IBM. The company can provide customers with a whole set of solutions in hardware, software, finance and services, by realizing the combination from hardware to software, finance and services to enhance its capability to satisfy customers' needs.

Third, enterprises should be transformed from manufacturers into service providers. For example, Li & Fung Group, which has neither factory nor manufacturing equipment, cooperates with about 7,500 suppliers from more than 40 countries. Once it gets its order, the company conducts industrial chain management and outsources every phase to the best manufacturer. For example, in making a dress, the lining may be produced in China's Taiwan Province but the zipper may be produced in Thailand, and the dress may be assembled in mainland China. In this way, the number of actual workers behind the 10 thousand Li & Fung Group staff reaches more than 1.5 million. At present, the business of Li & Fung Group reaches almost every corner of the world and the company cooperates with more than 300 multinational firms.

The no-border and virtual production mode not only guarantees the quality of the products, but controls the cost to the lowest level. In today's world, all the outstanding manufacturing enterprises are service oriented enterprises. The manufacturing service is the new source for increasing enterprise revenue, and the realization of product innovation is an ongoing process.

Third, develop the 'Internet Plus' action plan. China is at the crucial stage of industrialization and the Internet can be superimposed on any industry. In 'Internet Plus', new generation of information technology and platforms is used to advance the optimization of related industries; industrial development is planned and designed with a mindset oriented to the internet. As enterprises are the key actors in the Internet Plus, they should treat the internet with an open mind and increase their efforts to fulfill the goal of self transformation.

Internet Plus should be the combination of cyber-economy and real economy, and also the combination of Internet enterprises and real economy enterprises. The socialized, digitalized-networking industrial service requires the use of industrial networks to develop modern intelligent logistics and electronic commerce so as to greatly reduce manufacturing costs and conduct full life-cycle services. In this way, consumers can enjoy a hassle-free service and further stimulate consumption. Remote monitoring and online maintenance ensure long term and smooth operation. The socialized, digitalized-networking manufacturing supply chain and sales will adapt themselves to changes of new manufacturing mode to ensure rapid development of a productive service industry.

4. Rationalize the income distribution mechanism, and improve the income distribution structure. With certain amount of national income, the first distribution of national income is about how to coordinate the distribution relationship between the state and individuals, and substantially, how to deal with a rational proportion of accumulation to consumption. Government should play its role of regulation to the fullest to adjust citizen income distribution. The main factors that limited the expansion of urban-rural residents' demand for consumption are: first, the increase of disposable income of urban-rural residents lags behind overall economic growth with residents' income accounting for a low proportion of national income. Second, establishment of security systems is underdeveloped. Residents have a strong precautionary motivation and a lower marginal propensity to consume due to the inadequate basic public service provided by the government. Third, there is an apparent disparity of people's income distribution. The marginal propensity of consumption of high income groups decreases progressively, while the lower income groups are unable to increase their consumption, thus leading to a relative stagnation of the growth of the consuming volume.

In order to truly broaden the consuming demand of the citizens, we need to focus greater efforts on the strategy of fundamental solutions on the basis of providing temporary solutions, at the same time as implementing a series of effective consumption stimulus policies. We need to formulate and improve the institutional assurance base for the sustained consuming demand as follows: we will gradually increase the share of personal income in the distribution of national income, properly adjust the relation of national distribution, increase the share of resident's income and decrease the proportion of government's income, so as to enlarge consuming by increasing resident's income. We need to accelerate the progress of building a social security system, and advance the equalization of basic public services.

We will improve our social security system, and broaden its coverage and gradually promote the standard of social security. We will combine the reform of financial and taxation system with the transformation of government functions, pursue greater spending in fiscal on public services and goods, and dispel any further misgivings of the masses after expanding consuming. We will gradually narrow the income gap among our social members.

By adopting an economic means of tax revenue and transfer payment, we will adjust the income distribution structure among different stratums and regions, and between urban and rural areas. We will increase the income of medium-to-low earners who account the majority of the entire population, strengthen our assistance to those disadvantaged groups, and progressively expand the magnitude of middle-income class. At the same time, industrialization creates supply and urbanization generates demand. Therefore, we should pay special attention to the progress of growth in consumption demand through advancing the progress of urbanization, in a moderate way. We will accelerate reforms in the census register, finance, lands and social security systems, so as to promote the citizenization of rural migrant workers living and working in cities - especially in medium and small cities. We want, by allowing the rural migrant workers, who contribute greatly in the national modernization, to live and work in peace and contentment, to enable them to create a huge industrial capacity and at the same time to promote the sustained growth of effective demand.

Apart from the above, the government needs to adjust financial resources toward the economically less developed areas or poor areas through fiscal transfer payments, so as to change the situation of imbalances in regional development and strengthen the development capacity in less developed areas or poor areas. Not only should we pay attention to the initial distribution of national income, but also to its redistribution. The first distribution of national income needs to maintain the optimization of the income distribution structure of the state, enterprises and social consumption. The redistribution of national income should adjust the structure of national income distribution and remove the inappropriate part of the distribution structure through the redistribution of government finance to national income. Aimed both to protect low income and limit excessive income, we will adjust the residents' income distribution structure, and alleviate unfair social distribution. We will protect the income of low-income earners and the interests of disadvantaged groups, and raise taxes on high income earners. The focal point of these adjustments is to increase the income of the low-income earners so as to remit the unfairness in social distribution and narrow the gap between the rich and the poor. We should put equal emphasis on the fairness of residents' income distribution and on the equality of opportunities for individual development.

IV. Effective Implementation of the Innovation-driven Strategy

The new normal is the innovation-driven economy. The growth rate slows down, while the intelligent production, innovative manufacture, factor productivity and growth quality speed up. We should accelerate the transition from factor-driven and investment-driven growth to innovation-driven growth. The Fifth Plenary Session of the 18th CPC Central Committee stressed that China should highlight and implement the concepts of innovative development, coordinated development, green development, open development and shared development, and place innovation ahead of all other development concepts, in order to fulfill the goals of the 13th Five-Year Plan period, overcoming obstacles and sharpening its edge in development. Innovation-driven growth will be a key driving factor for the strategic restructuring of the economy. It will also be a basic support and key force in the overall plan for promoting all-round economic, political, cultural, social, and ecological progress. "We should stick to the innovation-driven development, centering on scientific and technological innovation, removing institutional obstacles as focal points and piloting reform in a systemic, integrated and coordinated way. While we should also promote coordinated innovation in science and technology, management, brand, industrial structure and model, speed up forming a new engine of our economic society to strongly support the construction of an innovation-oriented country."[1]

1. The new normal is the economy driven by innovation. The previous external and extensive development model is not sustainable, as it is driven by factors and investment. We need to transform the mode from excessive dependence on factor increase to deepening reform, promoting market expansion, market deepening and system innovation, so that it can yield system-wide dividends. Innovative capability and system arrangement must be put at the centre of the new normal in order to promote endogenous growth. Outwardly, the new normal is the change of pace in economic growth. Essentially, it is the transformation of the driving force of economic growth which will lead to industrial restructuring. Seen from the aspect of driving force for development, the constant rise of production costs, increasingly scarce resources as well as environment restraint and the weakened driving force of factors, determine that we should depend more on human capital quality as well as technological progress, and improve innovative ability. We should create a new economic growth point through an innovative drive to stimulate consumer demands.

Innovation-driven growth generates new competitive advantages and brings about a new driving force. Hence, we need to foster a new development driving force and speed up its pace of transformation. We should optimize factors such as workforce, capital, land, technology, and management. Firstly, we should stimulate the vitality of innovation and entrepreneurship, promote the massive entrepreneurship and innovation by all, and release new demand. Adam Smith believed the driving force of economic growth in human society is dependent on the improvement of labor productivity and market deepening, as well as the extension brought about by specialization of labor and profession. Specialization of labor improves the labor productivity, and thus promotes economic growth. Specialization and capital allocation, which contribute much to the improvement of labor productivity, will be naturally initiated and effectively achieved under the function of market forces. The government's mission is to maintain a stable legal system and market order, and provide institutional guarantees for economic growth. 'The father of GNP' - Kuznets - holds that economic growth mainly depends on the increase

---

[1] When presiding over the 12th leading group session of the Central Committee of the CPC on Comprehensively Deepening the Reform, Xi Jinping stressed that we need to grasp, serve and submit to the whole situation of reform, so that we can jointly improve the comprehensive deepening of reform. www.people.com.cn May 6, 2015.

of such factors as population, resources, and the transformation of economic structure from agricultural production in the leading role, to manufacturing industry playing the key role.

In his 'Diamond Model', Michael Porter, the founder of country competitiveness, analyzes the reason why a certain industry in one country will show strong international competitiveness. He points out that the difference between competitiveness of countries and regions lies in the divergence of superior factors of production, such as modern communication, information and highly educated human resources, and research. The reform of the market economy should attend to superior factors of production related to innovation activities, including competent personnel, technology, finance, education and brands. They need to be expanded and deepened in the market. To acquire persistent competitiveness, we must make industries that are based on primary factors of production, rise to superior factors of production and speed up their marketization. If we can make a breakthrough in this field, we can promote the substantial progress of innovation-driven growth and enable the shift of our growth mode. The creation and destruction is mainly achieved by competition of innovation rather than the competition of price. A high level of innovation will displace old technology but establish new production systems.

The new normal indicates that the growth model is shifting gear from a widespread model that emphasizes scale and speed, to a more intensive one emphasizing quality and efficiency, and from being driven by investment in production factors to being driven by innovation, which forms the basic logic of economic development. In this context, innovation-driven strategy becomes the inexhaustible impetus for industrial upgrading. Enterprise is not only the market entity, but also the innovation entity. The government should support innovative, as well as vital small and medium sized enterprises, and promote the upgrading of traditional industries; and form a new source of economic growth and industrial driving force under the new normal of economy - as soon as possible.

We should foster and develop strategic emerging industries, contrive an innovation chain serving the needs of strategic emerging industries, remove technological bottlenecks and secure key technology, so as to speed up the research, development and application of new technologies, products and production processes, strengthen innovation in integration of technologies and develop new business models; advanced technology should be applied to improve traditional industries. In key industries, we need to build a platform for technological innovation. We should speed up the transformation and application of scientific and technological achievements and improve innovation as well as the development ability of traditional industries; we need to emphasize the centrality of enterprises' technological innovation. We should establish a system of technological innovation in which enterprises play the leading role, the market directs the way, and enterprises, universities and research institutes work together. Innovative systems and mechanisms should be built to make enterprises lead the research of industrial technology. We should facilitate innovative factors such as technology and supply of competent personnel to R&D institutions of enterprises, and foster innovative enterprises.

We should implement an innovation-driven strategy and take steps to promote innovation to catch up with global advances. We should increase our capacity to make original innovations and to integrate innovation; and to make further innovation on the basis of absorbing fruits of overseas scientific and technological advances, and place greater emphasis on making innovation through collaboration. We need to carry out the transformation of scientific and technological findings and promote the integration of science and technology, as well as finance. We should strengthen the creation, utilization, protection and management of intellectual property rights, and intensify legal protection of innovation activities as well as achievements of science and technology so that it can ensure the realization of innovation in science and technology; we should establish sound norms for scientific research and strengthen education on scientific research integrity and scientific ethics. We need to build a relaxing and positive atmosphere and create an environment of innovation; we should speed up the construction of a national innovation system that is led by enterprises and guided by the market and that combines the efforts of enterprises, universities and research institutes. We should build a road towards endogenous growth driven by innovation and form a new pattern of innovation by the people and innovation by all.

To implement innovation, we need to create new supply and promote the rapid development of new technologies, industries, and formats of business. Based on innovation, we must develop mechanisms to promote innovation, drive more pioneering development on innovation and bring the first-mover advantages into full play. We need to foster new foreign economic advantages with technology, standard, brand, quality and service as the core. We should improve the added value and technology of labor-intensive products, create new advantages of capital intensive industries and technology intensive industries, and improve the status of China's industries in the global value chain.

In reality, innovation-driven strategy is essentially driven by talent. We should give full play to science and technology as the primary productive force and competent personnel as the primary resource, remove institutional barriers that impede the development of an innovation-driven strategy, and establish an favorable policy environment, as well as institutions which are most conducive to the optimization of innovation. We should realize the goal proposed by General Secretary Xi Jinping, "To carry out the innovation-driven strategy, the basic thing for us is to enhance our self-initiated innovation ability and the most urgent thing in this regard is to remove institutional barriers so as to unleash to the greater extent the huge potential of science and technology as the primary productive force."[1]

We need to deepen structural and institutional reforms, make breakthroughs in aspects such as government administration, taxation, finance, competent personnel, education, and equity incentive, and provide institutional innovation for innovation-driven development. For instance, we can deregulate market access for emerging industries and develop the system for innovative competent personnel and the corresponding educational system. We can implement a tax system of angel investment, promote innovation by commercial banks and financial services and create an equity intensive system for innovation by state-owned enterprises and public institutions. In this way, we can further promote massive entrepreneurship and innovation by all, build new driving forces and create strong new engines of China's economy. And we can create ecological innovation as well as entrepreneurship and form an innovative economy based on creation, circulation and application of knowledge.

2. The key lies in the innovation of institutional mechanisms

The Fifth Plenary Session of the 18th CPC Central Committee proposed that, "In pursuing innovative development, innovation should be placed at the heart of China's development and promoted it in every field, from theory

---

[1] Transition to Innovation-driven Growth (June 9, 2014). *The Governance of China*, Eng. ed. Foreign Languages Press. Oct 2014. p.133-134.
  Note: This is the speech delivered by President Xi Jinping at the 17th General Assembly of the Members of the Chinese Academy of Sciences and the 12th General Assembly of the Members of the Chinese Academy of Engineering on June 10, 2014.

to institutions, science, technology, and culture. Innovation should permeate all work of the party and the country and become an inherent part of the society."[1] The present mechanism of government administration fails to meet the needs of innovation-driven development. It basically behaves in the following aspects: firstly, the ability of government to make and implement innovative policy needs to be improved. For instance, there are more 'penalty kick' policies promoting innovation, but fewer inclusive policies; there are more policies on the supply side, but fewer policies on the demand side; there are more direct subsidy policies, but fewer policies on society leading. The coordination of policies by government is inadequate. Secondly, the government still adopts a traditional mode of thinking in evaluating innovative activities via GDP, in its assessment of government and economic activities. The innovative and personnel value cannot be reflected by reform in science and technology through factor value. And the country cannot strive for success simultaneously from the aspects of economic development as well as social development. Thirdly, there are some problems in market mechanisms for transforming scientific and technological achievements. For instance, knowledge needs to be updated, management system of intangible assets should be improved, the institutions for finding, transforming, assessing, and benefit-allocating of scientific and technological achievements in market have not been soundly established, so improvement is required. Fourthly, society lacks an environment that is tolerant of inclusive and open entrepreneurship and innovation. The whole society is in want of an atmosphere respecting innovation and tolerating failures, and an environment encouraging innovation and the service system of entrepreneurship and innovation. For instance, there are few professional service institutions and competent personnel, insufficient openness as well as coordination among universities, scientific research institutions and enterprises and inadequate flow of innovative factors. Fifthly, services around social innovation need to be improved. For instance, public resources of the government are scattered, lacking a top-level design and overall planning. There are some problems in the scientific research investment and quitting mechanism especially around enterprises. Small and medium sized enterprises and young startups are underfunded by social capital. All these factors have a negative impact on the innovative mechanism and the vitality of enterprises and personnel.

  Douglass Cecil North regards systemic factors as the source of economic

---

[1] Central Committee of the CPC: Recommendations for the 13th Five-Year Plan for Economic and Social Development. Xinhuanet. November 3, 2015.

growth, so he links economic growth with system changes. He believes that we should study the incentive structure behind the new growth that derived from systems and drives up economic growth. This incentive structure can reduce transaction costs so as to promote the property rights behind economic growth, including the innovation in the state system, government management methods, and the incentive mechanism of property rights, as well as enterprise organization. How should we deepen the market mechanism and establish the market culture of contracts, integrity and equality? How to strengthen the protection of intellectual property rights and encourage innovation and promote the capitalization of capital in rural areas and marketization of interest rate; how to take advanced technology from laboratories and apply them to the production line? How can the whole market system, which includes financing, scientific research, manufacturing and consumption, operate in light of a modern economic model? Furthermore, there are obstacles between capital and technology, technology and industries, industries and market, and domestic resources and foreign resources. And only through changes in the system can we remove these obstacles.

The practice of innovation-driven development indicates that innovative activities should conform to not only the law of scientific and technological activities but also to the internal requirements of the market economy, given the fact that enterprises take the lead in self-initiated innovation. We should enhance intellectual property protection to ensure the rights of innovators; we should create an open innovative environment to encourage innovation and entrepreneurship. Through institutional innovation, we can guarantee innovation in technology as well as the operating model of enterprises. Sustainable innovation needs help from sustainable innovation of enterprises, so innovation of technology, organization and the commercial model needs to be integrated, to ensure the launch of technological innovative activities with innovative achievements by system and organizations.

In reality, it is the mechanism or policy barrier rather than technology that hinders the sustainable development of the economy. Therefore, to enhance our self-initiated innovation capacity, the most urgent thing in this regard is to remove institutional barriers so as to unleash to the greatest extent the huge potential of science and technology as the primary productive force. Compared to the advantages of low costs, technological innovation has high added value and is not easily imitated, which results in its long-lasting and strongly competitive innovative advantages. We should achieve the organic unity and coordinated development of scientific and technological innovation, institutional innovation and open innovation. We should seek speed, sustainability as well as efficiency from scientific and technological innovation and focus more on quality and efficiency, so as to improve core competitiveness of all enterprises.

3. The method and model of innovation-driven strategy. Seen from the perspective of global emerging industries and their development of new models as well as new conditions, and as part of the wave of emerging new productive forces, the essential driving forces are technology, market and institution. The first factor is technology-driven strategy. It means that, with unprecedented new products and services, enterprises can create new requirements as well as market space, that is, using provision to create requirement. For example, after the birth of 3D printing technology, a start-up named Shapeways created '3D cloud printing mode' in 2007. After users upload a product design (or buy 3D design on the company's website), choose raw material and pay for it, Shapeways can print the finished product. Users can also exhibit and sell products online, and the website charges 3.5% of the profit as commission. The second factor is market-driven strategy. With new commercial models, enterprises can meet market requirements and conform to market competition through much lower costs, more convenient service and rapid response. For instance, in 2014, with (US)$568 million, Alibaba merged Sina Weibo and acquired 18% of its shares, and a new model of 'social network + commerce + third-party payment' is being developed. The third factor is system-driven strategy. It changes the relationship of interests among market entities through systematic adjustment or creation to provide huge development space for new models or new conditions of emerging industries. For example, the trade system of international carbon emissions gives rise to the global carbon trade market with a value of €140bn, and promotes the rapid development of new models and new conditions related to carbon trade, carbon finance, carbon audit and carbon intermediaries.

To establish an innovation-driven model, we need to do the following things: firstly, workforce factors and capital factors need to be upgraded. We should deepen the reform of higher education. Universities should integrate elite education with innovation, as well as with entrepreneurship education in an effort to build talents that include excellent insights and skills. Universities should improve the system of vocational skills training and cultivate many high standard skillful workers who can adapt to industrial upgrades and the development of emerging industries. We need to improve the multi-level capital market, promote the role of the capital market in capital flow, and support innovation as well as spread risk and optimize the configuration of labor elements as well as the element of capital. We should enhance the protection of intellectual property rights, protect the legitimate rights of innovators and improve the added value of intellectual property rights. We need to promote the reform of governmental management systems and establish a public service system which is conducive to innovation;

Secondly, we should promote the implementation of innovation-driven strategy in light of the industrial upgrading target to ensure the industrial chain leads the innovation chain and the innovation chain supports the industrial chain. We should remove institutional barriers impeding optimal configuration and integration, as well any that impede the interaction of industrial chain and innovation chain, to achieve innovative resource sharing. We should establish a mechanism in which industries as well as innovation elements are rationally distributed and optimally allocated upstream as well as downstream and all linkages can interact organically. Through the promotion of industrial innovation, we can create a sound industrial ecosystem and build an innovative service platform to promote the gathering as well as sharing of knowledge elements and innovation elements such as capital, talented personnel, scientific research, information, internet and data.

Thirdly, move forward in a coordinated way and concentrate on the key and common technology in the development in the industrial field. Targeting key industrial fields, through fiscal policies, tax revenue, finance and other methods, we should integrate the R&D system of kernel and common technology formed by existing scientific research institutions and enterprises and reform its management system and performance appraisal mechanism, so as to give full play to the advantages in research and development of those key and common technologies.

4. A sound ecological innovative environment is the basis of innovation. Innovation requires a suitable environment. The ecological environment is the key element to the cultivation of innovative entrepreneurs. Freedom, protection of property rights, rules of law and culture are of great importance to innovation. Innovation requires free thinking and protection by law. In the absence of strong protection of property rights and sound rules of law, there will still be arbitrage entrepreneurs, but the outcome of developing innovative ones is impossible.

Innovation needs freedom. It is impossible that you can innovate unless you take risks for your thought. Real innovation requires the strong protection of patent, or the motive power of innovation will be exhausted. A thorough analysis shows that all kinds of innovations are relative to opportunities and are an integral whole composed of research, trials, mistakes and repetitions. They are full of odd coincidences. Everyone can innovate. However, only a small group of people can achieve success and the probability is low. It lies in not only the innovative capacity of a person or a team, but also the innovative ecological environment. For example, what kind of resources can you use? What kind of personnel can you communicate with? Can you find relative resources and opportunities in every step you take when you innovate? Can other people give you enough feedback?

If we compare innovators to frogs, the innovative environment to a pond and success to reaching the other side of the pond: then, all kinds of exterior elements can be compared to the lotus leaves. When the frogs want to reach the other side of the pond, they must draw support from these lotus leaves. However, they never know what they will encounter when they jump on a particular lotus leaf, and they have no idea about what leaves may lie ahead. The only thing that is certain is that the closer and the shorter the distance between lotus leaves, the more likely they are to arrive at the other side of the pond. Given a constant degree of innovative capacity, the one who can draw more support from external elements has the greater possibility to succeed.

The creation of an innovative ecological environment calls for an innovative governance system. We should achieve innovation in government regulation, and the commercial environment as well as in innovation policy and focus on a 4-T environment which is relevant to an innovation-driven development, namely Tax, Trade, Technology and Talent. The reason for this is that technological innovation is about openness, freedom, persistent research and market competition rather than regulation. The top priority for the government is deregulation. As for the service function that can be achieved by the market mechanism or replaced by social institutions, the government should practice transformation and provide room for development as well as necessary support. The second thing the government should do is to refrain from intervention. As for the innovative activities that are guided by the market, the government should minimize its intervention on the choice of detailed program and enterprise innovation.

The third thing government should do is to move forward. The government should further strengthen coordination on different aspects and planning at the top level and focus on strategies, key points, the frontier and the foundation. The government should strengthen the innovation policy design, and change the arrangement of innovative policies on the supply side for its marginal utility is obviously diminishing. So it needs to implement a systematic plan and move forward in a coordinated way at a higher level. Speaking of innovative policy, the government should focus more on inclusive policy. Giving more is inferior to taking less. For example, we should implement the three inclusive policies, namely policies for weighted deduction of research and development expenses, recognition of hi-tech enterprises and advanced technology service enterprises; the innovative system aspeccts of government should have specific, stable definition, to ensure that there be rules for the elements of administration to follow. For example, every four to five years, the European Union will adjust the emission standard of automobiles and promote it throughout Europe and the public is informed five years ahead of schedule. All these measures force the auto industry to upgrade its technology.

Technological innovation is of utmost urgency and requires consistent efforts of the government. The government and society should keep the organic balance of overt achievements and covert achievements, translate the development model into sustainable development and allocate elements in response to innovation-driven development. The government should put more emphasis on the utilization of elements such as technology and regard technological innovation as the key benchmark of regions, industries and enterprises. To implement the innovation-driven strategy, we should respect technological innovation and the rule of industrialization of technological achievements, and establish an open, unified, fair and competitive market environment. We should establish a sound service system of scientific and technological innovation and industrial development, and a functional platform which supports innovation. We should build innovation parks with distinctive themes and platforms and build an innovative culture as well as the social environment that encourages innovation while tolerating well-intentioned failures. Furthermore, through institutional innovation, we should provide guarantees for innovation in enterprises' technology as well as their operating model, encourage more people to innovate and start up businesses, and create an open environment for innovation and entrepreneurship.

We should establish an low-cost, convenient, total-factor and open entrepreneur services organization through market-oriented mechanism, specialized service and capitalization approach. Technological intermediary services and technological finance are becoming increasingly important to the technological service industry. In economic structure, private small and medium-sized enterprises become the main body of innovation. In response to the needs of the establishment of an innovative ecological system, we should develop technological service industry and emphasize marketization, specialization and socialization. We should develop group innovation space, guide private enterprises and social capital to become involved in the establishment as well as the operation of business incubators, and improve the entrepreneurship incubator chain which consists of young science and technology entrepreneurship programs, and incubatory apparatus as well as entrepreneurship accelerators.

The angel investment system should be facilitated and an entrepreneurship investment fund should be set up. We should offer some preferential tax policies to support them. We should provide a public service facility which is low-cost as well as innovative and reduce the cost of enterprises; we should reduce the operating cost of innovative and entrepreneurial enterprises, and institute preferential policies of tax exemption relative to scientific and technological innovation. We should help scientific and technological innovators to reduce labor costs. For example, we can have a policy of subsidy of social insurance and low-cost dormitory. We can provide revenue subsidy policies for enterprises that employ local college graduates or attract talents. We should establish a market-oriented mechanism for technological innovation and make sure that technological research and development direction, route selection, resources and elements are optimally allocated in light of market orientation.

Chapter 2

Advance All-round and Deeper-level Reform

Reform and Opening up is a long-term and arduous cause, and people need to work on it generation after generation. We should carry out reform to improve the socialist market economy of China, and adhere to the basic state policy of opening up to the outside world. We must further reform in key sectors with greater political courage and vision, and forge ahead steadily in the direction determined by the 18th CPC National Congress.

— Main points of the speech at the second group study session of the Political Bureau of the 18th CPC Central Committee which General Secretary Xi Jinping presided over. (December 31, 2012)[1]

Since the 18th CPC National Congress, General Secretary Xi Jinping has made a series of remarks on comprehensively deepening reform and opening up, which are visionary, profound, rich in connotations and pertinent to the point. They are a new development and a breakthrough on reform, and opening up the theory of our party and provide fundamental guidelines for intensifying reform and opening up to a deeper level. It is of great significance in politics, theory and practice, to guide us to study and research General Secretary Xi Jinping's important speeches on reform and opening up.

I. Decisive Role of Reform and Opening Up in Determining the Destiny of Contemporary China

"Reform and opening up plays the decisive role in determining the destiny of contemporary China. It is also the key to realizing the Two Centenary Goals and the great rejuvenation of the Chinese nation. There are no bounds

---

[1] Reform and Opening up Is Always Ongoing and Will Never End (December 31, 2012). *The Governance of China*, Eng. ed. Foreign Languages Press. Oct 2014. p.119.

to practice and development, to freeing the people's minds, or to the reform and opening up effort. We will reach an impasse if we stall or go into reverse on our path; reform and opening up is always ongoing and will never end."[1]

Reform and opening up is of great significance to our party, to our people, to our nation and even to the international communist movement. General Secretary Xi Jinping has deemed reform and opening up as "the decisive role in determining the destiny of contemporary China and it is also the key to realizing the Two Centenary Goals and the great rejuvenation of the Chinese nation", which is appropriate, without exaggeration.

Reform and opening up is a new great revolution of the Chinese people led by our party in the new era. The reason why reform and opening up has been elevated to a 'revolutionary' level can be understood from the following three dimensions. The first dimension is self-improvement and development in the socialist system. Things are moving, changing and developing, which is the fundamental viewpoint of Marxism and holds true for the socialist system. Engels had addressed this point in his letter to Otto Von Boenigk as early as in 1890. He stated, "To my mind, the so called 'socialist society' is not anything immutable. Like all other social formations, it should be conceived in a state of constant flux and change." In the international communist movement, the rigid and closed developing model of socialism, in the USSR and Eastern Europe in particular, eventually led to the subversion and sabotage of the socialist system in these countries, as well as leading the setback and low-point in the international communist movement, which in turn confirmed the correctness of Engel's viewpoint. In the early days of the PRC, soon after its foundation, the CPC followed and indiscriminately copied the Soviet model of socialism construction under the 'one-sided' policy. Some fatal problems involving the whole nation had been created, such as 'being larger in size and having a higher degree of public ownership', 'equalitarianism and indiscriminate requisition of manpower, land, draught animals, farm tools and funds', and unilaterally pursuing 'purity' in relation to production. It even led to the 'Cultural Revolution', which weakened our national economy to the verge of collapse, and jeopardized the party, the country and the Chinese nation. The bitter historical facts taught a lesson to the CPC and the Chinese people, and later we changed our mode of learning from indiscriminately copying and mechanically imitating the Soviet Model, to reforming systems

---

[1] Explanatory Notes to the "Decision of the Central Committee of the CPC on Some Major Issues Concerning Comprehensively Continuing the Reform" (November 9,2013). *The Governance of China*, Eng. ed. Foreign Languages Press. Oct 2014. p. 77.

and institutions that are not suitable for our economic development or social realities. Hence, we started to explore socialism with Chinese characteristics, entering the great historical course of reform and opening up in accordance with our national conditions. This achieved self-improvement and led to the development of the socialist system which was then filled with new energy and vitality for further progress. It has proved that the practice of 35 years of reform and opening up has brought changes not only in the outlook of the CPC, Chinese people and the entire Chinese nation, but also in the historic destiny of Socialism and International Communist Movement. The second dimension is to liberate and develop social productivity. In the Preface to a *Contribution to the Critique of Political Economics*, Karl Marx stated that "In the social production of their existence, men inevitably enter into some relations which are independent of their will, namely, relations of production appropriate to a given stage in the development of their material forces of production. The totality of these relations of production constitutes the economic structure of society, the real foundation, on which arises a legal and political superstructure and to which correspond definite forms of social consciousness."[1] The basic conflicts of human society lie in the contradiction between productivity and production relations, and that between economic base and superstructure. Under different social and historical conditions, the two pairs of conflicts have different natures. Before socialist society, the two pairs of conflicts stood against each other, while in the socialist society they are compatible with each other. In different settings, the solutions differ accordingly. In the former society, a revolution conducted by one class served the purpose of overturning another one, while in the latter society, the ruling class consciously pushes ahead reforms by itself so as to liberate and develop productivity, by means of disposing of those parts of production relations and the superstructure that fail to accommodate corresponding productivity and the economic base. The cause of reform and opening up, led and pushed forward by our party, belongs to the latter practice. The third dimension is comprehensively intensifying reform to a deeper level, which means the reform is not conducted to repair minor faults by old systems and mechanisms, but to transform them all-round and to a deeper level. The economic base determines the superstructure. China's reform starts in the economic field and focuses on economic structural reform. However, the superstructure has an inverse effect on the economic base. Therefore, we must gradually extend the reform from the economic field to other areas,

---

[1] *Karl Marx and Friedrich Engels: Collected Works*, Vol.2, Eng. ed. Moscow: Progress Publishers. 1987, p. 263.

and further drive reform in systems of economy, politics, culture, society, and ecological progress as well as party building; so as to make the revolution deeper and more profound. Certainly, the reform of the economic system plays an important and leading role in that of other areas, as is expressed by the saying 'touching one part and affecting the whole'. Likewise, the speed of major reform in economic system determines the pace of reforms in other systems. As General Secretary Xi Jinping emphasized, "As we continue to reform comprehensively, we should keep our focus on economic reforms, and strive to make new breakthroughs in the reform of key fields, so that such breakthroughs will drive and stimulate reform in other areas."[1] In terms of the comprehensiveness and profundity of its contents and the difficulty of its implementation, this all-round and deeper-level reform is no less than a revolution.

Reform and opening up is a magic weapon that enables our party and people to keep pace with the times. Reform and opening up constitute the most salient feature of the new period. Since the Third Plenary Session of the 11th central Committee of CCP, we have been pushing forward reform and opening up from rural areas to cities, from economic fields to other fields and from the progressive reform to the reform of conquering harsh difficulties. Opening up has gone through a process from points to surfaces and from a shallow level to a deeper one, gradually impelling progress from the economic zones and coastal open cities, to cities along rivers and national borders, and from the eastern to the central and western regions. Melting into this tumultuous and irresistible tide, China has achieved rapid economic and social development, created miracles, and astonished the world with impressive accomplishments. First, productivity developed rapidly. Since the reform and opening up from 1978 to 2014, China's GDP has grown from Rmb364bn to Rmb63.65tr with an annual growth rate approaching to 10%, which is more than three times the world average. Second, China's overall national strength has developed substantially. China's GDP has risen to second place in the world by 2010. Moreover, China has become the world's largest exporter and possesses the largest foreign currency reserves. Through 30 years' reform and opening up, it has become an indisputable fact that China's overall national strength has greatly increased and the position and influence of our country have risen significantly in international politics. Third, the people's living standard has

---

[1] Align Our Thinking with the Guidelines of the Third Plenary Session of the 18th CPC Central Committee (November 12, 2013). *The Governance of China*, Eng. ed. Foreign Languages Press. Oct 2014. p. 105.

improved rapidly. Over the past three decades since the introduction of the reform and opening-up policy, we have provided 1.3 billion people with adequate food and clothing, and gradually marched towards a moderately prosperous society. Significant changes have been achieved in the per capita income. From 1978 to 2014, the urban per capita disposable income increased from Rmb343.4 to Rmb29,500, and rural per capita disposable income increased from Rmb133.6 to Rmb9,892. By and large, during the past thirty years, the driving force behind the improvement of the Chinese people's life, the advancement of our socialist country, the progress of our party, and the important international status we have attained is none other than our perseverance in carrying forward the reform and opening-up policy. As General Secretary Xi Jinping said, "What has helped our party inspire the people, unify them and pull their strength together over the past 35 years? What have we been relying on to stimulate the creativity and vitality of our people, realize rapid economic and social development and win a competitive advantage over capitalism? The answer has always been reform and opening up."[1]

Reform and opening up plays the decisive role in realizing the Two Centenary Goals and the great rejuvenation of the Chinese nation. As General Secretary Xi Jinping points out, "Without reform and opening up, China would not be what it is today, nor would it have the prospects for a brighter future."[2] The 18th National Congress of the CPC established a goal of building a moderately prosperous society in all respects by the centenary of the CPC (around 2020), and a further goal of building a prosperous, strong, democratic, culturally-advanced and harmonious modern socialist country by the centenary of the PRC (around 2050). Facing these glorious and arduous historical missions, we must continue reform, comprehensively striving for solutions to all kinds of problems and conflicts that challenge China's economic and social development, and work tirelessly to promote self-improvement and progress of socialism with Chinese characteristics. We should be keenly aware that our country was, and will be, confronted with extensive and profound changes domestically and internationally, and that China is still confronted with a series of prominent dilemmas and challenges in economic and social

---

[1] Explanatory Notes to the "Decision of the Central Committee of the CPC on Some Major Issues Concerning Comprehensively Continuing the Reform" (November 9, 2013). *The Governance of China*, Eng. ed. Foreign Languages Press. Oct 2014. p.97.

[2] Reform and Opening up Is Always Ongoing and Will Never End (December 31, 2012). *The Governance of China,* Eng. ed. Foreign Languages Press. Oct 2014. p. 75.

development, which poses a number of difficulties and problems on the path of development to realize the Two Centenary Goals. For example, the world economy is progressing slowly, and is still in the course of profound adjustment. International competition becomes more intensified; economic growth, particularly at home, has eased from high speed to medium-high speed. There is still much room for improvement in the socialist market economy. Unbalanced, uncoordinated and unsustainable development remains a prominent problem. Our capacity for scientific and technological innovation is far from sufficient. There remain issues such as unbalanced industrial structure and extensive development mode. We are confronting challenging tasks in deepening reform and development and transforming economic development mode. The development gap between urban and rural areas is still large. So are income disparities among individuals. Social conflicts have increased greatly, and many problems remain unresolved concerning people's vital interests in the areas of education, employment, social security, medical care and housing. Some people still live hard lives. The development of culture, economy and society cannot cater to the people's growing intellectual and cultural needs. The role of culture in improving the cultural and ethical quality of the whole nation needs to be enhanced. There is a lack of ethic standards and honest conduct in some fields of work. The education of socialist core values needs to be strengthened and the construction of cultural soft power demands great efforts. Water contamination, air pollution, and solid waste pollution stand out as major problems and seriously threaten people's work and life. Thus, the task of ecological progress is a demanding one. Formalism, bureaucratism, hedonism, and extravagance are serious and major problems. Corruption and other types of misconduct are likely to occur in some sectors, more frequently in some than in others, posing a serious challenge for us to combat corruption. There is no alternative but to continue reform and opening up, if we are to resolve all sorts of difficult problems that hinder our development, defuse risks and tackle challenges in all types of work.

Reform was pushed ahead by confronting new problems and was deepened by resolving problems. In a transitional period between the past and the future, General Secretary Xi Jinping emphasized, "Reform and opening up plays the decisive role in determining the destiny of contemporary China. It is also the key to realizing the Two Centenary Goals and the great rejuvenation of the Chinese nation. There are no bounds to practice and development, to freeing the people's minds, or to the reform and opening-up effort. We will reach an impasse if we stall or go into reverse on our path; reform and opening up is always ongoing and will never end."[1]

II. The Targets and Tasks of Reform

From the process of developing a more mature and well-defined system, we have walked half way on the path of socialism, in which the main historical mission is to establish the socialist system and carry out reform. Now, we have established a sound and solid foundation. In the second half, our main historical task is to improve and develop the socialist system with Chinese characteristics, and provide a set of more complete, more stable and more effective systems for the development of the party and nation, the wellbeing of the people, social harmony and stability, and the enduring prosperity and stability of the country.[2]

Comprehensively deepening reform, is to coordinate the reform of all fields. And the top priority is to establish a general goal as well as specific targets in all sectors. General Secretary Xi Jinping pointed out that in the past, we also initiated various objectives of reform. In general they were mostly targeted at specific areas. For example, in various earlier historical periods, the overall goals of political system reform were to consolidate the socialist system, to develop the productive forces of socialist society, to promote socialist democracy, and to mobilize the enthusiasm of the masses. In 1992, the party's 14th National Congress stipulated that China's economic reform should aim at establishing a socialist market economy. The Third Plenary Session of the 18th CPC Central Committee pointed out that the general goal is to continue the reform to a deeper level, and confirmed the sub-goals of deepening reform in the economic system, political system, cultural system, and social structural system; and of ecological environment management and the party building system under the command of the general goal.

With regard to the general goal, General Secretary Xi Jinping pointed out that to continue the reform comprehensively, we must improve and develop

---

[1] Explanatory Notes to the "Decision of the Central Committee of the CPC on Some Major Issues Concerning Comprehensively Continuing the Reform" (November 9, 2013). *The Governance of China*, Eng. ed. Foreign Languages Press. Oct 2014. p.77.

[2] The Speech at the Seminar Which Studies and Implements the Spirit of the Comprehensive Deepening of Reform in the Third Plenary Session of the 18th CPC Central Committee among Leading Officials at Provincial and Ministerial Level (February 17, 2014). *Excerpts of Xi Jinping's Remarks on the Overall Deepening of Reform*. Central Party Literature Press. 2014. p. 27.

the socialist system with Chinese characteristics and modernize our national governance system and capability. The general goal of continuing the reform comprehensively consists of two aspects: the fundamental guidance of reform (to improve and develop the socialist system with Chinese characteristics), and the basic approach to reform (to modernize our national governance system and capability). In this way, the two aspects are dialectically integrated, in guidance and approach. The experience of development of socialism with Chinese characteristics and the practice of reform and opening up over the past 30 years have fully proved that the prerequisite and guarantee for modernizing our national governance system and capability is to persistently improve and develop the socialist system with Chinese characteristics. To effectively respond to and cope with all kinds of conflicts and problems emerging in the practice of socialism with Chinese characteristics, and to accomplish new victories, we should make headway modernizing our national governance system and capacity.

Establishment of the general goal of continuing reform to a deeper level and in an all-round way is an objective requirement put forth during the process of pushing forward reform, which reflects our party's deep and systematic understanding of the reform and the development law that applies in socialist construction, and represents the new measures for the governance of China taken by the new Central Party Committee. In the history of the international communist movement, the classical Marxist authors failed to provide systematic answers for questions about how to develop and improve a socialist system appropriate to a country's conditions, and especially about how to effectively govern a new socialist society. Practices from Paris Commune to Soviet Union and to eastern European socialist countries, did not address these questions successfully. The CPC led the people in carrying on the arduous exploration to resolve these problems. Especially during the great historical course of reform and opening up, we have accumulated rich experience and achieved great success in improving the socialist system with Chinese characteristics, and our governance system and capacity. Even so, we should realize that compared against China's needs for social and economic development and our people's expectations, against today's increasingly intense international competition, and against the need to ensure permanent stability at home, we still have great scope to make our system more mature, with a sophisticated model. We have room to enhance our national governance system and capacity. System operation and governing capacity have increasingly become our 'short slab' or 'short leg'. Therefore, to address these problems, we have put forward the general goal of comprehensively continuing the reform, which has become a primary requirement for us to understand and to advance reform to a deeper level and in an all-round way. We must work hard to improve and develop socialism with Chinese characteristics, and establish a set of more complete, more stable and more effective systems for the development of the party and the nation, the wellbeing of the people, social harmony and stability, and the enduring prosperity and stability of the country. As General Secretary Xi Jinping pointed out, "This is a grand project. Neither piecemeal adjustment nor fragmented mending will do. It entails carrying out all-round and systematic reform, and integrating reforms in various fields to promote the overall modernization of our national governance system and capability."[1]

In terms of the sub-goals of deepening reform in all sectors, General Secretary Xi Jinping has made a systematic elaboration on the primary mission and major initiatives with regard to economy, politics, culture, society, ecological progress, national defense, and the army; and on opening up to the outside world. For instance, on deepening the economic structural reform - the central task of reform - we should adhere to the objective of a sound socialist market economy. We should strike a proper balance between the role of the government and that of the market as a key issue, and make the market play a decisive role in allocating resources, enabling the government to play its due role more effectively. As to deepening the political structural reform, we should uphold correct political guidance, and keep to the socialist path of making political progress with Chinese characteristics. To do so, we should ensure the unity of the leadership of the party, and the position of the people as masters of the country and law-based governance, so as to guarantee the fundamental position of the people. So doing, we will reach the goal of enhancing the vitality of the party and the country and keeping the people fully motivated, to expand socialist democracy and to promote socialist political progress. As to deepening reform in the cultural sector, we should take the path of socialism with Chinese characteristics, carry forward advanced socialist culture, greatly develop and enrich socialist culture, stimulate the cultural creativity of the whole nation and encourage the free flow of cultural inspiration from all sources. As to deepening social structural reform, we should promote social fairness and justice as well as the improvement of the people's lives as the

---

[1] The Speech at the Seminar Which Studies and Implements the Spirit of the Comprehensive Deepening of Reform in the Third Plenary Session of the 18th CPC Central Committee among Leading Officials at Provincial and Ministerial Level (February 17, 2014). *Excerpts of Xi Jinping's Remarks on the Overall Deepening of Reform*. Central Party Literature Press. 2014. p. 27.

starting point and ultimate goal. We should ensure that our development is for the people and by the people and that the fruits of development are shared among the people. We should make institutional arrangements more effective, regarding matters at the core of social reform, such as education, employment, income distribution, social security, medicine and public health, housing, food safety and safety in production. As to deepening the reform of ecological progress, we should pursue green development, remain committed to the basic state policy of resource conservation and environmental protection, and strike a balance between economic growth and environmental protection. We should improve the evaluation norms for economic and social development and the country's natural resource management. We should implement control of the amount and the application of energy consumption, of water consumption and of land for construction, and improve the ecological compensation mechanism in key ecological functional zones. As to deepening the reform of national defense and armed forces, we should strive to accomplish the goal of "building powerful armed forces that follow the command of the party, are able to win battles, and have fine conduct" under new circumstances. We should speed up military reform in key areas, further emancipate and develop fighting capacity, further liberate and enhance the vitality of the armed forces, and provide mechanisms and policy system security for achieving the goal of strengthening the military. We will build a new system of open economy by implementing a more proactive opening up strategy and improving the open economy so that it promotes mutual benefit and is diversified, balanced, secure and efficient. We should encourage coastal, inland and border areas to draw on each other's strengths in opening up; develop open areas that take the lead in global economic cooperation and competition; and establish leading zones for opening up that drive regional development.

All in all, reform and opening up is an in-depth and all-round social transformation. We must sincerely learn and research into a series of works by General Secretary Xi Jinping regarding top level design and overall planning, closely follow the guidance and strive for targets, and have a clear understanding about tasks and requirements. We should highlight core and key links, and at the same time focus on both the all-round progress and the coordination of all sectors. We should undertake a further study on the relationship between reforms in all fields, the compatibility of different targeted measures and the feasibility of approaches to reform. We should understand the significance of comprehensively continuing reform to make joint efforts in furthering reform to a deeper level, and wider opening up, in order to ensure meeting the targets and achieving the tasks of reform.

China (Shanghai) Pilot Free Trade Zone, located in Shanghai Pudong New Area District, is a regional free trade zone set in Shanghai by the Chinese government. (Xinhua News Agency)

III. Fundamental Issues and Drastic Mistakes

China is a big country. We cannot afford any drastic mistakes on issues of fundamental importance, as damage from such mistakes will be beyond remedy. Our position is that we must be both bold enough to explore and advance, and prudent in carefully planning our actions. We will keep to the correct direction and press ahead with reform and opening up. We will have the courage to crack the 'hard nuts,' navigate the uncharted waters and take on the deep-rooted problems that have accumulated over the years. We must not stop our pursuit of reform and opening up – not for one moment.[1]

A month before the opening of the Third Plenary Session of the 18th CPC Central Committee, General Secretary Xi Jinping made a speech on the 2003 APEC CEO Summit, and pointed out, "China is a big country. We cannot

---
[1] Work Together for a Better Asia Pacific (October 7, 2013). *The Governance of China*, Eng. ed. Foreign Languages Press. Oct 2014.p384.

afford any drastic mistake on issues of fundamental importance, as damage from such mistakes will be beyond remedy". The meaning and connotation of the statement is quite clear. French historian Alexis de Tocqueville once incisively claimed that "the goal of small countries is to realize free, rich and happy life for the people, while the goal of great powers is fated to create greatness and eternity and to take responsibilities and sufferings". China, with a population of 1.3 billion, is the only great power whose culture has never been appreciated like others among the world's Four Great Ancient Civilizations. China should assume the duties and responsibilities to continuously create 'greatness and eternity', all of which decide that we cannot afford the price of any drastic mistake, nor can the world.

What are the fundamental issues of importance? In a profound revolution, the direction and target, the theoretical guidance, and the starting point and ultimate goal of the reform and opening up are the issues of fundamental importance. What are drastic mistakes? Principled, fundamental and global mistakes are drastic mistakes. Reform and opening up concerns the self-improvement and development of China's socialist system, so we cannot afford any drastic mistake on issues of fundamental importance. In order to comprehensively deepen the reform, we are required to hold high the great banner of socialism with Chinese characteristics, to uphold the direction of reform towards the socialist market economy, and to put the promotion of social fairness, justice and improvement of people's lives as the starting point and ultimate goal. We should also further free our minds, continue to stimulate and develop productive forces, release and strengthen the vigor of the society, and eliminate defects in various systems and mechanisms so as to accomplish self-improvement and development of socialism with Chinese characteristics and strive to open up broader prospects for this great cause.

The direction decides the road and the road decides the destiny. Since China is a socialist country with Chinese characteristics, we must adhere to socialist direction and keep to the party's basic line, no matter what approaches we may adopt to drive reform and opening up. We should always combine the principle of taking economic development as the central task, with both the Four Cardinal Principles and the reform and opening-up policy, so as to achieve the organic unity of 'one central task, two basic points'. The Decision of the Third Plenary Session of the 18th CPC Central Committee pointed out clearly, "The success of reform and opening up has provided us with important experience for comprehensively deepening reform. We have to adhere to it in the long term. What is most important is to uphold the leadership of the party, adhere to the party's basic line, reject both the old and rigid closed-door policy and any attempt to abandon socialism and take an erroneous path, firmly keep to the road of socialism with Chinese characteristics and ensure that our reform is in the right direction".

The great success of reform and opening up over the past 30 years can be ascribed to the practice of reform and opening up of a socialist nature and to the resolution to consolidate and develop socialism. Over the past 30 years, our party has been unswervingly adhering to the its basic line and to making efforts to realize the organic integration and dialectical unification of 'one central task, two basic points' while promoting the grand cause of socialism with Chinese characteristics. Moreover, our party has effectively withstood all risks, challenges and tests both at home and abroad, giving life and vitality to socialism with Chinese characteristics, as well as to the international communist movement. Though some big parties, and veteran parties, of other socialist countries in the world also promote 'reform' of the parties themselves, as well as their countries, their 'new thinking' deviates from socialist principles and direction, and their practice is bound to lead socialism to go astray and suffer setbacks and even failures. Their painful lesson is thought-provoking and must be taken as a warning. At present, some radical thoughts and ideological trends in society should indicate the need for continued attention and vigilance. For instance, some people take the political views and values of some western countries as the criterion by which to judge reform and opening up oriented towards western 'universal values' and political system. Some hostile forces and people with ulterior motives in this area make a spectacle, create public opinion and confuse public opinion. Those people, with all kinds of complex motives, 'predict' and anticipate the changes that China will make concerning some 'fundamental issues' and even hope for some subversion. In face of a complicated situation and numerous challenges, we should maintain our political composure, clarify the goals and directions of the reform and be aware of what we will reform and what we shall not. For example, the general goal of comprehensively deepening reform is to improve and develop socialism with Chinese characteristics and to promote the modernization of the national governance system and capacity. It is essential that we completely understand and grasp this. Of the two components of the general goal in the sentence immediately above, the former regulates the fundamental direction of all-round and deeper-level reform, while the latter specifics the clear direction as to how to improve and develop socialist system with Chinese characteristics. Our national governance system is to be improved and refined, but how to do it? The answer lies in our historical inheritance, cultural traditions, economic and social development level as well as the will of the Chinese people. These are the decisive factors, rather than a blind worship or a mechanical copy of any other country's institutional model. Otherwise, "none of the practical problems can be solved, and serious consequences will be brought about due to non-acclimatization. Just as an old saying goes, some set out to be tigers but end up as dogs—failure to achieve what one plans to get."[1] We must stay clear-minded about the direction of reform and the substantial issues concerning what to change and what to retain. We should "have courage to crack the 'hard nuts', navigate the uncharted waters and take on the deep-rooted problems that have accumulated over the years. We must not stop our pursuit of reform and opening up — not for one moment". Also, we should "be both bold enough to explore and advance, and be prudent in carefully planning our actions". Matters that must not be reformed include the basic line, basic principles, basic experience, and basic requirements of socialism with Chinese characteristics. They are not to be changed now, nor in the future. We should always keep to the correct direction of reform and opening up, and uphold and improve the party's leadership and the socialist system with Chinese characteristics. We should ensure we maintain the right tempo of reform in complicated situations and seek the right approaches to reform from varied opinions without swaying back and forth, relaxing our efforts or getting sidetracked.

While keeping firmly to socialist reform and opening up, we must always be vigilant against, and prevent, incorrect understanding or defective thinking from negating reform and opening up and socialism with the Chinese characteristics. During his inspection tour to the South in 1992, Deng Xiaoping mentioned that China should maintain vigilance against the 'Right' but primarily against the 'Left'. Leftist mistakes have brought many serious losses to the party's cause, and even almost completely ruined the Chinese revolution. Leftist bias has never disappeared in the history of our party. In the historical process of reform and opening up, there have always been various criticisms and negative voices against this cause. Some extremists deliberately distort and exaggerate the conflicts, difficulties and problems in the China's development course since reform and opening up.

---

[1] The Speech at the Seminar Which Studies and Implements the Spirit of the Comprehensive Deepening of Reform in the Third Plenary Session of the 18th CPC Central Committee among Leading Officials at Provincial and Ministerial Level (February 17, 2014). *Excerpts of Xi Jinping's Remarks on the Overall Deepening of Reform*. Central Party Literature Press. 2014. p. 22.

They condemn China's reform as shifting public ownership to private, and as transforming socialism to capitalism, denying the reform and opening-up policy and the path of socialism with Chinese characteristic. Instead, they propose to completely alter the process, to 'thoroughly set wrong things right again' as in the past; and to make China take the old path of implementing a rigid closed-door policy. Deng Xiaoping once said, "If we do not adhere to socialism, implement the policy of reform and opening up to the outside world, develop the economy and raise the people's living standards, we would find ourselves in a blind alley." At present, China's reform is sailing in uncharted waters and there are tough challenges. As noted by General Secretary Xi Jinping, "Having been pushed ahead for more than 30 years, China's reform has entered a deep-water zone. It can be said that the easy part of the job has been done to the satisfaction of all. What is left are tough bones that are hard to chew."[1] At this time, it is extremely important that we press ahead without letting up, and "We will reach an impasse if we stall or go into reverse on our path". If we hesitate and become indecisive, waver in our faith and even give up reform, all our previous gains in the 35 years of reform and opening up may be totally ruined. Reform and opening up accord with the aspirations of the party membership and the people, and keep up with the trend of the times. Only through reform and opening up can we properly develop China, socialism and Marxism.

In short, as long as there is no drastic mistake, China will be able to maintain a good momentum for reform and opening up and national rejuvenation. The Chinese Dream will certainly come true.

IV. Methodology Adopted for Reform and Opening up

We should take the pulse of reform from the complex outcomes, in the light of the inherent laws of comprehensively deepening the reform and, especially, pay attention to some major relationships during the process of reform. We should also cope well with the relationship between freeing up the mind and seeking truth from facts, between promoting all-round progress and making breakthroughs in key areas, between making top-level design and "wading across the river by feeling for the stone", and between holding courage and staying prudent.[2]

---

[1] Push Ahead with Reform Despite More Difficulties (February 7, 2014). *The Governance of China*, Eng. ed. Foreign Languages Press. Oct 2014. p. 113.

[2] The Speech by Xi Jinping at an Investigation Tour of Reform and Development Work in Hubei (from July 21 to 23, 2013). *Excerpts of Xi Jinping's Remarks on the Overall Deepening of Reform*. Central Party Literature Press. 2014. p. 37.

The issue of approaches is like a bridge or a boat crossing a river. Reform and opening up is a brand-new cause that has never been pursued before, so we should adopt a correct methodology. From the in-depth exploration and the inherent laws of reform and opening up, General Secretary Xi Jinping acutely revealed some of the major relationships in deepening the reform comprehensively, and made some new methodological explorations in the approaches to reform and opening up. In particular, he proposed that we should pay attention to both wading across the river by feeling for the stones, and to top-level design, to promoting an all-round progress and making breakthroughs in key areas, and to courageous exploration and steady advancement.

We should not only free our minds but also seek truth from facts, for the thought is the forerunner of action. The main theme throughout 30 years of reform and opening up is emancipating the mind. There are no bounds to practice and development or to freeing up the people's minds. Though we have accomplished a lot during the past 30 years of reform and opening up, we still need new thoughts for guidance with the emancipation of the mind as the leading principle. Without great ideological emancipation, there would be no major reform initiatives and great achievements in reform. To free up the mind is to eradicate backward understanding so that we can become more practical and realistic rather than unrealistic or overwhelmed with wild fantasies. It requires us to promote the development of reform based on China's national realities and conditions. We should always bear in mind the people's interests and expectations, and we must dare to explore and be down to earth to constantly promote theoretical and practical innovation, and to effectively resolve various risks and challenges on the way forward. We should continually push forward reform and opening up so as to keep ahead of the times.

We should promote both all-round progress and breakthroughs at key points. Reform and opening up is an in-depth and all-round social transformation and is a systematic project. Every reform will have great impact on others, and all reforms support each other and interact positively. Therefore, "It should be pushed forward in an all-round way with all kinds of reforms well coordinated."[1] If the overall situation is not handled well and the overall promotion is not made, many concrete reforms are too difficult

---

[1] Part of the speech at the second group study session of the Political Bureau of the 18th CPC Central Committee (December 31, 2012). *Excerpts of Xi Jinping's Remarks on the Overall Deepening of Reform.* Central Party Literature Press. 2014.p. 35.

to conduct. Therefore, we must promote reforms in the context of the overall situation, and intensively study the relevance of the reforms in various fields and the correlation among various reform initiatives, to make sure that "they can work well with each other on policy orientation, facilitate each other in the process of implementation, and complement each other in the effectiveness of reform."[1] However, the whole advancement of reform does not mean making equal efforts in every field and having no key focus of work. We must ensure the unification of the central task and the two points, as well as that of the whole advancement and of key breakthroughs. In the process of comprehensively promoting reform, we should clearly recognize the principal conflict and its main aspects, and learn to set priorities. With greater political courage and vision, we should strive to make breakthroughs in key sectors and key parts of reform so as to promote the all-round advancement and deeper-level development of reform and opening up.

We should consider both the whole and individual parts. The whole is composed of every single part, and each belongs to the whole. Without the whole, there wouldn't be any part to depend on, and vice versa. Therefore, we can't replace the whole with any part or only consider the whole while ignoring the parts. As to the reform measures, we must develop a holistic view and act in the overall interests of the country. Every plan for reform should be made in accordance with the overall situation. Meanwhile, we should also take the specific situation of each part into account and act accordingly to conduct reform. Considering the interests that the reform may affect, we should not only aim at serving the overall, holistic and long-term interests of the people, but also the sectional, private and immediate interests of the people. In all, we should appropriately handle the relationship between the whole and parts.

We should both 'wade across the river by feeling for the stones' and conduct the top-level design. China's reform and opening up is a great innovative cause that has never before been pursued, for which we have no ready-made answers or experience to learn from, so we have to advance cautiously; like, 'wading across the river by feeling for the stones.' General Secretary Xi Jinping once said that "wading across the river by feeling for the stones is a reform method with Chinese characteristics and in line with the prevailing conditions in China. Wading across the river by feeling for

---

[1] Part of the speech at the second group study session of the Third Plenary Session of the 18th CPC Central Committee (November 12, 2013) *Excerpts of Xi Jinping's Remarks on the Overall Deepening of Reform*. Central Party Literature Press. 2014.p. 44-45.

the stones, we can identify the laws that apply."[1] The path of socialism with Chinese characteristic has been explored through 'wading across the river by feeling for the stones.' This gradual reform can help us avoid social unrest caused by unknown situations or improper measures, and provides a guarantee to steadily advance the reform and achieve the goal smoothly. However, with the deepening of reform and opening up, complexity and difficulty have been increasing day by day. Against this backdrop, we need to keep wading across the river by feeling for the stones and still encourage bold experiments and breakthroughs. At the same time, we need to strengthen our macroscopic thinking and top-level design, and make sure that the reform is systematic, integrated and coordinated, and strive to make real progress in deepening the reform in an all-round way. The Belt and Road Initiative proposed by General Secretary Xi Jinping is a marvelous work out of the top-level design.

We must push reform forward boldly and steadily. At present, our country's reform has entered a deep-water zone with tough challenges. The reform has been impeded by the barriers of old notions, the fences erected by interest groups, and the inertia of operating systems. The arduousness, complexity and risks of reform have become more noticeable. "The inherent difficulty of reform entails extraordinary courage, and only persistent efforts befit this commendable cause." General Secretary Xi Jinping required that even knowing that it is hard to solve, we should have courage and backbone, dare to face tough choices, to crack hard nuts and chart a path through the treacherous river, and advance reform continuously to a higher level. Meanwhile, General Secretary Xi Jinping has tirelessly told the whole party that "Reform is a gradual process. We should make bold breakthroughs while steadily advancing step by step."[2] Confronted with the arduousness and complexity of comprehensive reform, we must keep a positive and steady pace, based on practice, seriously explore the laws of reform, and be prudent in carefully planning our action so as to ensure the attainment of the goals of the reform.

We should accelerate development through reform, maintain stability

---

[1] Part of the speech at the second group study session of the Political Bureau of the 18th CPC Central Committee (December 31, 2012). *Excerpts of Xi Jinping's Remarks on the Overall Deepening of Reform.* Central Party Literature Press. 2014.p. 34.

[2] The Speech at the Seminar Which Studies and Implements the Spirit of the Comprehensive Deepening of Reform in the Third Plenary Session of the 18th CPC Central Committee among Leading Officials at Provincial and Ministerial Level (February 17, 2014). *Excerpts of Xi Jinping's Remarks on the Overall Deepening of Reform.* Central Party Literature Press. 2014.p.151.

through development and promote reform and development through social stability. Reform, development and stability are important points in the construction of China's socialist modernization. To properly handle the relationship of the three and achieve their unity are important guiding principles for the overall situation of China's drive for socialist modernization. Only development will make a difference, and it is the basic purpose of reform, development and stability and the key to solve the economic and social problems. Stability is the critical task; it is a prerequisite of, and fundamental to, reform and development. Reform is the great ability providing a strong driving force for development and stability. Relying on each other, supporting each other, taking advantage of each other, these three form a relation in a closed loop. To properly handle the relationship among the three, we should take into full consideration the momentum of reform, the speed of development, and the capacity of the general public to sustain change. Further, we should coordinate the three to promote and facilitate each other so as to ensure that the people can live and work in peace with happiness and that our country can maintain social and political stability and realize enduring peace and stability.

V. The Principal Position of the People to Advance Reform

Reform and opening up is a cause involving billions of Chinese people. We must respect the people's pioneering spirit and advance this cause under the leadership of the party. Reform and opening up put into effect the requirements of the people and the proposals of the party. The people are the makers of history and the practitioners of reform and opening up. Therefore, we must adhere to the principles of position of the people as masters of the country and the leadership of the party, and closely rely on the people to push forward reform and opening up.[1]

The people constitute the main force of reform. We should adhere to and respect their position as masters of the country, give free rein to their creativity, and promote reform with the close support of the people. We have to follow this basic principle to deepen reform comprehensively.

General Secretary Xi Jinping pointed out that "The fundamental reason why our reform and opening up has won the people's wholehearted support

---

[1] Part of the speech at the second group study session of the Political Bureau of the 18th CPC Central Committee (December 31, 2012). *Excerpts of Xi Jinping's Remarks on the Overall Deepening of Reform*. Central Party Literature Press. 2014.p. 138.

and vigorous participation all along lies in the fact that from the very beginning we let the cause strike deep roots among the people."[1] Looking back on the process of reform and opening up over the past 30 years, we have witnessed a series of reforms from the exploration of big contracts to the overall spread of contract system with remuneration linked to output, from emerging township enterprise to prevailing private economy, and from the expansion of the enterprises' decision-making power to state-run enterprise reform. From the whole process, we can discover that it is the people's great creativity and wisdom that contribute to each breakthrough and innovation concerning knowledge and practice, to each emergence and development of new things and to the creation and accumulation of reform experience in multiple fields of many aspects. The willing support and active participation of the people is the source of power leading to the accomplishments of reform. The valuable experiences of our reform and opening up lie in our practices of putting people first, respecting their principal position in the country, giving free rein to their creativity, and promoting reform with the close support of the people.

As extensive and profound changes are taking place domestically and internationally, China faces a series of prominent dilemmas and challenges, and there are quite a number of problems and difficulties on its path of development. To solve these problems, the key lies in deepening reform. However, "having been pushed ahead for more than 30 years, China's reform has entered a deep-water zone. It can be said that the easy part of the job has been done to the satisfaction of all. What is left are tough bones that are hard to chew."[2] Facing the difficulties and obstacles on the road of reform, only the close support of the people as well as their endorsement and participation can lead us to victory by conquering challenges one after another.

As General Secretary Xi Jinping has said again and again in addresses to the press, the people's aspiration for a better life is our goal, so "We should focus on serving the people and make realizing, safeguarding and developing the fundamental interests of the overwhelming majority of the people our starting point and goal."[3] While conducting the all-round and deeper-level

---

[1] Align our Thinking with the Guidelines of the Third Plenary Session of the 18th CPC Central Committee (November 12, 2013). *The Governance of China*, Eng. ed. Foreign Languages Press. Oct2014.p.109

[2] Push Ahead with Reform Despite More Difficulties (Feb.7, 2014). *The Governance of China*, Eng. ed. Foreign Languages Press. Oct 2014. p.113.

[3] Enhance Publicity and Theoretical Work. *The Governance of China*, Eng. ed. Foreign Languages Press. Oct 2014. p.172-173.

reform, we should stick to the principle above and take people's satisfaction as the basic standard against which the reform is measured. To push forward any key reform, we must have the major issues concerning the reform examined and addressed from the people's standpoint, while formulating guidelines and measures based on the people's interests. We must always worry about the people's security and kept their wellbeing at heart, understand the people's thoughts, hopes, sorrows and worries in a timely and accurate way, and make efforts to resolve the problems that most concern the people in relation to their most direct and practical interests. Changes should be made in areas that the masses look forward to the most, and to the constraints and the most prominent issues of economic and social development. We should adhere to the shared development concept so that the whole society can experience the real achievements of reform and development and the people can get real fruits and naturally gain a stronger sense of benefit. At the same time, we should appropriately handle the relationship among the fundamental interests of the majority of the people, the common interests of the masses at this stage and the special interests of different groups so as "to make all the Chinese who live in our great country in this great age share the opportunity to pursue excellence, realize our dreams, and develop ourselves along with our country."[1]

The people are the creators of material wealth and spiritual wealth, and they are the main body and the decisive force in reforming the society, so we must adhere to the principal position of the people. Dating back to 1944, comrade Mao Zedong has pointed out in *The United Front of Cultural Work* that our cultural workers must "link themselves with the masses, not divorce themselves from the masses. In order to do so, they must act in accordance with the needs and wishes of the masses. All work done for the masses must start from their needs and not from the desire of any individual. ... There are two principles here: one is the actual needs of the masses rather than what we fancy they need, and the other is the wishes of the masses who can make up their own minds instead of we making up their minds for them."[2] We make plans, decisions and do things out of an impulsive rush, with a closed mind, or by relying on the masses, to get close to them, mobilize their initiatives and pool their wisdoms. Different choices lead to completely different results. We should take the masses' proposals, because on the one hand, we gain their

---

[1] Addre*ss to the First Session of the 12th National People's Congress (March 17, 2013). The Governance of China*, Eng. ed. Foreign Languages Press. Oct 2014. p.42.

[2] The United Front in Cultural Work (October 30, 1944). *Selected Works of Mao Zedong*, Vol.III, Eng. ed. 2006. p. P236-237

support by adopting their proposals, and on the other hand, even if different opinions emerge, we can rely on the masses to persuade. Conversely, if the government works out decisions from its own point of view, on the one hand, we may find that the people may not willingly support them. On the other hand we will find it difficult to convince the people, even through experts' evaluation and persuasion, which may incur a reverse response. Therefore, the party members and officials must develop a sound attitude towards the people and firmly stand by the people. We must take maintaining close ties with the people and finding out what the people think and want as our basic work method and style, as well as the basic content and form of the work of the party and government. Reform and opening up is the common cause of all the people, who are the source of strength, and most often the people from the grassroots come up with solutions to many problems. Party members and officials must earnestly seek advice, needs and comments on administration from the people, instead of paying lip service or working behind closed doors, not to mention acting out of fancies and whims. As a saying goes, 'the roc soars lithely not because of the lightness of one of its feathers; the steed funs fast not because of the strength of one of its legs.' Only by mobilizing the masses and relying on them can we achieve success in reform. As General Secretary Xi Jinping stated, "We should fully mobilize their enthusiasm, initiative and creativity, bring their wisdom and strength to the cause of reform, and work with them to move the cause forward."[1]

---

[1] Align our Thinking with the Guidelines of the Third Plenary Session of the 18th CPC Central Committee (November 12, 2013). *The Governance of China*, Eng. ed. Foreign Languages Press. Oct, 2014.p.110.

Chapter 3

Develop a Law-based Country

Comprehensively implementing the Constitution is the primary task and groundwork for developing a law-based socialist country. The Constitution is the fundamental law of the state and the general program for managing state affairs; enjoying supreme legal status, legal authority and legal validity, it is fundamental and consistent, and is of overall and long-term importance. ...No organization or individual is privileged to act beyond the Constitution or the law. All acts in violation of the Constitution or the law must be investigated.

— from Xi Jinping's Speech at the Meeting of the People from All Walks of Life in Beijing to Commemorate the 30th Anniversary of the Promulgation and Implementation of the Current Constitution (December 4, 2012).

Since the 18th National Congress of the CPC, General Secretary Xi Jinping has published a series of important works on the rule of law in China. During the Fourth Plenary Session of the 18th National Congress, the CPC for the first time made an important decision with the theme of the rule of law, which performed critical deployments to comprehensively promote the rule of law, whereby the CPC launched the most significant campaign for the rule of law with the most far-reaching influence since the founding of the PRC. General Secretary Xi Jinping's important talks on the rule of law are highly comprehensive and profound, covering all aspects of the rule of law. They provide direct answers to many perplexing problems on the rule of law in the society today and have corrected a number of misunderstandings, thereby serving as a beacon for the smooth advancement of the rule of law along the right path. Studying these important talks by General Secretary Xi Jinping provides excellent guidance to deepening our understanding of the party's new strategy of law-based governance.

I. The Rule of Law: the Basic Way of Governance

General Secretary Xi Jinping's strategic decision to elevate law-based governance to the basic strategies and approaches to governance is fully compatible with the scientific view on the law of development of human society. More than 2000 years ago, the ancient Greek philosopher Plato divided political systems into two categories of 'ruled by law' and 'not ruled by law,' each being subdivided into autocracy (monarchy), oligarchy (aristocracy) and democracy and thus arrived at six political systems. Of the six political systems, Plato believes that "a tyranny is the most wretched form of government, and the rule of a king is the happiest." When bound by positive regulations or laws, the monarchy is the best of all; when uncurbed by law, it becomes tyranny, the most merciless and insufferable of all.[1] Though we may disagree with Plato on his views of monarchy, aristocracy and democracy, we can discern his advocacy of rule of law. It seems to Plato that the degree of centralization of powers is variable but the rule of law is absolute. In a word, 'rule of law' is the cardinal truth. In this era, the rule of law should naturally be the basis of a modern state, an indispensable and unshakable cornerstone of the national governance system and the modernization of capacity for governance.

1. Rule of law is indispensable for deepening reforms

The comprehensive advancement of the rule of law is an integral part of the 'Four-Pronged Comprehensive Strategy.' At the opening ceremony of a seminar of provincial or ministerial-level leading officials on the implementation of the guiding principles of Fourth Plenary Session of the 18th CPC Central Committee and the comprehensive advancement of the rule of law, organized by the Party School of the Central Committee of CPC, Xi Jinping has pointed out that comprehensively building a moderately prosperous society in all respects is our strategic goal. Meanwhile our three strategic measures are; to drive reform to a deeper level comprehensively; to implement the comprehensive rule of law; and to exercise strict discipline in running the party, respectively. These 'Four-Pronged Comprehensive Strategies' are mutually complementary and beneficial, creating improved synergy. To accurately grasp the spiritual nature of the comprehensive rule of law, we need to put it against the backdrop of our strategic planning of 'Four-Pronged Comprehensive Strategies.' Specifically, we need to have a thorough understanding of the relationship between 'comprehensive rule of law' and

---

[1] Plato. (2002). *Republic*. http://www.idph.net/conteudos/ebooks/republic.pdf. P437.

'comprehensive deepening of reform.' After the strategic deployment of 'driving reform to a deeper level' was issued during the Third Plenary Session of the National Security Commission, the strategic deployment of 'comprehensive rule of law' was subsequently approved at the Fourth Plenary Session. This amply proves that reform and rule of law are both sides of a coin, both wings of a bird, or both wheels of a bicycle. They are the two basic approaches to the strategic target of completing the building of a moderately prosperous society in all respects. However, in practice today, some comrades still hold erroneous beliefs regarding the relationship between these two elements, that is, that reform and rule of law are fundamentally contradictory to each other, for reform itself entails breaking the confines of law. This conception is wrong, for reform and rule of law are a dialectic unity. During the Second Meeting of the Central Leading Group for Comprehensively Continuing the Reform on February 28, 2014, Xi stressed that all major reforms should have a legal basis. He said that we should attach great importance to the application of law-based thinking and approaches during the whole process of reform, build on the guidance and promotion of rule of law, strengthen the alignment and complementary aspects of related legislative efforts, and ensure that reforms be advanced on the track of law. Good rule of law itself leaves much room for flexible regulations and innovation. At this critical stage of reform, we can authorize the reform entities through legislation so that they can give full play to the proactive innovation of reforms without breaking basic standards of activities. Even when faced with major institutional obstacles, as long as we conduct scientific evaluation and democratic procedures, we can still unleash reforms through timely revisions of laws. In this way, we can coordinate our legislative work with our decisions on reform to ensure that all of our major reforms have a legal basis, and that legislative work is carried out proactively to meet the needs of reform, economic development, and social progress. Practices that are proven effective should be promptly enacted into laws. By contrast, immature practices that need to be piloted should be authorized for trial through legal procedures. We should promptly modify or abolish laws and regulations that do not conform to the needs of reform. The guarantee of the rule of law is indispensable for comprehensively deepening reforms.

2. Economic development is inseparable from the rule of law

It is pointed out in the resolution of the Fourth Plenary Session of the 18th CPC Central Committee that in essence, the socialist market economy is a law-based economy. To ensure the decisive role of the market in resource allocation and better promote the role of the government, we must improve the legal system of the socialist market economy with basic orientations to protecting property rights, guaranteeing contracts, coordinating markets, and safeguarding equal exchange, fair competition and effective supervision. Without the rule of law, there would be no rules to follow in market transactions, and market competition would lead to a vicious circle. The scandals of tainted milk powder and recycled cooking oil are essentially a logical result of the profit-oriented market competition. So it is in the Chinese society today, so had it been in the Western society. Marx pointed out in *Capital* that "... enumerated multiple methods of adulteration. He named 6 for sugar, 9 for olive oil, 10 for butter, 12 for salt, 19 for milk, 20 for bread, 23 for brandy, 24 for meat, 28 for chocolate, 30 for wine, 32 for coffee." "...he had to eat daily in his bread a certain quantity of human perspiration mixed with the discharge of abscesses, cobwebs, dead cockroaches and putrid German yeast, not to mention alum, sand and other agreeable mineral ingredients." "It did not, however, prevent them, during 10 years, from spinning silk 10 hours a day out of the blood of little children who had to be placed upon stools for the performance of their work."[1] History has proven long ago that in the era of market economy, without prevention, and without legal restrictions on basic standards, market competitions are prone to become gates to hell. The only way to address the potential aftermaths of market competition is to enhance the rule of law so that the market economy will develop healthily under the constraint and guidance of law.

3. Social governance is inseparable from the rule of law

During the fourth group study session of the Political Bureau of the Party Central Committee held on February 23, 2013, General Secretary Xi Jinping pointed out that we should promote the socialist rule of law, encourage all the people to obey the law, solve problems with the law and develop a positive atmosphere that honors compliance. We should adhere to the combination of legal education with legal practice, carry forward law-based governance extensively and enhance the application of law in social governance. Once a rural society, China is now in the process of rapid urbanization. The agricultural production model and the rural way of life that were inherited throughout several millennia have contributed to the making of an 'acquaintance community' whereas the industrial production model and the urban way of life have led to a 'strangers' community.' The former is necessarily organized upon powers and relations while the latter

---

[1] Marx, Karl. (2012) *Capital, Volume One: A Critique of Political Economy*. Translated by Samuel Moore & Edward Aveling. New York: Dover Publications. p. 275.

is inevitably ruled by law and contracts. In other words, an acquaintance community can be governed with imperial edicts, a strangers' community has to be ruled by law. In the acquaintance community in which everybody is related to each other, mutual familiarity enables the community to curb one's behaviors with imperial edicts, family rules and folk customs. However, once this social fabric is torn, the explosion of social mobility alienates one from another, hence the society is rife with the soaring ethical risks of 'hit-and-run' mentality. With fast-growing deregulation, the law as the basic standard for governance has risen to be the critical stabilizer of the society. The process of urbanization in China is irreversible. So is the process of law-based governance in China. With respect to the application of law to social governance, it was amply explained in the decision at the Fourth Plenary Session of the 18th CPC Central Committee that we should strengthen the awareness of rules, promote the spirit of agreement, deepen the law-based governance by the local authorities, organizations and industries, and support the self-governance and management of all social entities. We should promote the active role of social norms that comprise resident codes of conduct, industry rules and regulations, and charters of organizations in social governance, enhance the active role of public groups and social organizations in building a law-based society, and help industry associations and guilds to provide industry self-discipline and professional services. The modernization of social governance is inseparable from the rule of law.

Many journalists from different media were reporting about the first case held at the First Circuit Court of the Supreme People's Court.(Xinhua News Agency)

4. The development of democracy is inseparable from the rule of law

It is pointed out in the resolution of the Fourth Plenary Session of the 18th CPC Central Committee that clearly defined systems, standards, and procedures are the fundamental guarantee of socialist democracy. Democracy and the rule of law comprise a pair of twins, but each has its unique character. It can be concluded from Gustave Le Bon's discussion on the relationship between democracy and rule of law that without the support of democracy, the constitutional government would become the champion of an 'evil' legal system[1]. The constitutional government is the fruit of a revolution of democracy. However, without the restrictions of the Constitution, democracy is usually vulnerable to ephemeral impulses that even result in tyranny. Law-based governance results from the processes of democratic mediations. However, once the rule of law is built, it determines the rules and the basic standard of games of democracy. History shows that in the paradoxical myth of priority for democracy or law, the latter should indeed precede the former. The authoritarian dictatorship of Napoleon Bonaparte eventually brought about the immortal *Code Civil des France* in 1804. The long-standing dominance of the People's Action Party did not prevent Singapore from growing into a country truly ruled by law. Therefore it is possible that the initial establishment of law-based governance can be advanced by the conscious actions of the core politicians of the state. Once the basic standard of rule by law is set, the potential chaos resulting from trade-offs of democracy will be greatly reduced. In countries devoid of rule by law, democracy spread in such an unrestrained manner like floods breaking through dams, leading to catastrophic aftermaths. Since the 16th CPC National Congress, we concluded positive and negative lessons from history and stressed the leadership by the CPC and the organic unity between the people being the masters of the country; and the rule of China by law. This is a correct judgment based on keen insights into the inherent relationship between democracy and law.

5. National harmony is inseparable from the rule of law

During the Second CPC Central Committee Symposium on Xinjiang Issues in 2014, General Secretary Xi Jinping proposed the strategy of "ruling Xinjiang by law, stabilizing Xinjiang with unity and developing Xinjiang with

---

[1] Le Bon, Gustave. *The Psychology of Revolution*. Translated by Tong Dezhi & Liu Xunlian. Guangzhou: Guangdong People's Publishing House. 2012. p. 20.

long-standing efforts." During the 6th CPC Central Committee Symposium on Tibet Issues, General Secretary Xi Jinping proposed the strategy of "ruling Tibet by law, invigorating Tibet by making Tibetans rich, and developing Tibet with long-standing efforts." Xinjiang and Tibet are the forefronts of anti-separatist activities and anti-terrorism efforts. How to practice good governance there and safeguard the unity of the state and national harmony? This is thus a key challenge that deserves careful reflection by the whole party and the whole country. The talks by General Secretary Xi Jinping clearly accorded top priority to the rule by law, which reflects his profound understanding of the basic and strategic role of rule by law in safeguarding national harmony. Every country in the world has its own untouchable basic standards. Fixing these principles in the form of laws constitutes the basic standard of rule by law of the country. To such a 'worldly state' as China, safeguarding national unity and opposing separatist activities conform to the supreme interest of the nation and the state. Anybody that dares to touch or violate this basic standard will suffer severe legal punishments. With no leeway for its basic standards, a country under rule of law must defend the dignity of law with utmost resoluteness and preclude any words or behaviors that dare to challenge this unchallengeable certitude. Before gaining independence in 1964, Singapore witnessed two severe ethnical clashes between the Malays and Chinese, causing hundreds of casualties. Since independence, the government of Singapore adopted various means of curbing the harm of ethnical or religious factors on national unity, including harsh legal penalties. For example, in 1990, the Maintenance of Religious Harmony Act was issued by the government of Singapore to delimit the spheres of religious activities and give the Minister of Internal Affairs the mandate to make restraining orders. The Minister may "make a restraining order against any priest, monk, pastor, imam, elder, office-bearer or any other person who is in a position of authority in any religious group or institution…" who has "committed or is attempting to commit any of the following acts: (a) causing feelings of enmity, hatred, ill-will or hostility between different religious groups; (b) carrying out activities to promote a political cause, or a cause of any political party while, or under the guise of, propagating or practising any religious belief; (c) carrying out subversive activities under the guise of propagating or practising any religious belief; or (d) exciting disaffection against the President or the Government of Singapore while, or under the guise of, propagating or practising any religious belief," restraining the said person's words and behaviors. The local court can also punish offenders. Under the heavy pressure of law, the ethnic and religious factors of Singapore are strictly limited within the rule of law. For more than two decades, no one has dared challenge this law in Singapore. The government has basically achieved ethnic and religious harmony. The history and personal stories can serve as mirrors for reflection. In the same vein, the anti-separatist activities in China are inseparable from the basic role of the law.

6. Combating corruption and promoting integrity is inseparable from the rule of law

At the Second Plenary Session of the 18th Central Discipline Inspection Commission held on January 22, 2013, General Secretary Xi Jinping pointed out that we should strengthen national legislation against corruption, step up the construction of anti-corruption rules and regulations within the party, deepen the reform in areas and procedures that are prone to corruption, and ensure that government agencies exercise their powers in accordance with legal mandates and procedures. To strengthen the restriction and supervision of the operation of power, we should keep power within the confines of systemic checks, develop a disciplinary mechanism in which no one dares to become corrupt, a preventive mechanism in which no one can become corrupt, and a guarantee system in which no one is prone to corruption. It was reiterated in the Fifth Plenary Session of the 18th CPC Central Committee that we should rule the party by law in a comprehensive and strict manner, deepen the party integrity initiative and restraints against corruption, strengthen the achievements of campaigns against corruption, and seek to build a mechanism in which no one dares to be, can be, or even wants to become corrupt. History shows that the unique geopolitical structure has contributed to a strong tradition of administrative centralization since ancient times in China. To effectively curb the abuse of administrative centralization, Chinese society has naturally developed the counterpart system of imperial censorship. For over two millennia, the imperial censorship system had remained one of the pillars of the Chinese system with its basic function remaining constant - as a dedicated supervisory body affiliated with the supreme ruler. It was independent of the administrative system and exercised strong supervision over the latter. Aside from being the top official of the Censorship Office, the supervisory censors were usually given low ranks and few administrative powers. However, they enjoyed such high discretion and powers in terms of supervision and impeachment that even Prime Ministers were afraid of them. In a sense, the Control Yuan of Taiwan (China); the Corrupt Practices Investigation Bureau (CPIB) of Singapore; the Independent Commission Against Corruption (ICAC) of Hong Kong; and the Central Commission for Discipline Inspection System of China's mainland are modern versions of this censorship tradition. However, these inherited traditions should undergo rigid legal transformations in the era of law. In a sense, CPIB and ICAC's successful transformation helped build the top two clean societies in Asia. However powerful in their discretion while performing tasks, both CIPB and ICAC have acted in strict compliance with legal procedures and contents without the least departure from those principles. In particular, they are also powerfully restrained by prosecutorial and judicial functions. These mark a fundamental distinction between these modern systems and the traditional censorship system acting upon 'gossips and hearsay' in the ancient ruled-by-man tradition. They are also far superior to the secret police system such as secret police (*jin yi wei*) of the Ming Dynasty. The world has witnessed the current remarkable progress in China's anti-corruption struggles. If there is any possible room for further improvement, that would be the expectation that the application of law in anti-corruption efforts will be further enhanced. Struggles against corruption beyond the curbs of law will not stand up to scrutiny in the modern society and their failures are doomed.

II. The Organic Integration of the Leadership of the party and the Law-based Governance

During the seminar of provincial or ministerial-level leading officials on the implementation of the guiding principles of Fourth Plenary Session of the 18th CPC Central Committee and the comprehensive advancement of the rule of law, General Secretary Xi Jinping once again expounded the core issue of the relationship between party's leadership and law-based governance. He pointed out that as the core leadership of the socialist cause with Chinese characteristics, the CPC plays the role of central control and coordination. The socialist rule of law should be based on party's leadership while the latter also depends on the former.

Whether law-based governance requires adherence to party's leadership is a key issue in building rule of law in China and plays a major role in the formation of social consensus. To understand the issue correctly, we need to introduce the theory of systems science. In his book *Republic*, the ancient Greek philosopher Plato wrote that "or that [the best-ordered State] which most nearly approaches to the condition of the individual - as in the body, when but a finger of one of us is hurt, the whole frame, drawn towards the soul as a center and forming one kingdom under the ruling power therein, feels the hurt and sympathizes all together with the part affected, and we say that the man has a pain in his finger; and the same expression is used about any other part of the body, which has a sensation of pain at suffering or of pleasure at the alleviation of suffering."[1] Using the simplest language, Plato expounded the theory of systems science. According to this theory, each life system is a common destiny with the integral whole composed of different elements in a hierarchy. It also states that the goal of development of each social system is to evolve into an advanced quasi-life system. Within the social 'common destiny', society is composed of discrete elements in a hierarchy that constitutes an integral whole in which they work on the basis of division of labor and face the common destiny.

If this argument is valid, then it is easy to understand that it can be compared to the human body working under the command of the brain. However, when the body is injured, the signal will be relayed to the brain through the neural system so that the brain will give due attention and work out a solution. In the same vein, the society also has its own 'brain,' 'body' and 'neural system', or the legal system, which connects the former two. In this sense, a society with the rule of law is just like a person without the neural system — one cannot feel when or where an injury happens and how serious it is. The grievous aftermath that results would be simply beyond our imagination. Moreover, the systems science holds that an advanced system of life is an organic whole in which each subsystem has its own capacity for 'self-organization.' When one goes to sleep, one never worries if the heart and breathing might stop, because the capacity for 'self-organization' of the heart and lung subsystems enables them to operate automatically on their own rhythms. In spite of being the most advanced system of supervision, the brain cannot give orders to the heart and the lungs at every moment. In a sense, the rule of law is manifested in the self-organization capacity of subsystems of the society.

Let us further elaborate on this issue by taking the relationship between party's leadership and rule of law. Needless to say, some people in the society have been trumpeting 'judicial independence' in China as the ultimate indicator of law-based governance. In fact, we prefer 'independent judiciary' rather than 'judicial independence.' This is by no means a word game, for the word 'judicial' in 'judicial independence' is a modifier denoting the concept of independence of the subject whereas the word 'judiciary' in 'independent judiciary' is a word of action that denotes functional independence. Hereby

---

[1] Plato. (2002). *Republic*. http://www.idph.net/conteudos/ebooks/republic.pdf. p. 320.

lies the fundamental difference between the two. From the perspective of systems science, the 'party's leadership' can be compared to the 'brain system' of a country or a society, for it embodies the soul and the will thereof. 'Independent judiciary' can be compared to the liver and kidney system of a country and a society, which is responsible for the 'removal of waste products of metabolism', or the mediation of social conflicts and disputes. Obviously, the liver and kidney system cannot exist while being independent of the body, and therefore sheer 'judicial independence' is an inherent fallacy. Even the so-called 'judicial independence' in the Western society is inherently a verbal expression of the concept of functional independence. However, given the exclusive capacity of the liver and kidneys for removing waste products of metabolism, even the brain cannot take their place and fulfill their duties, or else it would be poisoned by toxins. Therefore we can see that a real law-based society must effectively ward off the interference of political power in regular judicial activities, especially in certain case investigations. During the Conference on Politics and Law of the CPC Central Committee on January 7, 2014, General Secretary Xi Jinping stressed that we should handle the relationship between adherence to the party's leadership properly and ensure the exercise of power by the judicial bodies legally, independently and unbiasedly. Party organizations and leaders of all levels should support all agencies of the political and legal system in their operation based on individual responsibility and coordination in compliance with the Constitution and laws. The decisions of the Fourth Plenary Session of the 18th CPC Central Committee also unequivocally require that party and government organizations and leaders of all levels should support the Court and the Procuratorate in their exercise of power legally and independently. We should establish a system for recording and reporting leaders' interference in judicial activities and specific cases and holding them accountable. No leader in party organizations and governments of any level should order the judicial body to act beyond their legal responsibilities and against judicial justice. No judicial body should comply with demands of leaders of party organizations and governments that illegally interfere with judicial activities. It is thus expressed very clearly that the party's leadership has shown maximum respect for the functional independence of the judicial system.

Meanwhile, the functional independence of the judiciary does not deny the leadership of the party's leadership. Let's return to the human body analogy. If a person develops a fatty liver, the brain must give orders to diet and exercise regularly and, if necessary, take some medicine. Then what if the person knows about a tumor in his liver or kidney? The brain will probably make a critical decision to undergo a surgical operation at the right time. During the third and fourth plenary sessions of the 18th CPC Central Committee, careful strategic deployments were made in judicial reforms. The range of coverage and the influence of reform measures on the old system were unprecedented over scores of years. In a sense, the importance and level of difficulty of this judicial reform makes it comparable to a surgical operation on the judicial system. This surgical reform is obviously not initiated by the judicial system itself, and must rely on the strong political will of the political core as well as the excellent political consciousness of being accountable to the history and the people. Without the strong leadership of the party, all reforms, including judicial reform, could become a mirage, like the moon in water or flowers in the mirror. Of course, whether through diet, medicine or surgical operations, the ultimate goal of the brain's so-called 'interference' in the operation of the liver and kidneys is to help them to regain their independent functions for self-organization. Once they are fully recovered, the brain will make no further intervention, nor can it interfere with their independent operation. This is the scientific relationship between the control system and subsystems in systems science. It can also be used to help us understand the organic unity between the party's leadership and the rule of law.

III. The Synergy between the Rule of Law and the Rule of Virtue

It is pointed out in the Fourth Plenary Session of the 18th CPC Central Committee that we must persist in a joint commitment to the rule of law and the rule of virtue. Effective national and social governance demands a combination of law and morality. We need to lay emphasis on both the rule of law and the rule of virtue. It is imperative that we vigorously promote our core socialist values; carry forward traditional Chinese virtues; and cultivate social morality, professional ethics, family values, and the moral integrity of individuals. We should not only highlight the normative function of law but also value the educational function of virtue. The rule of law gives expression to moral values and the law better promotes the cultivation of morality. We must draw on virtue as a means of nurturing the rule of law and strengthen the role of morality as a pillar of the law-based culture, so that law and virtue promote each other, and the rule of law and the rule of virtue reinforce each other.

Whether rule of law should be combined with rule of virtue is a topic of controversy in academic circles in China. Some point out that while China's rule of law is a sign of progress, rule of virtue may give leeway to rule by man. This issue requires a comprehensive and dialectical perspective. In terms of restriction of power, the rule of law is indeed a cage for powers. At the Second Plenary Session of the 18th Central Discipline Inspection Commission held on January 22, 2013, General Secretary Xi Jinping pointed out that we should "strengthen the restriction and supervision of the operation of power, we should keep power within the confines of systemic checks." This statement by General Secretary Xi Jinping was so impressive that it soon caught on and became a classic remark on the rule of law and confines of power. In fact, keeping power within the confines of systemic checks has become a universal consensus in both China and the West. In *Essays on Freedom and Power* by Lord Acton, a 19th-century British historian, there is such a famous quote, "Power tends to corrupt, and absolute power corrupts absolutely." Realizing the risk of power and restricting it with the principles of democracy and law are indeed a laudable leap forward in the history of social development. In this regard, China still has a long way to go and needs to learn a great deal from other countries.

However, is keeping power within the confines of systemic checks alone enough? Just think about it. What do people usually cage in confines to protect their own security? They are probably two things – beasts in the zoo, and criminals in prison. We cage them because of their potential for harming us. But even when we cage them, dare we approach them? Can we expect them to serve us the people? Certainly not. However, we expect the power to serve us. Ultimately, the power is neither a beast nor a criminal, and thus should not be treated as our enemy. If the power were a latent foe, even when we caged it within the confines of the system, we would win half the battle and lose the other half. For 'keeping power within the confines of systemic checks' is half the story of rule of law, the other half being caging those good people with powers within the confines of systemic checks.

Then what is 'power'? Here is a quote from Mencius: there are two *ways* (*Tao*), the constant being routine while the changeable being power. It is good practice to follow the constant and curb the changeable. It is recorded in *Biography of Gong Yang in Spring and Autumn* (*chunqiu gongyang zhuan*) that: "What is 'power'? Power restores the routine and ushers in virtue." The relationship between the constant and the changeable and between the routine and the power reminds us of the one between law and power. Power lies in changes. The nature of power lies in the necessary room for discretion. However a society tries to curb and regulate powers with the institution, such room for discretion cannot be eliminated. This is one of the truths of power. The popular TV drama *House of Cards* may not be depicting the reality, but the political ecology that it reflects shows that even in a self-proclaimed law-based democracy such as the United States, the elite still have enormous room for discretion in exercising power. It thus can be seen that however sound the institution of a society is, given the permanent room for discretion, it should always resort to meritocracy. The rule of law should not only keep power within the confines of systemic checks, but also ensure that the necessary room for discretion should be reserved for the good people. The confines of systemic checks can prevent powers from deviating into great evil. But when powers are in the hands of good people, they not only ward off petty grievances but also serve the good of the people.

This issue touches upon the difference in political ideology between China and the West. The political ideology of the West centers upon skepticism, with the premise that all politicians are evil. The sentence that follows the famous quote of Lord Acton goes like this, "Great men are almost always bad men." However, the political ideology of China centers upon rule by virtue and benevolent governance, with the premise that politicians are virtuous people. Just as Confucius put it, "He who exercises government by means of his virtue may be compared to the north polar star, which keeps its place and all the stars turn towards it." These two ideologies bloom and prosper separately in the two ends of the Eurasian continent. With their separate historical origins and justifications of reason, they each help the West and China build political mansions that stand erect for thousands of years. Despite the fact that China is actively learning from the political ideologies of the West and fending off the abuse of power by learning to build the confines of systemic checks, Chinese people should never lose heart in their own political traditions and sway from one extreme to the other. However powerful the mechanism of checks with law and democracy, it can never deny the value of the moral consciousness of rulers. That is the fundamental reason why General Secretary Xi Jinping, while promoting the rule of law, still reiterates that we should "adhere to the supreme status of the people's interests, closely rely on the people, and serve the people heart and soul." During his inspection in Shandong in November 2013, General Secretary Xi Jinping pointed out that a nation cannot thrive without virtue, and a person cannot stand erect without virtue, either. We must strengthen the ideological and moral construction of the whole society, inspire people to develop positive moral will and sensibility, cultivate proper moral judgment and responsibility, enhance the capability for ethical practices, in particular the capability for conscious practice, guide people in their pursuit of a lifestyle that stresses, respects and observes moral values, and forge a positive attitude towards kindness. As long as generations of the Chinese nation pursue lofty moral standards, there is forever hope for our nation. In a sense, the rule of law and rule of virtue are to governance what both wings are to the bird or what both wheels are to a carriage. The core of a system lies in skepticism while the core of morality lies in trust. A good society should be a core of trust in a shell of skepticism. In this sense, 'law' indeed should go hand in hand with 'virtue,' creating synergy between rule of law and rule of virtue. In terms of the rule of law, Chinese civilization and Western civilization should be, as Gottfried Wilhelm Leibniz put it, "good if those two strengths can combine and draw upon each other, and enlighten each other."[1]

IV. The Legal Mentality and the Basic-standard Mentality in Governance

Since the 18th National Congress of the CPC, Comrade Xi has reiterated that we should always adhere to the basic-standard mentality, face up to conflicts instead of trying to conceal problems, and work for the best but prepare for the worst. Only in this way can we be always prepared for risks and contingencies and have a grip on the initiative. The new leaders of the CPC Central Committee such as Li Keqiang and Zhang Gaoli have also stressed adherence to the basic-standard mentality on various occasions. Subsequently, leaders of ministries of the CPC Central Committee and officials at all levels of the government recognized and underscored the importance of such mentality for their own work. The basic-standard mentality reminds us of the other mentality that has been stressed by the CPC Central Committee since the party's 18th National Congress – the legal mentality. The report of the 18th CPC National Congress points out that we must improve leading officials' capacity for applying the legal mentality and approaches to deepening reform, promoting development, resolving conflicts, and maintaining stability. So what is the basic-standard mentality? What is the legal mentality? What is the relationship between the two?

From the perspective of governance, the legal mentality and the basic-standard mentality are two different yet interacting modes of thinking. The legal mentality is the mainstream thinking mode of governance for leaders,

---

[1] Gottfried Wilhelm Leibniz. *Novissima Sinica*. Translated by Yang Baojun. Zhengzhou: Elephant Press. 2005. p. 2.

covering the three fields of reform, development and stability in today's society; the basic-standard mentality is one of the key thinking modes of governance by leaders, with a majority of its content incorporated in legal mentality but also has its unique denotations and connotations. For example, the basic standards for economic development and the rate of unemployment in specific periods, the certain basic standards of morality and discipline above the law for party officials. But generally, the majority of the content of basic-standard mentality is indeed incorporated by the legal mentality. Let's interpret the denotation of basic-standard mentality from the perspective of law and try to unveil its legal attributes.

1. The rigid basic-standard mentality

The basic standard of the law is a rigid and decisive line, the ultimate line of defense for the security of lives and possessions of a society. Once the law is made, the basic standard is set, nobody can break it under any excuse. It was written in China's Constitution that "All state organs, the armed forces, all political parties and public organizations and all enterprises and institutions must abide by the Constitution and the law. All acts in violation of the Constitution and the law must be investigated. No organization or individual is privileged to act beyond the Constitution or the law. For the purposes of law enforcement, the certainty and rigidity of this basic standard requires not only passive compliance but also proactive law enforcement."

This is the rigid basic-standard mentality of law-based governance. It has been proven with evidence that the more rigid this basic standard is, the greater deterring effect to criminals, and hence the lower costs of social management. By contrast, the less rigid this basic standard is, the greater becomes the opportunism mentality of criminals, and hence the higher costs of social management. From curbing violence to preventing corruption, from social management to the construction of a clean government, the rigid basic-standard mentality is an untouchable, unbreakable and indispensable 'high-voltage power cable' of the society. Any room for the discretion of power should be strictly limited within the sphere of compliance, and any deviation incurs severe punishment by law.

2. The basic-standard mentality of fairness

During the Central Economic Working Conference at the end of 2013, General Secretary Xi Jinping stressed that we must steadfastly follow the strategy of adhering to basic standards, highlighting some issues of focus, improving the institution and guiding public opinion; we should coordinate education, employment, income distribution, social security, medicine, housing, food safety and the safety of industrial production, and take concrete measures to improve people's standard of living. At the Fifth Plenary Session of the 18th CPC Central Committee, the concept of shared development was raised, requiring all people to participate in development, devote themselves to development, and share the fruits of development. It also requires steadfast adherence to basic standards, highlighting some issues of focus, improving the institution, guiding public anticipations, stressing equal opportunities, ensuring basic standard of living, and realizing a moderately prosperous society in all respects for all people. General Secretary Xi Jinping's speech and the decision of the CPC Central Committee show us clearly the perspective of how we look at people's standard of living and the equality of basic standards. As is known to all, recent years have witnessed a series of public security incidents targeting innocent civilians all over China.

In either killing sprees on school campuses or arsons on buses, criminals that deprived innocent people of their lives deserve the most severe punishment and the most vehement criticism. However, reflections on a law-based society should go beyond the phenomena per se. In the animal world, killings of herbivores by predatory animals are irrelevant to morality or law, for the supreme law of animals is survival. Life requires rules and regulations, but survival requires all means available. Being a kind of animal, human beings also have animal instincts that can lead us to kill each other for the sake of survival. However, human society differs from the animal society in that a basic standard has been accepted in the former—the part above it is called 'life' while the part below is called 'survival.' The part above belongs to the human society while the part below is categorized as the animal society. Just as is depicted by the film *Back to 1942* (2012) directed by Feng Xiaogang, the basic standard of living was completely shattered by a great famine that hit Henan Province in the year 1942. Under such circumstances, neither landlords with any storage of foodstuff or farming hands without a grain at home could protect their own lives or possessions in the whirls of chaos, because when the basic standard was broken, human society instantly reverted to animal society. In today's society where difference has become an indisputable reality but everybody lives above the basic standard, such a society can still maintain stability, and happiness that varies from person to person is largely determined by themselves. However, once someone falls below the basic standard into the state of subsistence, the happiness index of the whole society would probably be determined by the most unhappy people.

In a differentiated society, given the legal protection of individual rights of private property and rights of inheritance, the so-called propositions of 'justice at the starting point', or levelling the playing field, and 'justice of results' are in fact hard to prove. The most important justice worthy of pursuit in a differentiated society is the justice of basic standards, i.e., an irrevocable firm pledge to all members of the society that everyone can make a basic living with dignity. Only in this way can we prevent members of the society from losing heart in crisis and victimizing the society in desperation. As Maslow's pyramid of needs shows, survival and security are the most basic of human needs which in fact are the most basic standards for everyone. This ultimate standard ensures absolute fairness for everyone. In a differentiated society, though people differ in identity and wealth, they are equal in terms of the respect and protection of life. An ordinary commuter travelling in crowded subway trains may find a millionaire driving his luxury limousine acceptable, but would never accept it if the latter runs his car recklessly into pedestrians without getting punished. Such is the basic-standard mentality of fairness in a differentiated society. Once this basic standard of fairness is broken, the society would be plagued by turmoil and ultimately subverted.

The rule of law must guard this basic standard of fairness for society. However, this basic standard will not stay constant, but rather be adjusted in response to changes in times and conditions. As the old saying goes, 'When the river rises, the boat floats high.' If a society is finally free from such problems as subsistence and survival, then where should we set the basic standard of the society? In his speech at the Central Economic Working Conference at the end of 2013, General Secretary Xi Jinping has pointed out the direction for our efforts, and a good government should try their best to mobilize public resources and safeguard this basic standard of fairness for the society. It certainly needs to be noted that safeguarding this basic standard does not encourage loiterers to be parasitic on society, for the fairness of basic standards should be complemented by the fairness of opportunities. The value of the former lies in maintaining stability while the value of the latter lies in stimulating development. Ultimately, an unstable society cannot develop, and a society that does not develop eventually cannot remain stable. Therefore the perspective of fairness in a good society is like the letter T upside down – the horizontal stroke at the bottom represents the fairness of basic standards while the vertical stroke represents the fairness of opportunities. With basic standards and opportunities, there will be no real regret in life, and there will be no true failure in the society.

3. Mentality of reversed transmission by the basic standards

While talking with non-communist party personages on Sept. 17, 2013, Comrade Xi Jinping pointed out that reforms result from reversed transmission of problems but are deepened in constantly finding solutions. On Nov., 12, 2013, *Decision of the Central Committee of the CPC on Some Major Issues Concerning Comprehensively Continuing the Reform* was approved at the Third Plenary Session of the 18th CPC Central Committee, and resounded like a trumpet summoning all to comprehensively advance reform to a deeper level. In a sense, this comprehensive and profound reform resulted from reversed transmission by problems, just like the epic reform and opening up that started in 1978. Back in 1978, the turmoil of the Cultural Revolution had just ended in China, with the national economy towards the verge of collapse, and all fields were plagued with grave problems. The fate of China and the fate of the CPC were both upon the verge of death. One step backward, and China would have slipped into an apocalyptical abyss of history. Thus the Chinese people, unwilling to yield to doom and destruction, made a desperate attempt for development under the leadership of the CPC Central Committee centering upon Comrade Deng Xiaoping. The reversed transmission effect transformed problems into initiatives towards reform, leading to the successful establishment of the socialist market economy system. After three decades of arduous efforts, China has become the No. 2 economy of the world. The predicament of life-and-death did not deter the courage of the Chinese and the CPC, but rather gave rise to the initiative of reform. The same mentality that led to the reform and opening up in 1978 is once again driving reform to a deeper level. We call this the mentality of reversed transmission by the basic standards.

The mentality of reversed transmission by the basic standards is prevalent in all walks of life. A company cannot run well without the reversed transmission of the market mentality, for the market is the basic standard for the survival of a company; an army cannot be combative without the reversed transmission of the battlefield, and thus the battlefield is the basic standard of the army. In the same vein, good governance cannot be achieved without the reversed transmission of the legal mentality, and rule of law is the basic standard of the government. Rule of law stems from the will of the people, so a government that opposes the will of the people will eventually be dumped ruthlessly into the trash bin of history, just as will be companies that oppose the market rules, and armies that oppose the laws of the battlefield. Therefore companies must conscientiously follow the rules of the market and strive to produce goods that are popular on the market, if they seek survival; armies must consciously follow the laws of the battlefield in their drills, to develop real combative capacity, if they seek victory in the battlefield. In the same vein, if the government seeks to avoid being eliminated by the will of the people, it must conscientiously follow the requirements for rule of law, apply legal mentality and approaches to deepening reform, promoting development, resolving conflicts, and maintaining stability.

A conscientious government should respect the basic standard of rule of law. In fact, the reversed transmission by the basic standard of the will of the people may take many forms, the rule of law just being one of them. Such reversed transmission is inherently a constructive or systemic action. If a government rejects such reversed transmission from the rule of law, the will of the people would be realized through revolutions of violence, which in turn would still constitute reversed transmission to the government. However, this kind of transmission is destructive in nature. The regular cycle of dynasties in ancient China that was epitomized in such quotes as 'it rose robustly and fell abruptly' and 'the water that bears the boat is the same that swallows it up' is such destructive reversed transmission. Once the regular cycle of dynasties was applied, society had to pay a heavy price of total destruction. During the peasant uprising at the end of Qin Dynasty, "Xiang Yu led his troops to conquer the capital of Xianyang with a massacre, killing Ziying, the Qin king who surrendered, setting the Qin palaces on fire that did not extinguish until three months later, and trooping east with all the loots of goods, treasures and women." (from *Records of Xiang Yu, The Chronicles*). During the peasant uprising in the twilight of Tang Dynasty, Huang Chao twice conquered the capital of Chang'an, "allowing his soldiers to slaughter so wantonly that blood pooled into rivers, and hence the expression of 'bathing the city in blood.'" (Vol. 254, *History as a Mirror (Zi Zhi Tong Jian)*). By 2 AD, the total population of China in West Han Dynasty was 59.59 million, but by 57 AD of East Han Dynasty, a bloody civil war that lasted scores of years left China with a population only somewhat over 21 million. It was recorded that thousands of miles of fields were left barren, and nine households out of ten were exterminated. This was the horrible force of destructive reversed transmission by the regular cycle of dynasties. Only a profound understanding of its terrible destructive force can ultimately lead to the voluntary transmission of the institution. In this sense, the mentality of reversed transmission by the basic standards of rule of law is a real solution to the myth of the regular cycle of dynasties.

Therefore, the mentality of reversed transmission by the basic standards is dynamic in nature. Given the appalling aftermaths of breaking the basic standards, people must try their best to exceed basic standards instead of lingering upon their margins or even deliberately walking upon the tightrope. As the saying goes, if you often walk along the river, how can you avoid wetting your shoes? Walking upon the tightrope of basic standards, one is likely to fall off any time, incurring horrible aftermaths. Therefore the basic standard can be transfused into the starting line or the source of power for a conscientious government or official in their active pursuit of achievements through reversed transmission; for an unconscientious government or official, by contrast, the basic standard may well become the line that leads to their downfall. It is the mentality of reversed transmission by the basic standards of rule of law that defines the basic standard and drives up the awareness through reversed transmission. Therein lie the true elements of General Secretary Xi Jinping's statement of "working for the best while preparing for the worst."

Respecting the rigid basic standard, safeguarding its fairness, and complying with its reversed transmission - these constitute the basic-standard mentality in the landscape of rule of law. Only by firmly upholding the basic-standard mentality can modern officials and leaders be truly prepared against risks, stay calm in case of emergency, and have a firm hold of the initiative. Only in this way can they truly enhance their capacity for driving reform to a deeper level, resolving conflicts, promoting development and maintaining stability, thereby making their contributions to building a moderately prosperous society in all respects.

Chapter 4

Promote Deliberative Democracy

"Socialist deliberative democracy is a unique form and a distinctive strength of China's socialist democracy. It is an important embodiment of the party's mass line in the political field. It was stated at the 18th CPC National Congress that as China's socialist democracy progresses, we need to improve the institutions and mechanisms for deliberative democracy and promote its broad-based, multi-level, and institutionalized development. It was stressed at the Third Plenary Session of the 18th CPC Central Committee that with a focus on the major issues concerning economic and social development and the practical issues that affect people's immediate interests, the party should lead extensive deliberations throughout the whole of society and ensure that deliberations are conducted both before decisions are made and during their implementation. These important statements and plans have shown what the way forward will be for China's socialist deliberative democracy.

— Xi Jinping's keynote speech at the conference to celebrate the CPPCC's 65th anniversary, *People's Daily*, September 22, 2014.

'Deliberation' is a familiar word; 'democracy' is a word more familiar to us. When 'deliberation' and 'democracy' are combined, however, a 'new concept', namely 'deliberative democracy' is formulated, yet people find it 'fresh' and not easy to understand. Recently, the term 'deliberative democracy' has been emerging intensively and frequently, and has been interpreted variously. Since 1978 when the policy of reform and opening up to the outside world was implemented, people have been holding diversified views on deliberative democracy. Some note the discrepancy between paces of economic development (faster) and political development (slower). Some take the role of democratic parties as 'a decorative vase', deliberation among political parties standing as 'a show, full of empty rhetoric', and the united front and political participation for nothing but 'going through the motions'. All these voices are still very audible on certain occasions, because some people are still likely to 'repeat the past' and turn a blind eye and a deaf ear to objective reality. All these phenomena oblige us to interpret the scientific connotation, spiritual essence and practical measures of socialist deliberative democracy in a timely, thorough and accurate way. Theoretically and practically, we find it necessary and urgent to foster and intensify confidence in the construction of socialist democracy with Chinese characteristics.

I. Deliberation and Democracy

What is 'socialist deliberative democracy'? President Xi Jinping defined it precisely as, "socialist deliberative democracy is a unique form and a distinctive strength of China's socialist democracy. It is an important embodiment of the party's mass line in the political field." Fact is stranger than fiction. In the 'global village' where humans coexist, numerous examples show that some people pretend to be holding a 'democracy' banner or flaunt their 'deliberative democracy'. President Xi's concept of 'deliberative democracy', based on the precise and rigorous logical reasoning, is a complete scientific category. The modifier 'socialist' cannot be 'omitted', so it cannot be simplified as 'deliberative democracy'. 'Socialist deliberative democracy' profoundly reveals and manifests the essential socialist attribute and nature of deliberative democracy.

It has been president Xi Jinping's logical approach and methodology to stress the characteristics and essence of scientific categorisation. When we study the important speeches made by President Xi Jinping, we not only earnestly learn from the speeches' main contents and key thoughts, but also deeply comprehend the scientific thinking methods embedded in his speeches. It is important to grasp President Xi's scientific thinking method, in order to completely and accurately understand the spiritual essence of the speeches made by the President. Since the 18th National Congress of the CPC, Xi Jinping has been insisting the party "uphold and develop socialism with Chinese characteristics", and he also stressed in a straightforward way that "Socialism with Chinese characteristics is socialism rather than anything else. The basic principles of scientific socialism must not be abandoned; otherwise it is not socialism."[1] Socialist deliberative democracy is closely

---

[1] Xi Jinping's Speech at the Seminar of the Members and Alternate Members of the Newly-elected Central Committee of the CPC for Implementing the Guiding Principles of the 18th CPC National Congress. *People's Daily*. January 6, 2013

associated with the basic system of socialism. The word 'socialist' plays an indispensible part in 'socialist deliberative democracy', for it indicates the nature of our deliberative democracy.

The conference to celebrate the CPPCC's 65th anniversary was held in Beijing on September 21, 2014. (Xinhua News Agency)

1. Socialist deliberative democracy: a unique form and a distinctive strength of China's socialist democracy

"The people's democracy is the very life of socialism." "The position of people as masters of the country is the essence and core of socialist democracy." In a nutshell, adherence to people's democracy and the position of people as masters of the country ensures that the people can maintain their dominant position and that the country's power belongs to the people. The over-90-years' history of the CPC since it was founded in 1921, more than 60 years' development of the PRC since it was founded in 1949, and the achievements in reform and opening up and the socialist modernization over the past 30 years, all repeat the same fact that "the very purpose of the CPC's leadership of the people in developing people's democracy is to guarantee and support their position as masters of the country." "Guaranteeing and supporting the position of the people as masters of the country" is neither a 'slogan' nor 'lip service'. We must ensure its implementation in both the country's political and social activities, and guarantee the people's right to effectively manage state affairs, economic and cultural undertakings, and social affairs, in accordance with the law.

Chapter 4

"Only the wearer of the shoes knows if they fit or not." Xi Jinping's remark is concise, comprehensive, thought-provoking yet easy to understand. As the saying goes, 'we don't need the same shoes, for each of us needs one pair that fits best. Approaches to governance may diverge, but converge in the interests of the people.' Only the people are best qualified for judging if the development path they have chosen fits for their country or not. In the world, each country and their people are entitled to equal dignity. Therefore, Xi Jinping reiterates our steady refrain that, "We stand for … all countries, irrespective of size, strength and wealth, are equal. The right of the people to independently choose their development paths should be respected, interference in the internal affairs of other countries opposed and international fairness and justice maintained."[1] He also pointed out clearly, "The criterion of selecting the ideology is based on whether it can address historical problems that confront the country." The same applies regarding what type of democracy to choose, what path to follow and what doctrine to apply. ComradeXi Jinping's metaphor of 'shoes', simple but profound and powerful, is rich in philosophy. It is stated in plain words that have great appeal. This vivid metaphor conveys our firm confidence in continuously upholding and developing socialism with Chinese characteristics.

Xi Jinping stated frankly, "The reason why the political system of socialism with Chinese characteristics is feasible, dynamic and efficient is that it has been grown in the soil of Chinese society. The political system of socialism with Chinese characteristics, which was, and is, growing in the soil of Chinese society, must be deeply rooted in the soil of Chinese society for its thriving in the future."[2] Similarly, "guaranteeing and supporting the position of people as masters" as the basic requirement and content has to be implemented in corresponding forms and measures. Reality indicates there are a variety of approaches to democracy, so we should not follow any stereotype. "Further, we must recognize that there is no such a thing as a standard model that is universally acceptable." For this reason, it is extremely unreasonable, even irrational for one country to arbitrarily criticize or groundlessly rebuke the path of development and political system that other countries choose, or to impose its own approach to democracy on other countries.

---

[1] Xi Jinping. Part of the Speech at Moscow State Institute of International Relations. *People's Daily*. March 24, 2013.

[2] Xi Jinping. Part of the Speech at the Conference to Celebrate the 60th Anniversary of the National People's Congress. People's Daily. September 6, 2014.

The position of people as masters of the country is congruent with the rights that people duly enjoy. Election and ballots are tangible means of democracy. They are so evidently present in people's life that they intuitively take 'direct election' and 'public voting' for the standard by which to measure the process of democracy. Election and voting, which are indeed the key ways and means to practice democracy, are not the whole case. Whether the people enjoy democratic rights or not depends on "whether they have the right to vote in elections, as well as whether they have the right to constantly participate in everyday political activities." These two perspectives interrelate with and promote one another. The former is more 'obvious', while the latter is more 'profound'. "Socialist democracy requires not just a complete set of institutions and procedures, but also full participation." Based on this, Xi Jinping further explained the position of people as masters of the country with the following: it must be substantially and practically fulfilled through the exercise of the governance of the country by the party, through works of the party and government organizations at all levels in all sectors, and through the realization and development of the people's own interests.

In brief, "in light of the realities of each country, to guarantee and support the position of the people as the masters of the country", it is paramount that people's elected representatives participate in the management of state affairs and social activities, and it is equally important that the people participate in such activities through systems and methods other than election. In real life, we cannot take 'voting', mechanically and partially as the only way to democracy, or even as the 'best' one. Xi Jinping remarked frankly with great insight, "If the people merely have the right to vote but no right of extensive participation, in other words, if they are only awakened at election time but go into hibernation afterwards, then this kind of democracy will only be a formalistic one."

The experience with people's democracy in China shows that in such a vast and populous socialist country, extensive deliberation under the leadership of the CPC on major issues concerning the economy and the people's quality of life embodies the unity of democracy and centralism. Chinese socialist democracy takes two important forms, in one of which, the people exercise their right to vote in elections, and in the other, people from all sectors of society undertake extensive deliberations for reaching consensus on certain issues before major decisions are made. In China, these two forms do not cancel one another out, nor do they deny each other; they are complementary. They constitute institutional features and strengths of Chinese socialist democracy.

Xi Jinping stressed repeatedly, "The leadership of the CPC is the most essential feature of socialism with Chinese characteristics". China, the most populous developing country in the world, would fail to make progress and accomplish nothing in any cause without the core strength of the CPC's leadership. Both history and reality have constantly proved, and will prove completely, this incontrovertible scientific judgment. Both history and reality have proved, and will prove, that deliberative democracy has been integrated into the whole process of China's socialist democracy. The Chinese socialist deliberative democracy not only upholds the leadership of the CPC, but also gives expression to the positive role of all sides; it not only upholds the people's principal position in the country, but also implements the leadership system and organizational principle of democratic centralism; and it not only adheres to the principle of people's democracy, but also promotes unity and harmony. Therefore, the Chinese socialist system of deliberative democracy diversifies the forms and expands the channels of democracy, and enriches the connotation of democracy.

2. Socialist deliberative democracy is an important embodiment of the party's mass line in the political field

A song has it that "The common people are the earth, the common people are the sky, and they are forever the party's care. The common people are the mountains, the common people are the sea, and they are the lifespring of the party." As the vanguard of Chinese working class as well as Chinese people and Chinese nation, the party's tenet is to serve the people, heart and soul. This tenet is the basic requirement to uphold Marxist historical materialism. The people are the makers of history; the people are the driving force of historical progress. The people of all ethnic groups under the leadership of the CPC founded the PRC, and they are the masters of the country. The Constitution of the PRC stipulates that all power of the state belongs to the people, and all state organs and employees must rely on their support, keep in close touch with them, listen to their opinions and suggestions, accept their oversight, and work hard to serve them. Therefore, anytime and anywhere, China must closely rely on the people in governing the country and managing society.

Following Marxist historical materialism, the CPC implements mass line in its work. Mass line is the CPC's key achievement in theoretical innovation and practice by integrating basic principles of Marxism and Chinese concrete realities. The party systematically applied the Marxism-Leninism's principle of the people being the creators of history to its all activities and formed its basic work route of mass line. Mass line is "the basic work route to achieve the party's ideological line, political line and organizational line."[1] Historical experience shows that mass line is in accordance with 'seeking truth from facts' and 'keeping the initiative in our own hands', which is the very soul of Mao Zedong's thoughts.

The party's mass line cannot be randomly simplified as 'from the masses, to the masses'. *Constitution of the CPC* stipulates, "The party follows the mass line in its work, doing everything for the masses, relying on them in every task, carrying out the principle of 'from the masses, to the masses' and translating its correct views into action by the masses of their accord."[2] It is an organic integral of three parts: value endowment (doing everything for the masses, relying on them in every task), practice approach (from the masses to the masses) and goal orientation (translating its correct views into action by the masses of their own accord). Xi Jinping reiterated at the Working Conference of the party's Mass line Education and Practice, "Mass line is the lifeline and basic work route of our party." "Both history and reality show us that keeping close links with the masses is the embodiment of the party's nature and tenet, the distinctive sign that distinguishes the CPC from other political parties, and the main reason for the party's development and growth. Whether or not the party can maintain its close ties with the masses determines the success or failure of the cause of the party."[3]

Xi Jinping pointed out, "Serving the people wholeheartedly and always representing the fundamental interests of the greatest possible majority of the people are the important preconditions and foundation for the implementation and development of deliberative democracy." Since the moment it was founded, the CPC stated clearly that the CPC has no special interests of its own outside of the interests of the working class and the greatest possible majority of the people. The CPC and the state it leads represent the fundamental interests of the greatest possible majority of the people, and all of their theories, lines, principles, policies, and work plans should come from the people and should be formulated and implemented for the people's interests. With this as our major political premise, we have the obligation and

---

[1] *Selection of Important Documents on all the Plenary Sessions of the Central Committee of the Party's National Congress Since the Third Plenary Session of the 11th Central Committee of the CPC (the second half)*. Central Documents Press. 1997. p. 47.

[2] *Document Compilation of the 14th CPC National Congress*. People's Publishing House. 1992. p. 94.

[3] Xi Jinping. A Speech at the Working Conference of the Party's Mass Line Education and Practice. *People's Daily*. August 5, 2013.

ability to listen extensively to the people from all sectors of society for their comments and suggestions.

Experience has persuasively shown that we, under the CPC's unified leadership, are able to extensively listen to recommendations and suggestions, and accept criticism and oversight through various forms of deliberation, which reflects the unique strength of Chinese socialist deliberative democracy. Meanwhile, we are able to reach 'five possible goals' and fulfill 'five tasks effectively'. They are as follows: we are able to reach the broadest possible consensus on all decisions we make and on all our work, ensuring that factional rivalry and even bitter disagreement between parties and between interest groups can be avoided. We are able to have all the demands, on matters affecting the interests of all sides, heard before decisions are made so that political forces do not remain fixed in their own opinions or reject others with different views for the sake of their own interests. We are able to put in place broad-based mechanisms for recognizing and correcting errors so that decisions are not made without a clear understanding of the circumstances, or on the basis of belief in one's own blind pretension. We are able to build mechanisms for ensuing people's participation in administration and governance at all levels in order to effectively enable people's voices to be heard and their opinions to be incorporated in decision-making and governance. We are able to pool the wisdom and strength of the whole society to advance reform and development, effectively overcoming any problems with our decisions and work not being carried out for lack of consensus.

Socialist deliberative democracy is an important reflection of the party's mass line in the political field. It comprehensively shows that we should carry out the party's mass line in all work of the state, keeping close ties with the masses, listening to the voices of the people, responding to the expectations of the people, and constantly solving the most direct and practical problems that most concern the people, so as to pool the wisdom and strength of the vast majority of the people.

We are about to enter into the important historical period of the 13th Five-Year Plan for Economic and Social Development (the 13th Five-Year Plan). This is a decisive period to achieving the goal of making Chinese society moderately prosperous in all respects, which is the first of the Two Centenary Goals set by the CPC. In order to ensure that Chinese society becomes moderately prosperous in all respects within the set time frame, and to promote the sustainable and healthy development of economy and society, we must follow a series of important and basic principles in accordance with the situations of our country. Among them, first of all is 'upholding the people's principal position in the country.' *Central Committee of the CPC: Recommendations for the 13th Five-Year Plan for Economic and Social Development* (*Recommendations* for short) points out, "The people are the fundamental force that drives development, and realizing, safeguarding, and developing the fundamental interests of the largest possible majority of people is the fundamental purpose of development. We should adhere to a people-centered notion of development, make improving their wellbeing and promoting individuals' well-rounded development the starting point and ultimate goal of development." Hereby, the Central Committee proposed clearly that we should "develop the people's democracy, safeguard social equity and justice, protect the rights of the people to participate and develop on an equal footing, and give full rein to their enthusiasm, initiative, and creativity." Currently, we should inspire more citizens' orderly participation in political affairs at all levels and in all fields, and develop a more extensive, more complete and more robust people's democracy. We should further expand the people's democracy, strengthen the democratic system, enrich democratic forms and broaden democratic channels.

Completing the building of a moderately prosperous society in all respects, and achieving the Two Centenary Goals are central to the vital interests of billions of people and to the great rejuvenation of the Chinese nation. Hence, *Recommendations* points out emphatically that we should "motivate people to work together". "We should give full rein to democracy, implement the party's mass line, become better able to communicate with and organize the people, strengthen deliberation on major economic and social development issues as well as on issues that affect the vital interests of the people, protect all of their interests in accordance with the law, and inspire within every Chinese person a sense of contribution to their country's development." In practice, we should create new institutions, mechanisms, and approaches in our work with the public, and "properly handle problems among the people, so that, to the greatest possible extent, we can develop consensus and pool strength throughout China for the advancement of reform and development and the promotion of social harmony and stability."[1]

Socialist deliberative democracy is "a unique form and a distinctive strength of China's socialist democracy. Politically, it is an important

---

[1] *Central Committee of the CPC: Recommendations for the 13th Five-Year Plan for Economic and Social Development. People's Daily.* November 4,2015.

embodiment of the party's mass line". This statement has withstood the test of history and the test of practice. History and practice have convincingly shown that "socialist deliberative democracy is deeply rooted in China. It has its rich resources and is full of vitality. It is the great creation of the CPC and the Chinese people."[1]

II. Down-to-earth Democracy

1. Socialist deliberative democracy is not a matter of doing things for the sake of appearances; it must be carried out in a down-to-earth manner.

As Xi Jinping stated, "Democracy is not an ornament to be used for decoration; it is to be used to solve the problems that the people want to solve."[2] The CPC has always been practicing what it advocates and doing solid work. Neither engaging in formalism nor doing superficial writing is the intrinsic requirement of the party's ideological line. Socialist deliberative democracy should not be written on the paper, or shouted by mouth, nor hung on the wall. Instead, it should be applied to social life in a down-to-earth manner. In view of its development progress, "socialist democracy requires not just a complete set of institutions and procedures, but also full participation." The participation by billions of people, especially, their 'full' participation, has its basic requirements, that is, the position of the people as masters of the country must be given concrete and practical expression through the exercise of state power by the CPC and its governance of the country, in all aspects of the work of the party and government organizations at all levels, and through the realization and development of the people's own interests.

Further, real-world and difficult situations at home and abroad objectively require socialist deliberative democracy to be 'down-to-earth'. It cannot, even, is not allowed to, be a matter of doing things for show. From a domestic perspective, in the process of reform and opening up, the pattern of interests has undergone drastic changes and resulted in a new situation; new and old social problems are interwoven with one another; and notions and systems in market economy are diversified. From an international perspective, the competitive game of different political development paths

---

[1] Xi Jinping. Socialist Deliberative Democracy Takes Roots in China with Vitality. *People's Daily*. October 28, 2014.

[2] Xi Jinping. The Speech at the Conference to Celebrate the CPPCC's 65th Anniversary. *People's Daily*. September 22, 2014.

across the world presents new challenges. Thus, it is of great and far-reaching significance to carry out socialist deliberative democracy in a 'down-to-earth' manner for the following five purposes. It is conducive to attracting more citizens to participate in a orderly way in political life and to better realizing people's rights of being the masters of the country; to improve skills in scientific and democratic decision-making and accelerate the modernization of national governance system and capacity; to resolve conflicts and facilitate social harmony and stability; to maintain close ties between the party and the people and consolidate and enlarge the party's governing basis; to give full play to the advantages of our country's political system, and reinforce our confidence in the path, theories and system of socialism with Chinese characteristics.

'Democracy is not an ornament' drives the point home. It is the requirement for the development of socialist deliberative democracy, as well as the objective evaluation on the construction of socialist democracy with Chinese characteristics. Some ridicule those participatory parties as 'vases', while others simplify political consultation with Chinese characteristics as 'beckoning, raising hands, clapping, and waving', which is utter formalism and quite contrary to the reality. Frankly speaking, socialist deliberative democracy still needs to be improved and perfected in its development. However, it is even more necessary for us to affirm its achievements and to acknowledge its substantial contributions. 'Democracy is not an ornament to be used for decoration; it is to be used to solve the problems that the people want to solve.' This is a scientific conclusion.

Party consultation is a distinctive strength of socialist democracy with Chinese characteristics, which plays an indispensable role in the work of the party and the country. On the eve of the founding of the PRC, the first plenary session of the CPPCC was held. Representing the will of the people of all ethnic groups in China and performing the functions of the National People's Congress, that session adopted the *Common Program of the CPPCC* – a provisional kind of Constitution; the *Organizing Law of the CPPCC*; and the *Organizing Law of the Central People's Government of the People's Republic of China*. It adopted major resolutions on the capital, the national flag, the national anthem, and the calendar system of the PRC. In addition, the session elected the National Committee of the CPPCC and the Central People's Government Council of the PRC, and proclaimed the founding of the PRC. All these are the landmark achievements of democratic consultation, demonstrating significant and 'down-to-earth' contributions to the founding of the PRC made by the CPPCC.

Party consultation is another important part of the national governance system. Since the PRC was founded, the CPC has conducted extensive and in-depth consultation with the democratic parties on both domestic and foreign affairs, such as socialist transformation of capitalist industry and commerce, and the movement to resist US aggression and aid Korea (Korean War, 1950-1953). The CPC did not take actions until they reached a consensus, which was advocated and supported by all sectors of the society. At the initial stage of reform and opening up, in order to mobilize the business sector and motivate their enthusiasm to participate in economic construction, comrade Deng Xiaoping invited five leaders of the China Democratic National Construction Association, and All-China Federation of Industry and Commerce, to have an informal discussion. Their meeting called 'Five Seniors' Hotpot Feast' became a much-told story. Ji Fang, 92-year-old chairman of the Chinese Peasants and Workers Democratic Party, Hu Juewen, chairman of the Central Committee of the China Democratic National Construction Association, Hu Ziang, chairman of the All-China Federation of Industry and Commerce, jointly put forward *Proposals on the Promotion and Development of Chinese Medicine*, which was highly approved by the Central Committee of the CPC. The so-called 'Three Seniors' Proposal' is another much-told story in the history of multi-party cooperation.

Since the beginning of the 21st century, the central committees of the democratic parties participated in investigation of and proposals for revitalizing the old industrial bases in Northeast region, developing the Western Taiwan Straits Economic Zone, and establishing the Central Plains Economic Zone, which have become the significant strategies to drive our country's regional development. Since the 18th National Congress of the CPC, the central committees of democratic parties put forward many practical and efficient opinions and suggestions on issues such as promoting the coordinated development of Beijing, Tianjin and Hebei, and coping with the haze pollution. By means of party consultation and deliberation, the CPC set up an institutionalized platform for opinions, communication and consultation, widely pooling the wisdom and strength of all sectors of society, and boosting the scientific and democratic development of national governance decisions.

The great practice of building socialism with Chinese characteristics provides a broad stage for further stimulating and giving full play to the characteristics and advantages of each participatory party, and promoting multi-party cooperation and socialist deliberative democracy, so as to pool strengths and join hands to build a moderately prosperous society in all respects. The achievements of socialist deliberative democracy are highly valued by the party and the country, which have been transformed into policies and guidelines and put into practice. The ample and substantial fruits of investigation, participation in state affairs, and political consultation have been adopted and absorbed by the party, the government and the departments concerned.

When looking back to history and summarizing experiences of both past and present, we can clearly see that the diversified approaches and channels of socialist deliberative democracy have made tangible contributions of historic significance to rejuvenating and developing the economy, consolidating the newly founded people's government, giving impetus to social reforms, advancing the socialist revolution and development, building a moderately prosperous society in all respects, and constantly advancing socialist modernization. In the new historical development epochs and stages, the Party Central Committee with Comerade Xi Jinping as its core accurately understands the nature and position of the CPPCC, gives full play to its role as a main channel for deliberative democracy, and builds institutions regarding political consultation, democratic oversight, and participation in the deliberation and administration of state affairs, with the focus on the themes of unity and democracy. The CPPCC, along with the socialist deliberative democracy, has developed while carrying forward its fine traditions, and has kept making innovations throughout its development. It has concentrated on the central task of economic development, served the overall interests of the country, and made new positive contributions by developing consensus, drawing together people's energies, and making proposals on comprehensively deepening reform. All these are indisputable and obvious to all as solid facts.

In the light of dialectical materialism and historical materialism, we should recognize that socialist deliberative democracy has made significant 'down-to-earth' progress; meanwhile we should be aware that the deliberative democracy construction is a process requiring constant development. There are new problems, new challenges and new tasks under new circumstances, so in the new historical developmental epoch and new historical developmental stage, we should "support and encourage the exploration and innovation in deliberative democracy construction", respect people's initiatives, and attach importance to extracting and summarizing hands-on experience which can be developed into institutional norms in timely fashion. Efforts can be made in the following three aspects: We should strengthen leadership and organizational coordination, encourage exploration and innovation, implement extensive consultation by means of diversified mechanisms, channels and methods, and set up and perfect multiple consultative processes, including proposals, meetings, informal discussions, seminars, hearings, public notices, assessments, consulting, networks and public opinion polling. We should reinforce the construction of new think-tanks, establish and improve policy-making consulting system. We should advance theoretical research on deliberative democracy to constantly enrich and develop the theoretical system of socialist deliberative democracy.

2. We should establish a system of deliberative democracy with reasonable procedures while staying all-inclusive.

Xi Jinping stated that socialist deliberative democracy must be put into practice in all respects, and 'across the country at all levels'. It profoundly reveals that socialist deliberative democracy is a 'systematic engineering' composed of many elements, and emphasizes the significance and necessity of building a system of socialist deliberative democracy that is all-inclusive, with reasonable procedures.

As regards this issue, Xi Jinping, General Secretary of the CPC, put forward requirements clearly. They are to: expand the consultation channels of the organs of state power, committees of the Chinese People's Political Consultative Conference, political parties, and community-level and social organizations; conduct intensive deliberation on issues relating to legislation, administration, democracy, political participation and social problems; give full play to the important role of the united front in deliberative democracy; make the Chinese People's Political Consultative Conference serve as a major channel for conducting deliberative democracy; improve the systems of the CPPCC, standardize the contents and procedures for consultation, enrich the forms of deliberative democracy, and more actively carry out consultations on particular topics with specialists and representatives from all sectors of society and with the relevant government departments on the handling of proposals, to improve the intensity and effectiveness of the consultations.[1]

---

[1] Xi Jinping. Explanatory Notes to the "Decision of the Central Committee of the CPC on Some Major Issues Concerning Comprehensively Continuing the Reform." *People's Daily*. November 16, 2013.

The reason we lay emphasis on the CPPCC deliberative democracy and its requirements is that the CPPCC deliberative democracy is an important component of socialist deliberative democracy. Soon after *Opinions of the Central Committee of the CPC on Strengthening the Construction of Socialist Deliberative Democracy* was promulgated, on June 25, 2015, Xinhua News Agency published the full text of *Implementation Opinions on Strengthening the Construction of the CPPCC Deliberative Democracy* issued by the general office of the CPC Central Committee. The CPPCC deliberative democracy is an important democratic form. Under the leadership of the CPC, the political parties and groups, people of all ethnic groups and people from all walks of life have joined the CPPCC, perform their functions of political consultation, democratic oversight, and political participation in state affairs, and carry out extensive consultation and build consensus before and during decision-making with focusing on the major issues of reform, development and stability and the practical problems affecting the people's vital interests. The CPPCC functions on the basis of the China's Constitution, the CPPCC Charter, and relevant policies. It is guaranteed by the system of multiparty cooperation and political consultation under the leadership of the CPC and assumes the functions of deliberation, oversight, participation, and cooperation. It has become an important platform for political parties and groups, people of all ethnic groups and people from all walks of life to promote democracy, to participate in state affairs, to unite and cooperate. It is an institutional arrangement with distinctive Chinese characteristics suitable for China's national conditions. For a long time, the CPPCC, as an important channel for deliberative democracy, has played the role of an organization specializing in deliberation, and has made significant contributions to extensively soliciting advice and opinions, gathering consensus, making the decision-making of the party and the country scientific and democratic, better realizing the position of the people as the masters of the country, resolving conflicts and promoting social harmony and stability: so as to constantly advance the modernization of the national governance system and governance capacity.

Looking into the basic elements of socialist deliberative democracy system, we will find out that the logical framework of '3+3+1' is being built step by step in deepening the reform of the political system. The first '3' refers to the deliberation of political parties, government and the

CPPCC. The second '3' means the deliberation of the National People's Congress, people's organizations and community-level organizations. The last '1' is the deliberation of social organizations. It is worth careful study and understanding that, concerning the contents of the framework of '3+3+1', each implies a different focus of work. The first '3' is strengthening emphatically, and the second '3' is developing actively, while the last '1' is exploring gradually, which does not merely show differences in expressions, but embodies dialectical thinking of stratification and classification. In practice, the purpose of building and perfecting the logical system of '3+3+1' is to give full play to the advantages of deliberative channels and to adequately integrate them, so as to develop and improve the system of socialist deliberative democracy. What needs to be emphasized is that various forms of deliberation must determine the contents of their deliberation and methods in accordance with their respective characteristics and actual demands, enabling the people to enjoy the rights to know, participate, express and supervise, and participate jointly in democratic consultation via different democratic channels.

Based on the present levels of people's practice and understanding, in building the system of socialist deliberative democracy we need both to pay attention to the basic ways and channels of the framework of '3+3+1'. In accordance with reality and in line with the requirements of being scientific and reasonable, standardized and orderly, simple and convenient, and democratic and centralized, we need to formulate deliberation plans, clarify topics and contents for deliberation, determine members of deliberation, carry out deliberation activities and lay emphasis on the feedbacks on the deliberation achievements, so as to ensure the deliberation activities are orderly, practical and efficient.

It is necessary to point out that emphasis on 'in all respects' and 'across the country', essentially means that we need to firmly hold the view of putting the people ahead in the priority list for socialist deliberative democracy. We need to redouble our efforts in developing deliberative democracy at the community level, with a focus on conducting deliberations among the masses. All decisions that affect people's immediate interests must be made on the basis of opinions fully solicited from the people, as well as deliberations conducted with them through various means, on different levels, and from different sectors. We should improve the system by which community-level organizations maintain contact with the people, strengthen deliberation on community affairs, make a good job of two-way communication of information from the top-down to the bottom-up, and make sure the people manage their own affairs properly in accordance with the law. We should make the exercise of power more open and standardized, and increase transparency in the operations of the party, the government, and the judiciary, as well as in the administration of other fields. We should ensure that the people oversee the exercise of power and that it happens in broad daylight.

The *Central Committee of the CPC: Recommendations for the 13th Five-Year Plan for Economic and Social Development* was adopted at the Fifth Plenary Session of the 18th Central Committee of the CPC On October 29, 2015. *Recommendations* proposes, "We need to consolidate and expand the broadest possible patriotic united front; implement party policies on intellectuals, ethnic groups, religion, and work related to overseas Chinese; give full rein to the role of all other political parties, federations of industry and commerce, and public figures without party affiliation; substantially increase the people's awareness of the importance of ethnic unity and progress; and guide regions in adapting to China's socialist society. We need to foster harmony among political parties, ethnicities, religions, social strata, and Chinese both at home and abroad, consolidate unity among Chinese people of all ethnic groups, and strengthen unity among all the sons and daughters of China whether at home or overseas."[1] This functions as guiding principles for us to build a moderately prosperous society in all respects during the decisive period of the 13th Five-Year Plan, give full play to the important role of the united front in deliberative democracy, and achieve the Two Centenary Goals and the great rejuvenation of the Chinese nation.

3. Real deliberation requires deliberation both before and during the process of decision-making.

Xi Jinping stressed, "When we talk about deliberation, we mean real deliberation. Real deliberation requires deliberation both before and during the process of decision-making. It requires that decisions are made and work is adjusted on the basis of opinions and suggestions from all sectors. It also requires that institutions are in place to ensure that the results of deliberations are implemented, so that our decisions and work both better reflect public will and are more suitable to real-life conditions."[2] Implementing people's

---

[1] *Central Committee of the CPC: Recommendations for the 13th Five-Year Plan for Economic and Social Development. People's Daily.* November 4, 2015.

[2] Xi Jinping. The Speech at the Conference to Celebrate the CPPCC's 65th Anniversary. *People's Daily.* September 22, 2014.

democracy and ensuring the position of the people as the masters of the country require us to conduct extensive deliberation among people from all sectors of society in the governance of China. Extensive deliberation is the fine tradition of the CPC. Ranging from 'state affairs' to 'trifles', deliberation is indispensable. Therefore, Mao Zedong once said, "the relations between all aspects of the state need deliberation." He also said frankly and humorously that, "As you are familiar with the nature of our government – to do things through deliberation with the people, we may call it a deliberative government." Remarks of Mao Zedong are both witty and profound, and reveal the truth that the people's government is for the people. As a 'deliberative government', how to conduct deliberation is a 'question'. In consequence, Zhou Enlai clearly pointed out that "the spirit of deliberation is not in the final voting; it is mainly in the deliberations and repeated discussions that happen before a decision is made." With the passage of time, a lot of things may have changed, while the CPC's notions on deliberation before decision-making have been passed down from generation to generation, involving aspects such as; 'we should do things through deliberation with the people,' 'we should mainly conduct deliberations and repeated discussions before a decision is made,' and 'real deliberation requires deliberation both before and during the process of decision-making'.

Xi Jinping said, "The process of holding extensive deliberations among the people is the process of promoting democracy and drawing on collective wisdom, the process of unifying people's thinking and building consensus, the process of scientific and democratic decision-making, and the process of ensuring the position of the people as masters of the country. It is only in this way that we can have solid foundations for our country's governance and for social governance; it is only in this way that we are able to draw together powerful strength." For a long time, the CPC has been conducting deliberations, through various mechanisms, channels, and methods, on the major issues of reform, development, and stability, and especially on the issues that have a bearing on people's immediate interests. We need to respect the wishes of the majority of the people, and at the same time take into account the reasonable demands of those who are in minority. We should extensively solicit opinions and pool wisdom from society, expand consensus, and bolster cooperative strength.

The practice of socialist deliberative democracy vividly depicts the logical locus of 'to do things through deliberations' and 'to do things through effective deliberations'. Deliberation is not only of significance and necessity, but also of possibility and effectiveness. It shows that under China's socialist system, deliberations help effectively when a problem crops up, and matters involving many people are discussed by all those involved; to reach consensus on the wishes and needs of the whole of society is the essence of people's democracy. 'To conduct effective deliberation' means in the construction of socialism with Chinese characteristics, we can, and are able to, conduct deliberations on problems, by which we get things done to the utmost. We will make the 'people's government' a 'deliberative government'. The key of deliberation lies in repeated deliberations when we find and address issues. In a nutshell, the more numerous and in-depth deliberations we hold, the better the result can be.

It is worth noting that in practice, when we conduct deliberations on different contents, we need to take into consideration the scope of deliberation. That is to say, on matters that have a bearing on the interests of people of all our ethnic groups, deliberations will be held extensively throughout the whole of society; on matters that concern the interests of people in one specific area, deliberations will be held among the local people there; on matters that affect the interests of certain groups of people, deliberations will be held among those groups; and on matters that concern the interests of people at the community level, deliberations will be held within the community.

History and reality tell us repeatedly that "the process of holding extensive deliberations among the people is the process of promoting democracy and drawing on collective wisdom, the process of unifying people's thinking and building consensus, the process of scientific and democratic decision-making, and the process of ensuring the position of the people as masters of the country. It is only in this way that we can have solid foundations for our country's governance and for social governance; it is only in this way that we are able to draw together powerful strength."[1]

"Real deliberation requires deliberation both before and during the process of decision-making" indicates that there are two possibilities when conducting deliberation, one is real deliberation; the other is false deliberation. While "real deliberation requires deliberation both before and during the process of decision-making", false deliberation is likely to take place after decision-making. The emphasis on deliberation before and during decision-

---

[1] Xi Jinping. The Speech at the Conference to Celebrate the CPPCC's 65th Anniversary. *People's Daily*. September 22, 2014.

making is both profound and simple. As everyone understands, if deliberation is only carried out after decision-making, it is just like 'a Monday morning quarterback' or 'belated wisdom' – it is repellent 'formalism' and 'obscurantist policy' which does not respect the people but deceives the people.

Practice has proved that it is the important experience of deliberation among political parties that, on major policies and issues affecting the interests of the people, before and during the process of decision-making, they carry out extensive deliberation and make their efforts to build consensus to avoid making subversive mistakes in major issues. The party and the country conduct deliberations with democratic parties before establishing major policies and guidelines, and listen earnestly to suggestions from non-communist parties; while democratic parties prepare their opinions and suggestions from their particular perspectives, on major policies and issues affecting the interests of the people, demonstrating their participatory parties' advantages and functions. Furthermore, extensive deliberation before and during the process of decision-making is the process during which the party listens extensively to the suggestions of democratic parties; at the same time, it is the process by which democratic parties get to know and accept the party's political views and constantly enhance their confidence in the road, theory and system of socialism with Chinese characteristics.

'Real deliberation' before and during decision-making should be guaranteed by institutional construction. In recent years, the Central Committee has promulgated a series of documents on deliberative democracy, to make it more institutionalized, normalized and proceduralized. As for strengthening the deliberation among political parties, it is stipulated clearly that General Secretary of the CPC holds deliberative forums four time a year at regular intervals, conducting deliberations with the central committees of democratic parties and the representatives of the people without party affiliation, on the issues of economic development proposals, semi-annual economic work, Central Plenary documents, and Central Economic Work Conference documents. The forums enrich the contents and broaden the channels of socialist deliberative democracy to promote its broad-based, multi-level and institutionalized development.

III. Negations of 'Imported' Deliberative Democracy

As a saying goes, 'there is nowhere but Greece'. Once 'deliberative democracy' is mentioned, some people cannot help thinking about Greece, or they take some western scholars such as Rawls and Habermas as its 'initiators'. We have to know that during the process of human social development, countries in the world have developed diversified and varied democratic content and forms. We need to understand deliberative democracy in other countries, but we cannot simply and crudely conclude that our 'deliberative democracy' was invented by western countries, or that China's deliberative democracy was 'originated' from the West and 'transplanted' to China. In that interpretation, 'deliberative democracy' is 'imported'. Is this indeed the case?

Socialist deliberative democracy is the great creation of the CPC and the Chinese people with a unique form and the distinctive strength of China's socialist democracy. It is an important embodiment of the party's mass line in the political field. Socialist deliberative democracy is different from western deliberative democracy in theory and connotation. They have great differences in theoretical origins, institutional basis, political practice and cultural background. Socialist deliberative democracy finds its roots in Chinese history and culture, took its shape through the Chinese people's revolutionary struggle in modern times, and developed in the practice of socialism with Chinese characteristics. It is the important guarantee of the state's prosperity and strength, national rejuvenation and people's wellbeing.

Xi Jinping, General Secretary of the CPC, once summarized the major contents of socialist deliberative democracy, highlighting its Chinese characteristics, Chinese styles and Chinese manners. Socialist deliberative democracy is "a unique, particular and original form of Chinese socialist democracy. It derives from our nation's long-established inclusive political culture, in which we believe that all under heaven belongs to the people and we can seek common ground while putting aside differences. It derives from China's political evolution in modern times, from the long-term practical experience built as the CPC led the people through the course of revolution, development and reform. It derives from the great innovations made in our political institutions by all political parties, people's organizations, ethnic groups, and people from all social strata and different backgrounds after the PRC was founded. It derives from the continuous innovations in China's political system since the policy of reform and opening up was carried out. Hence, General Secretary Xi Jinping summarized strategically and concisely that socialist deliberative democracy "has firm cultural, theoretical, practical, and institutional foundations". All these reflect that fundamentally, our socialist deliberative democracy is not in any way copied or 'imported' from the western world.

1. Profound cultural foundation

China is a country that boasts thousands of years' cultural tradition, both extensive and profound. It not only contains the thoughts, theories, and institutional practice concerning political deliberation, but also embodies the cultural spirit and value orientation pertinent to deliberative democracy. Generally speaking, it includes the people-oriented thought, values, and spirit of harmony, expressed as 'the whole world as one community,' 'fully inclusive and equitable,' and 'seeking common ground while putting aside differences'. Other relevant notions, as 'the people are the basis of the country, and government serves the people', 'encouraging the people to advise, and listen to the people's suggestions', 'harmony in diversity', 'valuing justice above material gains', 'peaceful co-existence' and 'expostulation', have played a significant role in defining China's long-standing and well-established tradition of political deliberation.

2. Scientific theoretical foundation

Socialist deliberative democracy is the great creation and latest achievement of the basic tenets of Marxism, integrated with the actual conditions in China. It is the key content of the theoretical system of socialism with Chinese characteristics, and boasts a unique and firm theoretical foundation. It mainly consists of the following elements.

The first is the party theory, state theory, and democratic political theory in Marxism. Marxism puts forward the view that the proletarian party adhering to the leadership should unite other workers' parties, and contract an alliance with other democratic parties, the view on the origin and nature of the country, on proletariats seizing the power, and on how to apply the proletariat regime, and the view that though bourgeois revolution achieved the political democracy, it is based on private property, and in nature is false democracy for a minority of the people. All these views provide significant theoretical guidance for the construction of socialist deliberative democracy.

The second is the party's theory concerning the united front. The united front, as one of the 'three treasures', is important for the CPC to achieve victories in revolution, development, and reform and opening up. The essence of the united front is to unite with all available forces, and mobilize all positive forces to the utmost, which lies at the core and is a valuable experience of the CPC in its governance of China. Socialist deliberative democracy both adheres to the principle of people's democracy, and carries out the requirements of unity and harmony. It is a flexible application and creative development of the theory of the united front.

The third is the CPC's mass line theory. The CPC has been unswerving in upholding mass line, representing the fundamental interests of the greatest possible majority of the people, relying closely on the people in governing the country and managing society, listening extensively to the opinions and suggestions from all sectors of the people, and accepting their oversight. At a new historical starting point, the CPC highlights that socialist deliberative democracy is an important reflection of the party's mass line in the political field. Deliberation with the people and for the people reveals the value orientation of socialist deliberative democracy.

3. Solid practice foundation

Socialist deliberative democracy is deeply rooted in the vast territory of China. It is the inevitable result of the great practice of the Chinese people under the leadership of the CPC in their long-term struggle for revolution, development and reform, and in their exploration of a path for political development of socialism with Chinese characteristics. During the New Democratic Revolution Period, the CPC effectively implemented deliberative democracy in the construction of the 'three-three' democratic regime model, which was the initial stage of China's deliberative democracy. On April 30, 1948, the eve of May Day, in order to mobilize the people of all sectors of the country to achieve the glorious mission of building a new China, the CPC issued a commemorative 'May Day' slogan of great historical significance. It called upon democratic parties, people without party affiliation, and community leaders to hold the CPPCC promptly, which received a positive response from all sectors of the society, and started a prelude to the victory of the foundation of the new China, holding deliberative democracy deliberation with the people. In September, 1949, the first plenary session of the CPPCC was held for the establishment of the PRC and officially established the system of multiparty cooperation and political consultation under the leadership of the CPC, marking the nationwide implementation of deliberative democracy – a new democratic pattern in China.

It is worth noting that the CPPCC at this period played a 'special' role and had 'double' attributes. On the one hand, it was the organizational form of the people's democratic united front. On the other hand, it was the organizational form of the central state political power, a substitute of the National People's Congress – an organization of supreme state power. This is the CPPCC's special nature and historical function under the historical conditions at that time. In September, 1954, the first National People's Congress was held, marking the system by which the people's congress became the national fundamental political system. The CPPCC was no longer the substitute of the People's Congress. Then, the CPPCC had two 'prospects': one was to withdraw from the historical stage because it no longer played the roles of the People's Congress. While the other was to be kept as an organizational form of the people's democratic united front, although it didn't serve the function of the People's Congress any longer. The wise Chinese people and the CPC chose the latter, keeping the CPPCC. History has proved that this choice is correct. This choice of far-reaching significance opened up the road marking two forms of practice in terms of the people's democracy with Chinese characteristics.

Since the policy of reform and opening up was implemented, socialist deliberative democracy has been developing while inheriting, and improving, its traditions. The 13th National Congress of the CPC put forward the concept of building the 'system of social consultation and dialogue'. In 2007, *White Paper on China's Political Party System* firstly proposed the concepts of 'democratic election' and 'deliberative democracy'. The 18th National Congress of the CPC and the Third Plenary Session of the 18th CPC Central Committee put forward the strategic deployment of improving the system of socialist deliberative democracy, and promoting wide, multi-tiered and institutionalized deliberative democracy. Until now, China has gradually constructed the consultative channels that suit China's national conditions. Deliberative democracy has expanded its coverage from deliberation between political parties to social deliberation, from deliberation in the political field to the social and living areas, and from the state-level to the local and community-level.

4. Systemic foundation of institution

China has built its socialist deliberative democracy to be a relatively complete institutional system, protected by the Constitution, supported by the basic political system, and guided by the party's policies and guidelines.

Firstly, the Constitution, China's fundamental law, provides legal protection for the development and improvement of socialist deliberative democracy. From a legal perspective, it stresses the vital function and significance of upholding and developing the CPPCC, the united front and political consultation system.

Secondly, the basic political system and a series of important documents issued, are an important support to consolidate and develop socialist deliberative democracy. China has formed the deliberative democracy system with Chinese characteristics composed of state-level political deliberation, social deliberation between state and society, and society-level citizen deliberation. The process in brief is as follows. The deliberative government, founded in September 1949, marked the formal establishment of the multi-party cooperation system under the leadership of the CPC. At the end of 1989, the Central Committee of the CPC formulated the *Opinions on Sticking to and Improving the System of Multi-party Cooperation and Political Consultation under the Leadership of the CPC*, institutionalizing the multi-party cooperation system. In 1997, the 15th National Congress of the CPC brought it into the three basic programs of the primary stage of socialism. In 2005, the Central Committee of the CPC published the *Opinions on Further Strengthening the System of Multi-party Cooperation and Political Consultation under the Leadership of the CPC*, reiterating and intensifying this system. In 2012, the 18th National Congress of the CPC made an important decision to establish deliberative democracy as a major form of people's democracy through the congress of party representatives, so as to improve the system of socialist deliberative democracy. After the 18th National Congress of the CPC, the Central Committee of the CPC consecutively promulgated the *Opinions on Strengthening the Construction of Socialist Deliberative Democracy,* and *Opinions on Strengthening the Implementation of the People's Political Consultative Conference on the Construction of Deliberative Democracy*, providing theoretical and practical guidance for the construction of socialist deliberative democracy under the new circumstances.

Finally, a series of policies and guidelines of the CPC are the essential basis of the construction of socialist deliberative democracy. Currently, we have formulated clear requirements to improve the system of socialist deliberative democracy and promote its broad-based, multi-level, and institutionalized development, in terms of guiding thought, basic principles, measures, deliberative channels, procedures, and guarantees. They are the guides to actions and principles to follow to promote socialist deliberative democracy, and should be sincerely implemented in practice.

IV. 'Multi-Party Cooperation' instead of 'Multi-Party System' in Contemporary China

At the first sight, the two concepts of 'multi-party cooperation' and 'multi-party system' are 'similar', for both have a 'multi-party' modifier. Actually, they have a world of difference between them, especially in their nature. Across the world, each country has its respective national conditions. To choose a political system is to choose what development road to follow, which should be each country's independent choice. Similarly, in contemporary China, it is the Chinese people's independent choice to implement 'multi-party cooperation' instead of 'multi-party system'. It is the political system of socialism with Chinese characteristics, and also a basic political system in contemporary China. It is a great creation of the Marxist theory of political parties, the United Front Theory, and the theory of socialist democratic politics integrated with China's concrete practice. Meanwhile, an in-depth analysis of the nature of the 'multi-party system' in the West enables us to clarify that the 'multi-party system' does not suit China's national conditions, and then consolidate our confidence in following the political development road of socialism with Chinese characteristics. Indeed, we should not either exaggerate, or criticize the countries that implement 'multi-party system'. What matters is that 'multi-party cooperation' is not 'multi-party system', and 'one-party rule' is not 'one-party dictatorship'. The relations between the CPC and democratic parties are quite different from those between 'the party in power' and 'the party out of power', or between 'the party in power' and 'the opposition party'. Concerning these major theoretical issues, no 'sloppy' or 'vague' thinking whatsoever is permissible, even in the slightest.

That China cannot implement a 'multi-party system' is the choice of the people and also the choice of history. As Xi Jinping pointed out, "What political system to build in China has been a historical task that the Chinese people were faced [with] in modern times. To solve this historical task, the Chinese people have had a hard exploration."[1] The past is not easily forgotten. In modern Chinese history, a fair number of people conceived of the capitalist 'multi-party system' as the way to save the nation. After the Revolution of 1911, they followed the example of this western system, and hence political parties sprang up overnight, and at one point the number of parties reached more than 300. But at last, they all came to an end hastily,

---

[1] Xi Jinping. The Speech at the Conference to Celebrate the CPPCC's 65th Anniversary. *People's Daily*. September 22, 2014.

failing to change the backward situation of the Chinese nation. After the Chinese People's War of Resistance against Japanese Aggression (1937-1945), some people proposed 'a third way', under the banner of 'multi-party system'. However, the Kuo-min-tang with its autocratic dictatorship shattered the illusion of these people. History has proved time and again that 'multi-party system' does not work in China, which is the bitter experience at the cost of blood and life.

Xi Jinping made the following clear-cut judgments with his superb dialectical thinking, which are worth our earnest study and understanding. "Designing and developing a national political system, we should attach great importance to the organic unity of history and reality, theory and practice, and form and substance. We should insist on proceeding from China's national conditions and from the reality. We should grasp the long-term historical heritage, the development road we have followed, the accumulated political experience, the formulated political principles, and the realistic request to solve the realistic problems. We should not cut off history, and build a 'flying-peak' political system only based on imagination." He further stated, "The functions of political system are to regulate political relations, build political order, promote national development, and maintain national stability. It is out of the question to make abstract judgments by breaking away from the specific social and political conditions, to follow the same pattern and to be attributed to one standard." He stressed, "With regard to political system, we should not simply think whatever we do not have while other countries have is in deficiency, and then we are eager to bring it back. Or we should not simply think whatever we have while other countries do not have is redundant, and then we are eager to get rid of it. Both views are simplified and one-sided, so neither is correct."[1]

"The tasty orange, grown in southern China, would turn sour once it is grown in the north". China cannot copy the political system of other countries, because it would not fit us, it might even lead to catastrophic consequences, and it might even ruin the future of our country. Regardless of China's national conditions, it did not, does not and will not work to copy the development model of other countries. In a word, "a system, only rooted in its own national soil to absorb nutrients, is reliable and effective." "The political system of socialism with Chinese characteristics which was, and is,

---

[1] Xi Jinping. The Speech at the Conference to Celebrate the CPPCC's 65th Anniversary. *People's Daily*. September 22, 2014.

growing in the soil of Chinese society, must be deeply rooted in the soil of Chinese society for its prosperity in the future."[1] All these classical sayings should be kept in mind.

It should be shown clearly that 'multi-party cooperation' is only the shortened form of 'multi-party cooperation and political consultation under the leadership of the CPC'. It must be completely and clearly understood that, in particular, 'under the leadership of the CPC' cannot be omitted, though the complete name is much longer than the brief one. Xi Jinping clearly stated, "The leadership by the CPC is the common choice of the Chinese people, including the democratic parties, people's organizations, ethnic groups, social strata, and people from all sectors of society. It is the most essential feature of socialism with Chinese characteristics, and it provides the fundamental guarantee for the development and progress of the CPPCC."[1] In a word, the leadership by the CPC is the prime prerequisite and fundamental guarantee, and the core content of multi-party cooperation. The leadership by the CPC and multi-party cooperation, and the governance by the CPC and multi-party participation in politics are distinct features of the political party system of socialism with Chinese characteristics.

1. The implementation of the system of multi-party cooperation and political consultation under the leadership of the CPC is a requirement of the nature of socialist democracy. In the relations between different political parties, the CPC is in the leading position. This leadership is the correct choice of the Chinese people and democratic parties in their long-term practice of revolution, construction and reform, which suits China's national conditions. In contemporary China, no other political party can replace the CPC and become the core of leadership of 1.3 billion people. Democratic parties have a clear understanding of the importance, necessity, and practical significance of being under the leadership of the CPC, and an aspiration for sincere cooperation and common endeavor under the leadership of the CPC.

In the relations between political parties and state power, the CPC is the ruling party, and democratic parties participate in and deliberate on state affairs. The CPC's leadership is the choice of history, endowed and defined clearly by the Constitution. The actual role played by democratic parties in

---

[1] Xi Jinping. The Speech at the Conference to Celebrate the CPPCC's 65th Anniversary. *People's Daily*. September 22, 2014.

China's historical and contemporary political life determines their position as participant parties. Democratic parties, as the political alliances of socialist working people, builders of socialism and patriots who support socialism with whom they maintain ties, participate in the exercise of state power and the administration of state affairs under the leadership of the CPC, which is a major indication of people's democracy. It is different from a 'one-party system', 'two-party system' or 'multi-party system'. In China, the status and rights of democratic parties as participant parties are protected by laws. Democratic parties maintain wide and close cooperation with the CPC in participating in the exercise of state power and being responsible for the people. Members of democratic parties and some personages without party affiliation hold an appropriate number of posts in state organs at all levels. They also hold some leading posts in the People's Congress, governments, courts and procuratorates at all levels.

In relations between political parties and society, democratic parties in cooperation with the CPC jointly perform the function of social administration. In contemporary China, the CPC rules the country and performs the function of social administration. But with the deeper development of a market-oriented economy, social structure has been differentiated and reorganized, creating a variety of new social strata and groups. Democratic parties have historical, natural and close connections with many emerging social strata. In this way, the CPC representing the overwhelming majority of the people, and democratic parties and personages without party affiliation who represent some social strata and groups, jointly commit themselves to the cause of socialist construction. The system of multi-party cooperation and political consultation under the leadership of the CPC is conducive to giving play to the political advantages of democratic parties in maintaining ties with different social strata and groups, so as to cooperate with and assist the governing party to perform the function of social administration.

2. The implementation of the system of multi-party cooperation and political consultation under the leadership of the CPC facilitates the democratization of the state's political life. This basic political system is a key form to ensure the position of the people as masters of the country. It facilitates democratic parties and personages without party affiliation to participate extensively in state and social administration, makes decision-making democratic and scientific, and provides crucial guarantees for carrying forward socialist democracy and realizing democracy in state political life.

The system of multi-party cooperation and political consultation under the leadership of the CPC is an important practice of democratic consultation. As participating parties, democratic parties participate in the consultation on fundamental state policies and perform democratic oversight of state affairs. They cooperate with the CPC in each field to promote democratization in the state political life.

The implementation of the system of multi-party cooperation and political consultation under the leadership of the CPC plays an important role in maintaining social stability. History and reality have both proved that to push forward modernization in the largest developing country of the world, it is imperative to have the CPC as the strong core of leadership. Meanwhile, the change of the objective situations such as social transformation and interest diversification, requires more effective democratic involvement. Multi-party cooperation is conducive to developing channels for the expression of multiplicity of interests, mobilizing far-ranging social and political resources, settling and mitigating various conflicts involving interests, promoting social stability, fully arousing the enthusiasm and creativity of the people with whom democratic parties and personages without party affiliation maintain ties, duly handling disagreements among the people and coordinating diverse interest relationships.

3. The implementation of the system of multi-party cooperation and political consultation under the leadership of the CPC helps strengthen and improve the leadership of the CPC.

Mutual supervision among political parties, and especially, the oversight of democratic parties and personages without party affiliation over the CPC, enables the ruling party to listen to different opinions and criticisms at any time, so as to better accept the people's desires and demands, overcome and rectify bad practices such as bureaucracy and abuse of power for personal gains, and correct errors promptly. The supervising function of democratic parties is an important mechanism for the ruling party to guard against corruption. To strengthen and improve the leadership of the CPC, it is imperative for the CPC to improve its governing style, and establish and perfect the supervision mechanism of people's democracy that suits China's national conditions, so that the CPC and state organs can work better with the people's supervision. Certainly, the mutual supervision between the CPC and democratic parties is based on the Four Cardinal Principles, political supervision by putting forward criticisms, opinions, and suggestions, and by means of investigation and discussion. This is an important means of multi-party cooperation, whose purposes are to be better committed to the common cause and to achieve the common goal instead of undermining the opposite side. This mutual supervision is active, well-meaning and beneficent, completely different from that in Western countries where different parties fight against and cheat on each other. As Xi Jinping said, "We must uphold and improve the system of multi-party cooperation and political consultation under the leadership of the CPC, strengthen cooperation and coordination of various social forces, and feasibly guard against conflicts and in-fighting between parties." In a word, "we should adhere to the core of leadership of the CPC, coordinate leading forces from different sectors, improve the CPC's level of scientific governance, democratic governance and governance according to law, ensure effective governance of the country by the people under the leadership of the CPC, and feasibly guard against the state of disunity for lack of the leadership."[1]

---

[1] Xi Jinping. The Speech at the Conference to Celebrate the 60th Anniversary of the National People's Congress. *People's Daily*. September 6, 2014.

Chapter 5

Shape the Chinese Spirit

Our party has been consistently putting ideological building on the top agenda of the party building. We lay emphasis on the notion that 'the revolutionary ideal is higher than the sky', indicating the dialectics by which spirit can be transformed into material, and vice versa. We must not slacken any effort in ideal and belief in education, moral and ethical improvement, and ideological work. We must cultivate and disseminate the core socialist values to pool China's strength through the Chinese spirit, keeping pace with the times.

— A Speech stressed by Xi Jinping when he presided over the 20th group study session of the Political Bureau of the 18th CPC Central Committee (January 23, 2015)

Socialism with Chinese characteristics is the New Norm of socialism in all-round economic and social development, a key aspect of which is to develop socialist culture. Since the 18th CPC National Congress, Xi Jinping has been attaching great importance to promoting advanced culture and cultural and ethical progress. He put forward, in order to realize the Chinese dream of the rejuvenation of the Chinese nation, we should be greatly abundant not only in material wealth, but also in spiritual wealth. We must promote cultural and ethical progress with perseverance and consistency, intensify the exploration and interpretation of the excellent traditional Chinese culture, and achieve the creative transformation and innovative development of traditional Chinese virtues, providing firm ideological guarantees, powerful spiritual strength and rich moral nourishment for people of all ethnic groups to keep forging ahead. Only when the people hold to faith, can we enable the nation to stay hopeful and the country to grow powerful.

I. Ideological Progress: One of the Party's Top Priorities

Xi Jinping stated in the speech at a national meeting on publicity and theoretical work in 2013 (hereinafter shortened as August 19th Speech), "Economic development is the party's central task, and ideological progress is one of its top priorities." In this claim, Xi Jinping put ideological progress on a par with economic development, and stressed that ideological progress is more than important, but "one of top priorities", which reveals the core issue of socialist cultural advancement.

1. Ideological progress is one of the party's top priorities.

History and reality have told us that whether we can do well in ideological work is crucial for the party's future and fate, for the country's long-term stability, and for national cohesion and central force. A country should not only have hard power but also soft power, and it should not only feasibly accomplish the central task and provide a solid material foundation for ideological progress but also substantially accomplish ideological progress and provide forceful guarantees for the central task. We should neither neglect ideological progress because of the central task, nor make ideological progress away from the central task. Negligence of ideological progress would lead to endless trouble. There are profound lessons in this respect. Concerning the political disturbance that happened in Beijing in 1989, comrade Deng Xiaoping pointed out clearly that it was the consequence of errors in the political and ideological work within the party. Concerning international affairs, Deng said in a speech delivered in 1992, "The Soviet Union, once a strong country, collapsed in a few months. If China did not learn from this lesson, without noticing the symptoms of a trend, as Mikhail Gorbachev did not notice the 'new thinking' when it emerged, consequences would be disastrous."[1]

We should adhere to materialistic dialectics, and have a profound understanding of the decisive role of the economic base to the superstructure. Meanwhile we should thoroughly understand the reaction of the superstructure to the economic base. If we neglect ideological progress, we deny this reaction. Evidence has shown that if a country develops well, it is easy to carry out ideological progress and publicity and theoretical work. On the other hand, only with ideological progress and publicity and theoretical

---

[1] Wu Songying. *Record of Deng Xiaoping's Speeches in the South of China*. People's Publishing House. 2012. p. 66-67.

work done well, can a country develop well. Ideological progress is one part of promoting cultural and ethical progress. Only by promoting material, cultural and ethical progress, can we enhance the cause of Chinese socialism.

2. Ideological progress is confronted with unprecedented challenges and difficulties.

With regards to the actual status of ideological progress, Xi Jinping said, with his farsightedness, in his speech on August 19, 2013, "We are new to a battle with many new historic features. We are facing unprecedented challenges and difficulties. Therefore, we must continue to enhance and intensify the underlying trend of thought in our country, advocate the themes of the times, popularize positive energy, and encourage the whole country to strive as one for progress."

What does this mean by, "facing unprecedented challenges and difficulties"? This claim is based on the complex conditions in the current ideological sphere of China. China's reform has entered a deep water zone, and various social contradictions are intensified, driven by interest demands. People's value orientations present the tendency of 'independence, selectivity, variability and diversity.' Meanwhile, the hostile forces of the West have never stopped their efforts to achieve China's westernization, and their differentiation initiatives with cultural and ideological spheres as the key realm of their long-term penetration. Against this backdrop, together with the technical features of the network era, diversified interest demands, values and cultural pursuits, and even individual emotional release, all are transmitted and disseminated rapidly on the internet. Those who harbor grudges against the CPC, the basic system of socialism, and the achievements in building socialism with Chinese characteristics, may sabotage by means of slander, rumor-mongering and stigmatization through websites. The erroneous ideological trends represented by nihilism and neoliberalism are extremely obstinate, and spread unchecked from time to time. Concerning ideological leadership, there exists the problem of 'weakness and slackness' in varying degrees.

3. We must consolidate Marxism as the guiding ideology in China.

All sorts of problems point to the state of the ideological leadership, so does the primary solution. Xi Jinping stressed, "Our publicity and theoretical work aims to consolidate Marxism as the guiding ideology in China, and cement the shared ideological basis of the whole party and the people. Both party members and officials must hold a firm belief in Marxism and communism, make unremitting and pragmatic efforts to realize the party's basic program at the present stage, take every step needed for progress and pass the baton dutifully to our successors."

It is the 'relay race' of the CPC members, generation after generation to solve the problem of China's social development path and achieve the great rejuvenation of the Chinese nation under the guidance of Marxism. Marxism is our 'baton'. Xi Jinping sharply criticized a phenomenon, "Among the party members and officials, a lack of faith is a problem that needs attaching great importance to. Some even take criticizing and ridiculing Marxism as a 'fashion' or a 'gimmick.'"[1]

Therefore, Xi Jinping pays special attention to these officials – the "key minority". Officials, especially high-ranking ones, should master the basic theories of Marxism as their special skill and diligently study and learn their essence. Marxism must be a required course in party schools, executive leadership academies, academies of social sciences, institutes of higher learning and seminars for theoretical studies. These places should serve as the centers for studying, researching and disseminating Marxism. Officials should observe and solve problems from the Marxist stand, viewpoint and method, and become firm in their ideals and convictions.

4. We should stick to the principles of unity, stability and encouragement with a focus on positive publicity.

Above all, when it comes to major issues, including those of political principles, we must take the initiative. "The initiative" means we should maintain political sensitivity, have an insight into the situation, and help officials and the people draw a line between right and wrong and acquire a clear understanding in this regard. Especially we should absolutely say no to the political values dispersed by the western hostile forces, and to those who benefit from, but meanwhile undermine, the CPC's governance. Officials are in no way allowed to cherish the reputation of so-called 'enlightened gentleman', abandoning political principles. The departments concerned with publicity and theoretical work should play their part well, try their best, and improve their work, starting with their leaders and leading bodies.

---

[1] Central Commission for Discipline Inspection of the CPC; Party Literature Research Centre of the CPC Central Committee: *Excerpts of Xi Jinping's Exposition on the Construction of the Party Conduct and of an Honest and Clean Government and on the Struggle against Corruption*. Central Literature Publishing House& China Lianzheng Publishing House. 2015. p.17.

Secondly, we should both accumulate experience and become skillful at innovation in the fields of ideas, methodologies and grassroots work. In the current society featuring dynamic thoughts, concept collisions, daily progress of new technologies and new media such as the internet, only by sizing up the situation, making the best use of the circumstances, bringing forth new ideas and vehicles, and improving methods and styles, can we promote ideological, cultural and ethical progress with energy and vitality. The key to success lies in raising the quality and level of our publicity and theoretical work. We should have the proper timing, tempo and efficiency, make this work more attractive and influential, inform the people about what they love to hear, read and watch, and let positive publicity play its role in encouraging and inspiring the people.

We are reasonably confident that so long as the whole party devotes themselves to ideological progress – an extremely important work – we will achieve the Xi Jinping's outlook for 2015, "Faithful people, hopeful nation and powerful country."

II. Standing Firm in the Global Mingling and Clashing of Cultures

In the age of the Nation-state, culture is bound to have national attributes. In the era of globalization initiated by western modernity, the relationship between Chinese culture and western culture, as well as world culture, is an inescapable issue to confront. How to cope with it properly is important for promoting China's cultural development. In the relationship between western and Chinese cultures, what is the basic orientation of Chinese culture? Xi Jinping pointed out that to cultivate and disseminate core socialist values, we must draw on roots in traditional Chinese culture. Standing on the high ground of the history and sizing up the situation, Xi Jinping initially put forward the proposition of "the extensive, profound and outstanding traditional Chinese culture is the foundation for us to stand firm upon in the global mingling and clashing of cultures." Looking back on the history of relations between Chinese culture and western culture, we can say that Xi Jinping's proposition reverses the declining tendency of Chinese culture in modern times, so it is of extraordinary significance.

1. Chinese culture has been nourishing the Chinese nation.

The Chinese nation boasts a 5000-year history of civilization, and it has created a long-standing and well-established ancient culture. Why has the Chinese civilization never suffered from essential collapse while other ancient civilizations declined one after another? Xi Jinping has addressed this question in a series of his speeches. He said, "In the historical changes of the past thousands of years, the path of Chinese development has not always been smooth. It has undergone numerous difficulties and hardships, but we finally survived and made it. One of the key reasons is that the Chinese people, from generation to generation, have cultivated and developed the extensive, profound and outstanding Chinese culture with unique characteristics, which has provided formidable spiritual support for the Chinese nation to overcome difficulties and ensured the lineage, development and growth of the Chinese nation."[1] In the first place, Chinese culture has equipped the Chinese nation with the spirit of innovation. Our ancestors said that "Although Zhou was an ancient state, the ordinance which lighted on it was new", that, "As heaven maintains vigor through movements, a gentle man should constantly strive for self-perfection." and that, "If you can one day renovate yourself, do so from day to day. Let there be daily renovation." Hence it is safe to say the spirit of innovation has been the most distinct gift of the Chinese nation. In the course of more than 5000 years of development, the Chinese nation has created a highly advanced civilization. Our forefathers invented papermaking technology, gunpowder, the art of printing, and the compass. They also accomplished innumerable and remarkable achievements in a variety of fields such as astronomy, mathematics, medicine and agriculture, contributing countless scientific and technological innovations to the world and meanwhile exerting great influence on the progress of world civilization, so that China has long been in the list of world powers.

Secondly, Chinese culture is characterized by flexibility. In the course of more than 5000 years of development, the Chinese nation created an extensive, profound and outstanding culture. When Chinese culture holds fast to itself, the Chinese people realized long ago that "civilizations would become richer and more colorful with exchanges and mutual learning." During the long-term process of evolution, Chinese civilization absorbed abundant nourishment from its exchanges with other civilizations, and has made great contributions to the progress of human civilization. Vivid examples show exchanges and mutual learning between Chinese civilization and other civilizations, and they go as follows: China worked on the Silk Road leading to the Western Regions; large numbers of envoys from other

---

[1] Xi Jinping. A Speech at the Forum on Literature and Art Work (2014). *People's daily*. October 15, 2015.

countries were sent to China during the Sui and Tang dynasties; Xuanzang, the Tang monk, went on a pilgrimage to the west for Buddhist scriptures; and Zheng He, the famous navigator of China's Ming Dynasty, made seven expeditions to the Western Seas. As for various civilizations created by human beings, such as Chinese civilization, Greek civilization, Roman civilization, Egyptian civilization, Mesopotamian civilization, and Indian civilization in ancient times, or Asian civilization, African civilization, European civilization, American civilization and Oceania civilization at present, we should adopt the attitude of exchanges and mutual learning, so as to absorb their beneficial elements. By means of cultural exchanges and mutual learning, and with confidence in Chinese culture, the Chinese people's ideals and goals, and their values and inner world, are going to keep the same tempo with the times as society and history move forward, while they are deeply rooted in the soil of the splendid traditional Chinese culture.

2. The Chinese people are making the utmost efforts to achieve rejuvenation of the Chinese culture.

On account of the long-established ancient civilization it boasted, China ran ahead of the West in many aspects. Hence, in the relations between Chinese and western cultures, there once emerged a tendency of 'westward spread of Chinese culture' in the 18th century, with Chinese culture regarded as model civilization. However, in the 19th century, the West, driven by the industrial revolution, started its process of globalization. In 1840, the Opium War between China and the United Kingdom broke out. China was defeated on its own territory and forced to open up to the West. Facing the powerful western industrial civilization, people of insight in modern China chose to focus on and learn from the West. From the late 19th century to the early 20th century, no matter if we like it or not, traditional Chinese culture suffered a declining tendency. From the perspective of radical changes over one hundred years, we reach a conclusion after dialectic analysis of the decline of traditional Chinese culture: its positive significance is that the decline led to the modern development of Chinese civilization, while the negative influence is that the decline greatly damaged the Chinese people's confidence in Chinese culture.

Since the Opium War, after 170 years' exploration, as the world's second largest economy, China has achieved its rejuvenation, taking up over one-third of the world economy. China has been developing fast and the days when the Chinese nation was ridden roughshod over are gone forever. Currently, China has raised its international status and expanded its international influence, which demonstrates the respect won by the Chinese people striving over one hundred years.

From the perspective of cultural significance, China's rejuvenation marks the end of Chinese culture's decline. Chinese culture has stood on its own feet in the forests of world cultures. The age of 'there is nowhere but the West' is gone, and the Chinese should have a new cultural self-awareness.

3. The road of socialism with Chinese characteristics was determined by the Chinese historical inheritance and cultural tradition.

When he pondered on the historical path of the development road of China, Xi Jinping applied Marxist dialectics to his rational reflection on the Chinese ideological and cultural history in the past one hundred years. He affirmed the positive significance of western advanced culture to China's modernization and, meanwhile, he pointed out the other side under the surface. That is, although the outstanding traditional Chinese culture was once on the defensive, it never abandoned its tradition. Instead, it has been constantly rectifying the partiality of western culture, and opening up its own development path for China.

From the perspective of the relationship between culture and national development, Xi Jinping said, the traditional Chinese culture is our deepest cultural soft power and it is also the rich cultural soil in which the road of socialism with Chinese characteristics is deeply rooted. Each country and nation differs in their historical tradition, cultural accumulation, and basic national conditions, so their roads of development are bound to be with their own characteristics. For thousands of years, the Chinese nation has been taking a different development road of civilization from those in other countries and nations. The road of socialism with Chinese characteristics we opened up was not taken by chance, while it was determined by China's historical inheritance and cultural tradition.

What does it mean that, "the road of socialism with Chinese characteristics was determined by China's historical inheritance and cultural tradition"? Outwardly, the New Culture Movement in the early 20th century led to abandoning the dominant position of traditional Chinese culture and, meanwhile, openly absorbing western culture. However, during China's development, the potential influence of the outstanding traditional Chinese culture, along with its refusal of various westernization demands, has become the major theme of reality.

Xi Jinping pointed out, when looking back to the modern history of China, in order to save the nation from peril and achieve national rejuvenation, the Chinese people, and people with lofty ideals, persevered in seeking the model of political system that suited national conditions. Before the Revolution of 1911, the Taiping Rebellion, the Westernization Movement, the Hundred Days' Reform, the Boxer Uprising and the Late Qing Reform - all failed. After the Revolution of 1911, China tried constitutional monarchy, restoration of a dethroned monarch, a parliamentary system, multi-party system, and presidential system. Various political forces and their representatives came on stage one after another. However, none of them worked out the solution. Only the revolution led by the CPC fundamentally changed China's tragic fate of domestic strife, foreign aggression and being trampled upon at will in modern times. The revolution led by the CPC was squarely based on China's national conditions, and was an outcome of integrating Marxism with the outstanding traditional Chinese culture. In essence, Xi Jinping revealed that the Chinese revolution in the 20th century featured a high cultural self-awareness, under the guidance of which, the Chinese people correctly sought for China's road. The cultural significance of China's road lies in the reflection on westernization.

Nowadays, China is developing rapidly, but we have not yet completely realized the Chinese Dream of achieving the great rejuvenation of the Chinese nation. Neither have we fulfilled the task of comprehensively deepening reform. Therefore, to maintain China's development road with Chinese characteristics still requires our historical awareness. As Xi Jinping said, China is a country of over 9.6 million square kilometers of land with 56 ethnic groups. Whose model can we follow? Who can tell us what we should do? It does not work to copy political systems from other countries, which are unaccustomed to the climate of a new place. We will set out to be tigers but end up as dogs. In this way, we will ruin our country's future. Only the system which is deeply rooted in our country's soil and takes in its abundant nourishment, can be reliable and effective. We have to know that 'our country's soil' essentially refers to the outstanding traditional Chinese culture.

When taking into account Chinese history and the development road in China, do we have any reasons to doubt that Chinese culture is the foundation for us to stand firm upon in the global mingling and clashing of cultures? No.

III. Building the Core Socialist Values: A Significant Aspect of a Nation's Governing System and Capacity

In 2013, the Third Plenary Session of the 18th Central Committee of the CPC put forward the concept of 'modernizing the country's governance system and capacity', attracting lots of attention and giving rise to heated discussions in society. One tendency is to interpret it in reference to modern western political ideas, neglecting the Chinese historical and cultural background, deliberately or inadvertently. Xi Jinping emphasized the Chinese historical and cultural backgrounds and rectified certain partialities in his speech delivered on February 24, 2014.

1. Traditional Chinese political philosophy verifies Xi Jinping's proposal of 'Two Relations'.

Why is building the core socialist values a significant aspect of the national governance system and governance capacity? Xi Jinping said that to build core socialist values is connected with a country's social harmony and stability, as well as its long-term peace and order, namely the 'Two Relations', which has been verified by traditional Chinese political philosophy, above all by that in the Qin and Han dynasties.

In the history of China the Warring States Period, featuring constant chaotic warfare (476BC-221BC) was put to an end by the State of Qin which extinguished six states. In light of the Qin's way, which was to take the world with violence, the early rulers of the Han Dynasty (202BC-220 AD) had blind faith in the governing style of 'getting the world on horseback', disdaining to build values by applying the Confucian classics such as *Book of Odes and Book of History*. Until the reign of Emperor Wu (156 BC-87 BC) of the Han Dynasty, in order to achieve long-term national governance, Dong Zhongshu (917BC-104BC), a renowned scholar, took the Zhou and Qin dynasties as examples, saying that Zhou lost the world because of 'its complete loss of *Tao*'. So did Qin. He stated, "Nowadays there are different schools of thought with varied opinions. Different philosophers adopt different approaches, and have different pursuits and expectations. All these lead to the consequence that the imperial court fails to establish a fixed and uniform legal system. If the legal system changes frequently, the officials at lower levels and the plain folks are frustrated and don't know what to comply with. Therefore, I am holding such a humble view that anything that is out of the Six Liberal Arts and any doctrines and schools of thought that are different from those of Confucianism should not be allowed to publicize and disseminate, forbidding them to co-develop with Confucian thoughts. If the heretical thoughts are extinguished, national policies and guidelines can be established universally and the legal system will be formulated, with which people will know what to comply consistently." To be briefer, he meant that if there were no universal *Tao* in the society, namely values, the people would not know what to observe. To solve this problem required the uniform interpretation and promotion of *Tao*, making "heretical thoughts extinguish", then the people would know how to behave. This is Dong Zhongshu's well-known proposal: "to pay supreme tribute to Confucianism while banning all other schools of thought."[1]

Dong Zhongshu's suggestion was adopted by Emperor Wu of Han, solving the problem of governing by doing nothing in social governance. Meanwhile, it got over the rigid style of merely relying on political reign while neglecting to cultivate the people's ideology, and established the positive effect of building values on social stability and national governance and confirmed the core appeal for social values.

History has been proving that the Confucian values used to have positive significance for China's social governance, and even for the continuation of Chinese civilization. Helmut Schmidt, former German Chancellor, said in a recent dialogue with Chinese scholars that, besides China there were a couple of ancient civilizations 3000 years ago, such as Egypt, Iran, Greek, and Rome. Those civilizations have vanished, while China still exists and has achieved rejuvenation beyond our anticipation. He noticed that in the Chinese history of civilization, Confucianism covers almost half of its process.

Under the impact of the modern world trends, the cultural pattern of 'honoring Confucianism exclusively' faded away gradually in the late 19th century, while National rejuvenation and the revolution in pursuit of socialism became the major theme of China in the 20th century. A conspicuous fact is that although Confucian thoughts were criticized in the revolutionary process, when revolution was changing the old system and setting up the new one, the CPC inherited the tradition of attaching importance to building values and ensured the co-development of system revolution, and the transformation of humans with their raised moral standards. Maurice Meisner, a famous American scholar, wrote, "For the study of Chinese Communist ideology, it is a matter of special importance to understand the relationship between values

---

[1] *History of the Han Dynasty: Biography of Dong Zhongshu*

and goals and to understand how the former are made 'meaningful' in terms of the latter." He holds the view that one of the biggest and most significant features of the Maoist version of Marxism was "the recognition that economic development and the existence of 'socialist relations of production' do not by themselves automatically guarantee the future realization of communist goals. Communism cannot be achieved, it constantly has been emphasized, unless Marxist goals are consciously pursued, embryonic forms of communist social organization implemented, and the proper social values popularized and internalized *in the process*, and for the purpose, of creating the material prerequisite for the future communist society."[1]

It is fair to say that comrade Xi Jinping's argument inherited both the fine tradition of Chinese culture and the fine historic tradition of the CPC itself, consistent with the objective law of social governance.

2. The core values should be conducive to the modernization of a nation's governing system and capacity.

Society has always been developing throughout history. It is far from enough to acknowledge in a general way the significance of the core values in the national governance system and capacity. The Third Plenary Session of the 18th CPC Central Committee brought forward the notion of 'the modernization of the national governance system and capacity', leading to the consideration of how to build core values suitable for 'the modernization of the national governance system and capacity'.

On another occasion, Xi Jinping said, "to modernize our national governance system and capacity, we should foster and promote the core socialist values and the relevant system, and accelerate the building of a value system that fully reflects the characteristics of China, the Chinese nation and the times. We should delve deeper into and better elucidate China's excellent traditional culture, and make greater efforts to innovate and develop traditional Chinese virtues, promoting a cultural spirit that transcends time and national boundaries, and has eternal attraction and contemporary value. We should also present to the world China's contemporary creative cultural products that carry both our excellent traditional culture and contemporary spirit and that are based in China and oriented towards the outside world."[2]

---

[1] Maurice Meisner. *Marxism, Maosim and Utopianism*. China Remin University Press.2005, p.104.

[2] The Speech at a Provincial-level Officials' Seminar on Studying and Implementing the Decisions of the Third Plenary Session of the 18th CPC Central Committee on Continuing Reform. *People's Daily*. February 18, 2014.

That is to say, the core socialist values must modernize themselves in order to suit the modernization of the national governance system and capacity.

As for the inevitability of the modernization of the national governance system and capacity, Xi Jinping stated that a country's governance system and capacity are the major barometers of its system and that system's governing efficiency. The two are complementary. By and large, our governance system and capacity are good and have unique advantages, suitable for our national conditions and development needs. Nevertheless, our national governance system and capacity still have much room for improvement, and we should exert greater efforts to enhance our national governance capacity. It means that modernization should be realized in the "much room for improvement". Only with such improvement, can we say we have realized the modernization of our national governance system and capacity.

In the ideological system of Communists, the principles of democracy, which serves as a value category, are entirely in accordance with the value orientation of proletariats and the people. It reveals the requirements of democracy to take the majority as the starting point. Accordingly, the Third Plenary Session of the 18th Central Committee of the CPC highlighted maintaining the principal position of the people and developing socialist democracy, and stressed the principle of ensuring the position of people as the masters of the country as the foundation of a country's governance. It is imperative to make the design of the social fundamental system and the operation of the basic social institutions conducive to improving the democratic system and to diversifying democratic forms. Hence, what suits the democratic demands in the modernization of the national governance system and capacity is the core Socialist values, which can be condensed into 24 Chinese characters including '*minzhu*' (Chinese characters for democracy) in support of the modernization of a national system system with incorporation of modern values and ideology.

Indeed, the origins of the concepts such as democracy and liberty have a closer relation with western culture. 'Democracy' originated from the Greek 'demos', meaning the people. In western culture, the realization of democratic rights is closely linked to the free choices of individuals. The core socialist values affirm democracy and liberty, proving that its modernization is in agreement with the law of cultural development. Xi Jinping, taking account of a cultural spirit "that transcends time and national boundaries, and has eternal attraction and contemporary value", pointed out the requirement of "carrying forth both our excellent traditional culture and contemporary spirit, and being based in China and oriented towards the outside world." It means we should absorb categories widely accepted by the world civilization such as democracy and liberty, if our values are built to promote the underlying trend of the modern times and to be oriented to the outside world. However, China should not fall subject to foreign forces at their will because of this absorption, but instead it should insist on its own interpretation of democracy and liberty within the framework of socialism with Chinese characteristics.

IV. Saying 'No' to De-Sinicization

When inspecting Beijing Normal University on Dec. 9, 2014, Xi Jinping talked about the problem of scoring out classic poetry in textbooks and put forward the remark, "De-Sinicization is very pathetic". About one month later, at the Forum on Literature and Art work, Xi further stated clearly, "Strengthening cultural awareness and confidence is included within the practice of the confidence in our road, theories and system. If we take whatever from foreign countries as the exalted, the appreciable and the best to model after, aim to achieve overseas awards as our ultimate goal, ape others at every step, and are wild about '**De-ing**', such as 'De-thoughts', 'De-values', 'De-history', 'De-Sinicization', and 'De-mainstream', all these will absolutely lead us to nowhere."[1] It shows that Xi Jinping has penetrated the façade of the current global trend that there exists a cultural risk – following the lead of western culture, and taking great pride in 'De-Sinicization'. If things continue this way, the plots of westernization and differentiation will be achieved easily. In consequence, the Chinese Dream of achieving the great rejuvenation of the Chinese nation will be ruined.

1. We should face up to the impact of western culture on traditional Chinese culture.

Frankly speaking, since the policy of reform and opening up to the outside world was implemented, western cultural products have swarmed into China, having unprecedented impact on traditional Chinese culture. An essay from *The New York Times*, an American newspaper, on February 25, 2002 wrote:

"In the last few years, China's major cities have sprouted American stores and restaurants at prodigious rates, including Starbucks, PriceSmart, Pizza

---

[1] Xi Jinping. A Speech at the Forum on Literature and Art Work (2014). *People's Daily*. October 15, 2015.

Hut, McDonald's and Esprit clothing outlets. New housing compounds bear names like Orange County and Manhattan Gardens. A high-end Buick is a sought-after luxury car, a replacement for last year's Audi." "Europeans may be wont to view every Big Mac as a terrifying sign of American cultural imperialism, but Chinese have mostly welcomed the invasion - indeed they have internalized it."

Ten years has passed, but this tendency is by no means slowing down. Among the buildings in China, it is nothing new to mention some of them as 'Broadway in China', 'Hollywood in China', 'Thames in China' and 'Paris of the East'. It seems that without getting associated with the West, they were worthless.

In addition, another problem is the overemphasis on English at the cost of Chinese language. Due to the existing social institutions, from children in kindergartens to young and middle-aged professionals, all without exception study English assiduously leading to the emergence of an enormous English training industry, while their Chinese language capabilities degrade day by day. Even worse, in a country with Chinese language as its mother tongue, if an academic conference is held domestically but entitled 'international XX', English must be used as the working language. Against this backdrop, scoring out the ancient Chinese poetry is indeed an inevitable consequence of the wide-spreading 'De-Sinicization'

2. The collapse of vernacular culture is a tragedy for a nation.

How are we to understand the phenomenon of 'De-Sinicization' in the global era? Actually, the first to generalize and describe globalization should be Karl Marx and Friedrich Engels. They pointed out in *Manifesto of the Communist Party*, "The bourgeoisie has, through its exploitation of the world market, given a cosmopolitan character to production and consumption in every country. To the great chagrin of reactionaries, it has drawn from under the feet of industry the national ground on which it stood. All old-established national industries have been destroyed or are daily being destroyed. They are dislodged by new industries, whose introduction becomes a life and death question for all civilized nations, by industries that no longer work up indigenous raw material, but raw material drawn from the remotest zones; industries whose products are consumed, not only at home, but in every quarter of the globe. In place of old local and national seclusion and self-sufficiency, we have intercourse in every direction, universal inter-dependence of nations.

And as in material, so also in intellectual production. The intellectual creations of individual nations become common property. National one-sidedness and narrow-mindedness become more and more impossible, and from the numerous national and local literatures, there arises a world literature." "The bourgeoisie, by the rapid improvement of all instruments of production, by the immensely facilitated means of communication, draws all, even the most barbarian, nations into civilization. The cheap prices of commodities are the heavy artillery with which it forces the barbarians' intensely obstinate hatred of foreigners to capitulate. It compels all nations, on pain of extinction, to adopt the bourgeois mode of production; it compels them to introduce what it calls civilization into their midst, i.e., to become bourgeois themselves. In one word, it creates a world after its own image."[1]

That is to say, it is not a blessing for a nation that its culture is destroyed, neither is it neutral for a nation, but a tragedy for a nation, imposed on it by the western bourgeois. It would lead to the result that this nation is more apt to be enslaved and exploited by the West. In modern history, an ideological trend emerged of 'wholesale westernization'– in nature 'De-Sinicization'. One representative is Hu Shi, who said, "We have to acknowledge we are inferior to others in almost every aspect, from physical machinery, to political system, and to morality, knowledge, literature, music and arts, and even health."[2] Hence, we have to be 'hell-bent' on the western civilization.

3. Only by holding back 'De-Sinicization', can China achieve its great rejuvenation.

So to speak, without the revolution led by the CPC that in a practical way held back the promotion of 'De-Sinicization', it is impossible for China to achieve its rejuvenation. China today is closer to the goal of achieving rejuvenation of the Chinese nation than at any other period in its history. China is more confident and more competent to attain this goal, so it is more necessary to restrain 'De-Sinicization' than anytime before.

To the rejuvenation of the Chinese nation, the world cannot stay indifferent any longer. In 2009, Martin Jacques, a British scholar, published his new book *When China Rules the World*, causing a great stir in both the United Kingdom and the United States. "In the first half of the twenty-first century, Jacques speculates, Western rule will give way to a fragmented global order,

---

[1] *Karl Marx and Friedrich Engels: Collected Works*, Vol.2. People's Publishing House. 1972.p. 254-255.
[2] Hu Shi. An Introduction to My Thoughts. *Collected Works of Hu Shi*. Vol. 3. Anhui Education Press. 2003. p.667.

with multiple currency zones (dollar-, euro-, and renminbi-denominated) and spheres of economic/military influence (an American sphere in Europe, southwest Asia, and perhaps South Asia, and a Chinese sphere in East Asia and Africa), each dominated by its own cultural traditions (Euro-American, Confucian, and so on). But in the second half of the century, he predicts, numbers will tell; China will rule and the world will be Easternized. All over the world, people will forget the glories of the Euro-American past. They will learn Mandarin, not English, celebrate Zheng He, not Columbus, read Confucius instead of Plato, and marvel at Chinese Renaissance men such as Shen Kuo rather than Italians such as Leonardo."[1] To criticize 'De-Sinicization' is in nature to criticize 'wholesale westernization', and to break away from the western discourse hegemony, demonstrating the awareness of, and confidence in, 'Chinese characteristics'.

---

[1] Ian Morris. *Why the West Rules-for Now*. London: PROFILE BOOKS LTD. 2010. Available on http://www.doc88.com/p-9982181840436.html

Chapter 6

Improve People's Livelihood

Our people have an ardent love for life. They wish to have better education, more stable jobs, more income, greater social security, better medical and health care, improved housing conditions and a better environment. They want their children to have sound growth, have good jobs and lead a more enjoyable life. To meet their desire for a happy life is our mission.

— Part of a speech highlighted by Xi Jinping at the press conference by members of the Standing Committee of the Political Bureau of the 18th CPC Central Committee, *People's Daily*. Nov. 16, 2012.

Xi Jinping, General Secretary of the CPC Central Committee, puts special focus on improving people's livelihood and social construction. He has stressed the significance of people's livelihood many times. The improvement of people's livelihood involves many aspects. Employment is a fundamental one, so we should make great efforts to increase job opportunities. Income is a prominent one, so we should work hard to make the increase of labor remuneration keep pace with productivity improvement. Education is a long-term aspect, so we should strive to provide the education that satisfies the people. Social security is an inclusive aspect, so we should build a more equitable and sustainable social security system. Eliminating poverty is an urgent issue, so we should pay extra attention to people in straitened circumstances. The whole party must remain clear-minded, stay true to our principles, effectively avert, manage and respond to risks to our national security, and take up, cope with and resolve challenges to our social stability. We must follow the general trend of social development, respond to social voices and public concern, bring forth new ideas in social governance system and improve the level of social governance.

I. Outlook on People's Livelihood

Since the 18th CPC National Congress, General SecretaryXi Jinping, has expounded his 'outlook on people's livelihood' repeatedly, and put forward that the focus of people's livelihood lies in pooling the strength of the people for their pursuit of a happy life. On April 8, 2013, when inspecting Hainan province, Xi Jinping stressed that improving people's life means we must focus on the most direct and realistic issues of interest that concern the people most, working hard on them one by one and year after year and forging ahead with perseverance. People's livelihood refers to the people's lives, concerning their immediate interests that they most care about. It serves as the foundation of people's happiness and social harmony. [1]

People's livelihood is closely related to popular support that determines the fortune of a nation. The biggest challenge in governing a country is the issue of people's livelihood. Improving people's life is the biggest political task of the ruling party, and also concerns its most important political achievement. Officials at all levels must firmly establish the concept of political achievements oriented to people's livelihood and do a good job of attending to people's livelihood, with perseverance, to guarantee and improve people's lives. This is the basic requirement of the party's tenet of serving the people heart and soul, and the concrete embodiment of its governing concept of being built for public interests and exercising governance for the people. "We should make the improvement of the people's lives both the starting point and ultimate goal of all our work." We should make it our biggest achievement to do well in the improvement of people's livelihood and to make the people satisfied. We should share the people's sorrow and joy, do beneficial and practical things for the people, and help them solve problems. We should listen to the people's voices and evaluations, ensuring the people to have a greater 'sense of gain' in reform and development.

1. 'People's livelihood' is 'national economy', which is the foundation of the people at peace and a country in prosperity.

It has been a dream of the Chinese people since ancient times that the country is prosperous and the people live in peace. "With regard to the way of governance, nothing is more important than making the people live in peace; while the way to make people at peace lies in understanding

---

[1] Speed up the Construction of an International Tourism Island, Compose a Beautiful Chapter in Hainan, China. *People's Daily*. April 11, 2013.

their sufferings." Only by improving people's livelihood and solving the problems in their lives, can we achieve long-term peace and stability. The issue of people's livelihood is attracts unprecedented importance at present. It not only involves the people's fundamental interests, but also concerns the overall situation of national reform and development. The better this issue is addressed, the better the social economy develops. Therefore, we must ensure 'all people can benefit from the fruits of development'. *Recommendations for the 13th Five-Year Plan for Economic and Social Development* further stresses the concept of sharing, "We should ensure that development is for the people, that it is reliant on the people, and that its fruits are shared by the people. We should improve our institutions to ensure the people have a greater sense of gain as they contribute to and share in development."[1]

At present, the quality of people's life has experienced a general improvement, and people are free from worries about daily necessities. However, the rapid advance of marketization constantly amplifies all kinds of livelihood issues. The particular characteristics of market regulation, such as spontaneity, blindness and delay, make people both enjoy the happiness brought about by the rapid growth of the economy, and face a large number of new risks and uncertainties, which are continuously internalized into new bread-and-butter issues. For example, people are discontented with their jobs, and they have new higher requirements concerning the issues of educational equality, medical treatment, social security, and uneven distribution. We have to acknowledge that people's livelihood is, after all, a dynamic process with sustainable development, the intensity and extension of which will expand and upgrade constantly as the society develops and advances. The variety and complexity of demands of people's livelihood, in turn, make the government's task in effective supply more difficult. Hence, it has always been an important duty on the shoulders of the party and government to care for livelihood issues, which is the foundation and guarantee of social harmony. We can never be 'best' in the improvement of people's livelihood, but we can make it 'better'. On May 14, 2013, when inspecting Tianjin, Xi Jinping proposed that ensuring and improving people's wellbeing is a permanent job with continuous new starts, but without a end-point.

We should persevere in improving people's wellbeing, adept at transforming the work of improving people's livelihood into the 'engine' of

---

[1] *Central Committee of the CPC: Recommendations for the 13th Five-Year Plan for Economic and Social Development. Wen Hui Bao.*November 4, 2015.

economic development. Some local governments regard 'people's livelihood' as a 'burden' at work, holding the view that people's livelihood only means input and expenditure. They fail to understand the relationship between people's livelihood and development, making them contradictory to each other. Actually, if we think differently from another perspective, we can see the other side of the problem. According to the rationale of materialistic dialectics, people's livelihood and development have a positive interaction. Under China's 'new norm' condition, people's livelihood projects and engineering is another point of growth, both increasing investment and fuelling consumption. It is a new impetus with a multiplier effect. Meanwhile, coping with people's livelihood well is conducive to unifying the people and motivating the vitality of social startups, creativity and innovation. To this end, local governments at all levels should on one hand continuously increase the supply of public products and services; and enlarge their input in education, medical treatment and public health, and security housing. On the other hand, they should endeavor to boost public business and mass innovation, incubating and fostering new power for economic and social development.

2. People's livelihood is connected with people's wellbeing, which is the source of the progress of human civilization.

The pursuit of joy and happiness is the eternal theme of human society. It is also the ultimate goal for the government to pursue when they introduce public policies. David Hume, a Scottish philosopher once said, "The great end of all human industry is the attainment of happiness." What each pursues may differ in thousands of ways, but the ultimate goal that human beings strive for, in simple terms, is exactly the pursuit of happiness. The goal for the party and government to drive the development of the society should be the people's happiness as well. The ultimate purpose of economic growth is to benefit the public, as are 'good governance' and cultural development. Throughout almost the entire span of human history, it is not difficult to discover that people's happiness is not only an important aspect of a harmonious society but also the source of human civilization and the foundation for social harmony.

GDP, listed as one of the 'great inventions' by western economists, functions as a key criterion to evaluate the social development of countries worldwide. However, it cannot reflect the total real information regarding the status of a national people's livelihood. Neither can it offer complete information about public welfare. When GDP reaches a certain level, what determines the state of people's happiness is no longer the growth of material wealth, but other non-economic factors. GNH (Gross National Happiness) has received emphasis recently, becoming an important reference indicator to measure a country's stability and its people's happiness. GNH helps not only to monitor economic and social operation, but also to understand people's satisfaction with their lives. It serves as a 'barometer' of social operation and state of public life.

At present, there still exists a controversy around GNH, for happiness is a subjective assessment of people's satisfaction with life, and indeed it is hard to seek out objective measurements. As Leo Tolstoy once said, "All happy families resemble one another, each unhappy family is unhappy in its own way." The resemblance is that happiness, as a benign pleasure, is the ultimate goal of people's pursuit. Jigme Singye Wangchuck, King of Bhutan, was the first one to apply GNH in practice. He believed that government administration should be aimed at the attainment of happiness, focusing on the balanced development between the material and and the spiritual. Accordingly, in 1970, the Bhutan government treated economic growth, good governance, cultural development and environmental protection as four pillars of its national development. Today, GNH is gradually gaining recognition worldwide. For example, in 2008, Nicolas Sarkozy, French president, organized a panel of over 20 world-renowned experts, including Joseph E. Stiglitz, and Amartya Kumar Sen, two Nobel Laureates in economics, to conduct research entitled 'Happiness and Measuring Economic Progress'. This research suggests that reforms should be implemented in national economic accounting methods, GNH be listed into indicators measuring economic performance, and indicators such as subjective feeling of wellbeing, quality of life and distribution of income be applied to measure economic development.

Currently, a number of local governments in China have put forward an urban development strategy with 'happiness' as the ultimate goal. Social development should be in agreement with ensuring people can enjoy a happy life, which shows the progress in the governance concept. Certainly, local governments should not take building 'a happy city' as a show, follow suit, and fail to solve problems fundamentally. In order to make the people happy, building a happy city must be oriented to people's well-being. A happy city is not only a livable and workable place, but also one that can achieve full coverage in people's livelihood services.

The people can live and work in peace and contentment; meanwhile, the elderly can be looked after properly, the young can enjoy proper education, the poor and those in need can get help. In this way, people will attain their genuine 'happy life'.

On December 16, 2015, Feng Xinxing (front right in the picture), a low-income villager from Tangxia village, Wangqiao Town, Dongxiang County in Jiangxi province, together with other villagers was harvesting taros on the farms of Jiangxi Lvmu Agriculture Development Company Limited. This agricultural company adopts a cooperative pattern of 'company+cooperatives+farms+farmers' to plant over 1500 mu taro flowers, a well-known local product, by which it helps about 800 low-income families to alleviate their poverty. (Xinhua News Agency)

II. The Bottom Line of People's Livelihood

On Dec. 13, 2013, at the Central Economic Work Conference, Xi Jinping said we must do well in guaranteeing and improving people's livelihood, "we must continue to hold the bottom line, highlight the key points, perfect the system, guide public opinion, and plan as a whole in education, employment, income distribution, social security, medicine and health, housing, food safety, and safe production, substantially accomplishing various tasks in the improvement of people's livelihood."[1] On many other occasions, he

---

[1] The Central Economic Work Conference was held in Beijing. *People's Daily*. The front page. December 13, 2013.

repeatedly mentioned the livelihood work and the issue of holding the bottom line. We should accomplish the work of people's livelihood well in line with the principle of "holding the bottom line, highlighting the key points, perfecting the system and guiding public opinions." We must clarify the key point of the social security policies, so as to define the direction for comprehensively deepening the reform of people's livelihood. At the decisive stage to achieve the goal of building a moderately prosperous society in all respects during the 13th Five-Year Plan period, we should make sure that basic living needs are met, focus on key areas, improve systems and guide expectations. At the same time, we need to emphasize equal opportunity, guarantee basic living standards, and ensure that all our people enjoy moderate prosperity together."[1]

When paying close attention, and attaching great importance, to people's livelihood, and constantly guaranteeing and improving it, we must have a clear understanding of the most immediate and practical interests of the people's top concern, and know who needs help the most. We must solve their problems one by one, and forge ahead, with perseverance, year by year. The party officials must know in timely and accurately fashion what the people think of, hope for, worry about, and are concerned about, and do the mass work honestly, deeply, meticulously and thoroughly. Then, how can we best accomplish the work concerning people's livelihood? What counts is to hold the bottom line, namely 'social policies must be integrated'. It means that good social policies must be inclusive, everlasting and effective. 'Inclusive' means each should benefit from the achievements of development. People are different in their gifts, abilities, performance and opportunity, but the society should offer them basic livelihood protection. 'Everlasting' means the supply level of social welfare should be tailored to the practical development level. We should do our best and do it according to our abilities. We shouldn't make social welfare beyond our ability, but should avoid getting deep in debts and losing the trust of the people. 'Effective' means the supply of social security and social welfare should help formulate the mechanism to encourage people 'to live a better life through diligent work'. We should not practice egalitarianism and reward the lazy by punishing the diligent. Instead, we should maintain the vitality of society through establishment of the mechanism of fair competition.

---

[1] *Central Committee of the CPC: Recommendations for the 13th Five-Year Plan for Economic and Social Development. Wen Hui Bao,* November 4, 2015.

1. Holding the bottom line reflects the determination of the party and government to shoulder their responsibility for people's livelihood.

The 'bottom line' means that the government shoulders inescapable responsibilities, and must strive to match up to them. We all know how important a goalkeeper is in a football match. A good goalkeeper can be worth half of a football team. The task of a goalkeeper is to hold the gate (his bottom line). Once the line is broken, the game is a failure. Holding a bottom line stresses that we should stay on the alert and have a sense of responsibility at all times. We should have the awareness of crises and prevent any that are possible from arising. With regards to people's livelihood, holding the bottom line means to safeguard the minimum social equity, ensure the common people to live and work in peace and contentment, and provide the most basic needs for residents by means of a series of government social policies. For example, a number of issues, such as the subsistence security system which ensures the low-income group to have adequate food and clothing, the medical security system, and the compulsory education system, need to be dealt with by institutional guarantee and financial support. All these basic requirements belong to the inclusive livelihood rights and interests.

2. Holding the bottom line requires the joint efforts of all social powers to contribute to the improvement of people's livelihood.

In reality, giving play to the decisive role of the market in resource allocation is not incompatible with sticking to the bottom line in equity. The key lies in whether we can proceed from the weakest link of the market mechanism in resource allocation, 'preparing from the worst', and effectively resolve the problem of market failure. The teachers' fiscal subsidy mechanism should be established in the poor and remote areas. The Central Economic Working Conference repeatedly highlighted that large-scale enterprises should fulfill their social responsibility and increase the share allocated to labor elements, so they might participate in the distribution of wealth. The urban and rural insurance system for serious illness should raise its operational efficiency to be as good as a commercial insurance management system. The bottom line equity in these fields, such as education, income distribution, and social security, cannot do without strong national coordination, nor can it do without the multi-participation of enterprises, society and individuals. In fighting poverty, we need to "improve mechanisms for coordinating poverty reduction efforts between the western and eastern regions as well as mechanisms for party and government agencies, the military, people's organizations, and SOEs to support targeted poor areas. We should encourage enterprises and social organizations as well as individuals to pledge contributions to poverty reduction efforts."[1] For enterprises, establishing a staff welfare system is the effective human resource investment to enhance staff cohesion, as well as an effective supplement and response to the bottom line thinking. For individuals, they should cultivate sound values under the guidance of the social bottom line equity, getting rich by working hard instead of making a huge fortune overnight through speculation, against the law.

3. Holding the bottom line means making the low-income groups feel 'assured' of their life.

Holding the bottom line means to ensure a steady rise of people's living standard, especially that of the low-income groups. In order to increase support for low-income groups, in recent years, we have taken a series of measures, such as raising in succession minimum wages, basic pension and subsistence allowance standard, increasing the income of low- and middle-income groups, and lifting the threshold of personal income tax. Certainly, the minimum living standard of urban and rural areas should be adjusted in a timely way according to the local economic development level and financial positions, to ensure the basic living needs of the masses. We will take the treatment level of endowment insurance as an example. In recent years, enterprise retirees have enjoyed pension increases ten times in succession. At the same time there is a 10% increase in the risk of institutional sustainability. Experience from Germany shows that pension level should be linked to the consumer price index (CPI) to maintain purchasing power. Meanwhile, it should be linked to the social development level (like GDP growth rate), enabling all the citizens to enjoy the achievements of economic development. The bottom-line thinking is neither a rash advance nor the withdrawal of state responsibility. Instead, it is a moderate promotion based on institutional rationality.

4. Highlighting the key points means focusing on solving the urgent problems of people's livelihood.

Highlighting the key points means to grasp the most urgent problems of people's livelihood, for examples, paying attention to the stability

---

[1] *Central Committee of the CPC: Recommendations for the 13th Five-Year Plan for Economic and Social Development.Wen Hui Bao.* November 4, 2015.

and expansion of employment, doing a good job in youth employment with college graduates as the focus, and "increasing assistance for those who face difficulties in obtaining employment."[1] We need to perfect the employment service system, improve employment service capacity, treat well and support the development of small and micro enterprises, intensify the social responsibilities of large enterprises, continue to strengthen the construction and management of indemnificatory housing, and accelerate the transformation of shanty towns. Highlighting the key points makes clear that, under circumstances of limited financial resources, we need to solve the prominent problems, which are top concerns of the people and related to the people's wellbeing. General Secretary Xi Jinping said, "We should pay close attention to people in straitened circumstances, and extend care to them with respect and love", which reminds officials at all levels to care for the special groups. In late December 2012, General Secretary Xi Jinping, soon after he assumed office, regardless of the temperature of minus ten degrees Celsius, went to Fuping County, Hebei province, for a visit to people in straitened circumstances and an inspection of poverty-alleviation and development work. He stressed, "It is the essential requirement of socialism to eradicate poverty, improve the people's livelihood and achieve common prosperity."[2]

5. To perfect the system is to enable the system 'dividends' to benefit more people.

The bottom-line thinking requires us to constantly perfect system design. Specifically, in the field of people's livelihood, we need to continuously strengthen the responsibility for national institutional improvement and financial accountability, and shoulder three great responsibilities for transfer payment, public services and industrial strength. We will take the retirement pension system as an example. In 2012, we launched a pilot project on social endowment insurance system, and attempted to carry it forward for urban residents nationwide. However, because of the low basic level of endowment insurance, problems such as transfer to different places and connection inconvenience still make some people unsettled. How to perfect the system and make the system 'dividends' benefit more people is a direction for us to aspire to. In regard of services for the elderly and disabled, we need both to

---

[1] *Central Committee of the CPC: Recommendations for the 13th Five-Year Plan for Economic and Social Development. Wen Hui Bao.* November 4, 2015.

[2] Eliminate Poverty and Accelerate Development in Impoverished Areas. *People's Daily.* December 31, 2012.

offer subsidies to those in need by sticking to the bottom-line equity, and to 'strive for the best results' from a perspective in the long run, supporting and offering subsidies to the activities such as services for the elderly and nursing care for the disabled. In the process of system design, we need both to expand total government investment, and structurally to make clear the responsibility system of fiscal at all levels (central and local). We need to continuously perfect income guarantee systems, such as the subsistence security system and social insurance, and to further develop a series of public service systems such as compulsory education equity in underdeveloped areas, for example old revolutionary bases, areas with concentrations of ethnic minorities, border areas, and contiguous poor areas.

III. Promotion of Equity and Justice and Improvement of People's Living Standards

On July 23, 2013, when in Wuhan he presided over a forum of principals from some provinces and cities, Xi Jinping said we needed to achieve social fairness and justice and guarantee various rights and interests of the people by means of institutional arrangement. On the basis of joint efforts of all the people and continuous development of economic society, we need to safeguard rights and interests of the people by means of institutional arrangements and ensure all the people can enjoy rights and fulfill obligations equally according to law.[1] In *Recommendations for the 13th Five-Year Plan*, the Central Committee of the CPC stresses in particular the principal status of the people, and sets a requirement to "develop the people's democracy, safeguard social equity and justice, protect the rights of the people to participate and develop on an equal footing, and give full rein to their enthusiasm, initiative and creativity."[2]

The development and progress of human society, from a certain perspective, is reflected in the changes of two relations. The first is the relation between man and nature, that is, the issue of economic development. The second is the relation between individuals, namely, the issue of social equity and justice. The relation between man and nature mainly concerns human survival, the core of which is how to make conditions of existence increasingly better, in other words, how to enable people to live a happy life.

---

[1] Xi Jinping's Speech at the Forum in Wuhan with Heads of Some Provinces and Cities. *People's Daily*. July 25, 2013.

[2] *Central Committee of the CPC: Recommendations for the 13th Five-Year Plan for Economic and Social Development. Wen Hui Bao*. November 4, 2015

Conditions of existence are the bases for human development as well as for all social activities, which is the basic principle of Marxism that economic base determines superstructure. We must liberate and develop social productivity in order to improve the people's conditions of existence. As productivity develops, there is more and more wealth, giving rise to the problem of uneven possession of wealth, that is to say, the issue of social equity and justice. The greater is the accumulation of wealth, the more prominent is the equity problem. At all times and all over the world, the great turbulences, even changes of dynasties, in history, mostly resulted from serious conflicts associated with social inequity and a big gap between the wealthy and the poor, and escalating conflicts resulted in social revolutions.

1. Promoting equity and justice is an active response to increasingly strong social voices.

As China develops further and the people's living standards improve continually, public awareness of equity, of democracy and of rights and interests have been steadily enhanced, and hence people's resentment at injustice becomes more pronounced. For example, some get rich overnight by exploiting an advantage or through dishonest practices. Some get extremely rapid promotion due to prominent family background. Because of incomplete policies and systems, residents of different identities are treated differently in income, medical treatment, education and pension for the aged. Some suffer from unfair treatments. China's luxury consumption ranks second in the world, but still a large number of people live below the poverty line. In the past, awareness of unjust events and phenomena spread slowly, exerting little influence. Nowadays, the rapid development of the internet and mobile phones enables each individual to be a 'journalist'. Once an unjust event happens, knowledge of it will be spread rapidly. In addition, some people, when noticing unjust phenomena, are likely to be charged with with irrational and extreme emotions and deliberately hype or overstate the degree of inequity. 'Unfair things lead to unsettled minds, which result in irritability'. The issue of equity and justice becomes the focal point of many social conflicts, arousing people's top concern.

The issue of equity and justice, if not dealt with well, will not only reduce public confidence in reform and opening up but also undermine social harmony and stability. Therefore, *Recommendations for the 13th Five-Year Plan* puts forward, "We should make the social security system fairer and more sustainable. We need to ensure the social safety net essentially covers all people entitled by law. We should keep the social security system in actuarial balance, improve its funding mechanisms, and define the responsibilities of the government, enterprises, and individuals in this regard."[1] If we cannot bring practical benefits to the people and create a fairer social environment, we cannot keep the development sustainable. Then the reform we are carrying out will be meaningless. The issue of equity and justice is a big problem our party is confronted with. It concerns whether the party can stay in power permanently. We are still facing a tough test when dealing with this issue. Xi Jinping attached great importance to this issue. He saw through clearly that it is an issue related to the party's rise and fall. Hence, he warned the whole party, "This problem, if not resolved in good time, will reduce public confidence in our reform and opening up, and undermine social harmony and stability." In the *Report to the 18th CPC National Congress*, it is stressed that "We must establish in due course a system for guaranteeing fairness in society featuring, among other things, equal rights, equal opportunities and fair rules for all, and foster a fair social environment and ensure people's equal right to participation in governance and to development."[2] On the road to pursuing equity and justice, China must hold up the banner of reform.

2. The pursuit of equity and justice is a basic requirement of Marxism as well as the reflection of reform.

With regard to this old but often renewed topic of equity and justice, human beings have never stopped reflecting on and pursuing it tirelessly. From Plato to Aristotle, and then to early utopian socialism, ideologists have depicted a picture of society without exploitation and oppression but with equity and justice. However, because of historical limitations, they failed to find a route leading to their ideal society. Karl Marx and Friedrich Engels, based on the analysis of fundamental contradictions of capitalism, created the theory of scientific socialism by applying historical materialism and the doctrine of surplus value, making socialism a real social movement. Although capitalist mode of production created a large amount of social wealth, its system would inherently cause polarization between the rich and the poor. Therefore, it should be changed. Marx visualized an ideal society in the future which, whether at the lower stage of communism with distribution in accordance with labor; or at the advanced stage of communism with distribution

---

[1] *Central Committee of the CPC: Recommendations for the 13th Five-Year Plan for Economic and Social Development. Wen Hui Bao.* November 4, 2015.

[2] *Firmly March on the Path of Socialism with Chinese Characteristics and Strive to Complete the Building of a Moderately Prosperous Society in All Respects.* People's Publishing House. 2012.p.14-15.

according to one's needs; is based on the fundamental principles of equity and justice as well as human emancipation.

Reform is the self-improvement and development of the socialist system. On the basis of the reform and development achievements, we must attach importance to the requirements to improve social equity and justice and enhance people's living standards. In recent years, with the advance of reform in social fields, with regard to the people's livelihood construction, we have accomplished remarkable achievements. However, we must see, at the existing level of development, there are still many phenomena of violations of equity and justice. For example, there are wide income gaps between different occupations and different regions. In some places, violent law enforcement in the process of land expropriation and house demolition gives rise to tense relations between officials and the masses. Other serious issues such as environmental pollution, food safety, excessive-priced housing, difficulty of getting medical service, and high cost of getting medical treatment, mirror the social problems concerning justice. As China develops further and the people's living standards improve continually, public awareness of equity, democracy and of rights and interests has been steadily enhanced, and hence people's resentment at injustice becomes stronger. Deng Xiaoping was particularly concerned about the issue of equity and justice in his old age, stressing "How to make a population of 1.2 billion wealthy? How to distribute the wealth after they become rich? Both are big problems. They are the issues we should work on. It is more difficult to resolve these problems than to develop the country [to make it] stronger." If we cannot create a fairer social environment after China has developed well, or if the development leads to more injustice, reform will be meaningless. So to speak, promoting equity and justice is a serious problem that humans will not avoid or bypass.

3. We need to constantly explore the way to achieve equity and justice in practice.

At the initial stage of reform and opening up, our party realized the relation between equity and efficiency. Which is more important, 'to make the cake bigger' or 'to cut the cake fairly'? It is hard to decide, after all, for both of them are indispensable. At the initial stage of reform and opening up, under the pressure of development, people preferred efficiency, attaching more importance to make 'the cake' bigger, while after they get rich, they have more expectations for justice, which is inevitable. How to deal with it? It was pointed out in the *Decision of the Central Committee of the CPC on Some*

Major Issues Concerning Comprehensively Deepening the Reform at the Third Plenary Session of the 18th CPC Central Committee that, 'To deepen the reform comprehensively, we must put the promotion of social fairness, justice and improvement of people's lives as the starting point and ultimate goal.' If we fail to bring tangible benefits to the people and to create a fairer social environment, and even bring about more social injustice, reform will be meaningless and will not be sustainable. We must deepen reform, perfect the system, intensify supervision, and take comprehensive measures to form a feasible and orderly income-distribution structure, making the development achievements benefit all people more fairly.

How to correctly handle the relationship between justice and efficiency is a difficulty that each country is bound to encounter in its development. To address it well is conducive to both economic development and social harmony and stability. This issue, if not handled well, will bring about difficulties for economic development. Even if the economy may endure for a certain period, it cannot last long. Even worse, serious social chaos may take place. In general, China has done a good job on this issue in recent years. In particular, at the beginning of reform and opening up, the national economic and social development both improved efficiency and underscored fairness, and hence it greatly mobilized the initiative and creativity of the people, and liberated productivity to an unprecedented extent. Nowadays, we have gradually shaken off poverty and backwardness, and developed to be the world's second largest economy with per-capita income reaching the level of medium-developed countries. However, the large population and the wide gap between the urban and rural areas as well as that between different regions result in discrepancies of regional development.

4. We must guarantee the improvement of equity and justice by means of comprehensively deepening the reform.

The realization of social equity and justice is determined by a variety of factors, the most important of which is the level of economic and social development. At different levels of development and in different historical periods, people of different social status differ in their understanding of, and their demands for, social equity and justice. There exist phenomena of equity and justice violations at our present stage, most of which are consequential problems during the development process that can be solved through constant development by means of institutional arrangement, legal regulation and policy support. The improvement of social equity and justice must start from the fundamental interests of the majority of people. We must treat and deal with this issue from the perspectives of social development, overall social situation and concern about all the people. We must take economic development as the central task, promote sustained and sound growth and 'make the cake bigger,' thereby laying a more solid material foundation for greater social fairness and justice. Meanwhile, we must cut 'the cake' fairly by establishing a just and reasonable income-distribution system, striving to increase the proportion of residents' income in national income and of labor remuneration in primary distribution so as to achieve the residents' income growth at the same pace with economic development and labor remuneration growth at the same pace as labor productivity. We should accelerate the establishment of a reasonable and orderly national income-distribution structure, and practically narrow down income distribution gaps.

Proceeding from our national conditions, we must fundamentally rely on institutions to guarantee the improvement of social equity and justice. We should make great efforts to be innovative in institutional arrangements so as to eradicate social injustice and inequality caused by man-made factors, and ensure the people's equal rights to participate in governance and self-development. General Secretary Xi Jinping said, "We should take social fairness and justice and the living standards of the people as a mirror to examine our systems, mechanisms, policies and regulations in all respects, and introduce reforms accordingly by focusing on areas where the problems of injustice and inequality are most prevalent."[1] As for problems caused by unsound institutional arrangements, timely measures should be taken to better reflect the principle of fairness and justice in our socialist society and better realize, maintain and develop the fundamental interests of our people. On the basis of the joint efforts of all people and of economic and social development, we must accelerate building the institutions that may best guarantee social fairness and justice, and gradually establish a system to guarantee social justice by taking rights equity, opportunity equity and rule equity as major contents. We should strive to create a fair social environment and ensure our people's rights to equal participation and development. The core of building institutions is to reasonably address the issue of power disposition, improve the legal foundation to be beneficial to equity and justice, and avoid social injustice caused by abuse of rights. We need to transform government functions through reform, eliminate monopoly, break

---

[1] Xi Jinping. Align Our Thinking with the Guidelines of the Third Plenary Session of the 18th CPC Central Committee. *People's Daily*. January 1, 2014.

up any kind of special interest group, and offer each individual the equal opportunity to fulfill their dreams by their own efforts. We should provide rural residents, over half of the population, with freedom of migration through reform, and eradicate the injustice in social stratification caused by an unreasonable household registration system.

IV. Participation of Citizens and Social Organizations in Social Governance

On March 5, 2014, Xi Jinping stressed at the deliberation session of the Shanghai delegation at the Second Session of the 12th National People's Congress, that the key to strengthening and innovating social governance is institutional innovation with the people at the core. We must adhere to being people-oriented when solving social conflicts and problems, and firmly establish the concept of social governance for the people, in order to achieve the goal of serving people, being close to people, loving people and being favorable to people.[1] We must investigate and survey at grassroots level, satisfy the people's increasing needs, adapt ourselves to the situation that people's democratic and legal awareness has been enhanced, and attract each citizen to participate in social governance, so as to effectively solve all kinds of social conflicts and problems. In the *Recommendations for the 13th Five-Year Plan*, it is clearly stated, "We should further refine social governance and establish a structure of social governance which is exercised by the people and for the people. We should improve mechanisms for expressing, coordinating, and protecting interests, and guide people in exercising their rights, expressing their demands, and resolving their disputes in accordance with the law. We should make sure that communities provide better services and that there is positive interaction between government governance on the one hand and social regulation and resident self-governance on the other."[2]

There is currently a variety of social affairs issues. Practice has proved that the government, if it attempts to take on everything, cannot work well, and goes nowhere. Therefore, how to solve this problem? The best way is to attract citizens and social organizations to participate in social governance, and achieve the effective and integrated use of social resources by means of social coordination and public participation. On a world scale, modern social

---

[1] Xi Jinping. Advance the Development of Shanghai Free Trade Zone, Strengthen and Innovate the Social Governance of Megacities. *People's Daily*. March 6, 2014.

[2] *Central Committee of the CPC: Recommendations for the 13th Five-Year Plan for Economic and Social Development*. Wen Hui Bao. November 4, 2015.

governance is the collaborative governance in which, under the structure of normative public governance, citizens participate by interacting positively with the government. At present, our social organizations are developing rapidly, playing a significant role in maintaining social stability, providing public services and promoting the development of science, education, culture and health, and have become an important participant in social governance. Certainly, social organizations are at the initial stage in their development, hence improvements are still needed in quantity, scale and capacity. It is hard for them to give full play to their coordinative function in social governance. Therefore, government at different levels should conscientiously mobilize social organizations and general citizens to participate positively, and promote the capacity of social self-governance and public service.

1. Social organizations should adapt themselves to the current trend of social development, transform the old mindset and dare to take actions.

In modern society, social organizations, as an important force independent of government and market, play an irreplaceable role in rectifying the excessive concentration of government power and the tendency to a monopoly of market power. Our social organizations have been developing to certain extent in recent years; however, compared with those in western countries, they are far from sufficient. Each 10,000 people only have 3.2 social organizations, taking up 1/16 of that in the USA, 1/31 of Japan and 1/34 of France. In particular, the social organizations of some industries that society has urgent need of, such as science and technology, public interest and charity, urban and rural community services, need to speed up their development. Local governments are taking measures to actively foster and promote the growth of social organizations. Citizens and social organizations themselves should take initiatives to fulfill the function of social governance transferred by government. Besides carrying out more and better social service programs authorized by the government as contracts, they should exert subjective initiatives to shoulder the responsibility for social governance as a main force. They should fulfill the function of social governance transferred by the government, so as to accelerate the transformation and concession of governmental functions and realize the model of modern collaborative governance. For example, the senior citizen associations will gradually fulfill the community's function of serving the elderly. The associations for the disabled will gradually assume the role to serve the disabled. The youth and adolescence organizations will play a pioneering role, leading a new trend as volunteers.

2. Social organizations should strengthen their progress, normalize their internal governance and constantly promote their capacity.

Social organizations, as the undertakers of public services, should continuously perfect their internal governance, strengthen their organizational capacity and constantly improve the competitiveness of their own development. Many places have set out their strategic plan, aimed for long-term goals, and strengthened standardization management of social organizations so as to promote their sound development. For example, since 2002, Shanghai has formulated in succession a series of regulations. They are *Interim Measures for the Administration of the Industry Associations in Shanghai*, *Opinions on Further Promoting the Participation of Non-governmental Organizations in the Community Construction and Administration*, *Guiding Opinions on Further Strengthening the Construction of Social Organizations in Shanghai*, and *Guiding Opinions on Encouraging the Public Welfare Social Organizations to Participate in the Community Livelihood Service*. On the one hand, we should actively foster and encourage social organizations to participate in social governance. On the other hand, we should formulate and improve related laws, regulations and policies to support and guide their legal and orderly participation in social governance. We should strengthen and improve government supervision, establish information publication and an evaluation system of social organizations, and perfect and integrate a withdrawal mechanism, in order to ensure the organizations can carry out activities in accordance with standards. Social organizations must comply with requirements for clearly-stated status of legally-responsible persons, and have a complete internal governance structure, as well as their standardized management operation, enact regulations for their internal governance, implement democratic election, democratic decision-making, democratic management and democratic supervision, promote the specialization and professionalization of their teams, and improve their credibility and service capability.

3. Social organizations should offer specialized services, optimize social resource allocation, and realize social collaborative governance.

A basic way for social organizations to participate in social governance is to offer more specialized social services, which has a direct bearing on their survival and development. It is the basic requirement for them to offer public welfare services and non-profit services in modern society, in particular during the period of social transition. They should fulfill the service function and substantially represent and safeguard the legal interests and common interests of specific groups and members. At the same time, they can give full play to their advantages in mechanism, resources and talents to fulfill those public services that the government and market mechanism cannot offer, and play a supplementary role in the fields that the government and market are unable or unwilling to be involved in. For instance, urban communities may have access to plenty of undeveloped resources, unused facilities, and idle funds of residents. The government usually has no time to deal with the integration and distribution of these resources, while individuals are not powerful enough, so social organizations can put their capacity to good use, and their specialized services can meet the needs of community residents. Apart from their needs for life services and cultural recreation, with the improvement of living standards, residents increasingly put forward more sophisticated requirements. For instance, community residents require more specialized services in education (early childhood education), health (professional nursing), and law (elderly real estate disputes), and social organizations are characterized with wide coverage and flexibility, offering more meticulous and attentive services. By means of accepting commissions and participating in bidding, social organizations can undertake functions of social management and public services. Practice has proved that social organizations enjoy unique advantages in satisfying the needs of special groups and vulnerable groups and in resolving a variety of social problems. We should give full play to the advantages of all kinds of social organizations, which helps to develop the effective collaboration of government, market and social organizations, effectively distribute social resources, strengthen social coordination, defuse social conflicts, and meet the needs of society in an all-around way through specialized social services.

Chapter 7

Pursue Ecological Progress

Ecological progress is of vital importance to the wellbeing of the people and the future of the nation. It is an important element in the Chinese dream of the great rejuvenation of the Chinese nation. "We want both clean waters and green mountains as well as golden and silver mountains. And if we have to choose between the two, we would rather choose the former over the latter. In essence, clean waters and green mountains are golden and silver mountains."

— *A Series of Important Speeches by General Secretary Xi Jinping*. Beijing: Xuexi Publishing House. (the version of People's Publishing House). 2014. P.120.

I. Ecological Progress Boosts National Civilization

Xi Jinping stated that "Ecological progress boosts our national civilization, while ecological deterioration causes civilization declination." when he presided over the sixth group study session of the Political Bureau of the Central Committee of the CPC in May, 2013. This remark reveals the keen relationship between ecological environment and human civilization, and reflects the CPC's profound understandings on laws of nature, of the development of human civilization, and of economic and social development. Also, it shows the objective laws in the development of human civilization, embodies the very importance of ecological construction, and has enriched and developed the Marxist outlook on ecosystems.

Chinese civilization boasts a long-standing history of more than five thousand years with a rich accumulation of wisdom on the ecosystem. At one point in history, Confucians proposed that, "The benevolent regards all creatures as a whole"; Taoists claimed that "Man is an integral part of nature",

"The way (tao) accords to nature", and "Heaven, Earth and I came into being at the same time, and all things and I became an integral whole"; other classic verses went as 'Never shoot at birds in spring, for the infants are expecting their mothers' return'; and there are other familial precepts such as 'While taking a mouthful of congee or rice, or using any bit of resource, you should bear in mind that it is not easy to come by'. All of these sayings embody profound wisdom of ancient Chinese philosophers about the relationship between man and nature, and they still resonate with us in the depth of our hearts. The ecological environment is the natural precondition and material foundation for the existence and development of human civilization, without which there would not have been the formation and continuation of human civilization. Ecological environment has great influence on, and places constraints on, the historical process and development level of human civilization. From a historical perspective, the ebb of some ancient civilisations was closely related to the destruction of their eco-environment. Examples include the civilization of ancient Babylon, the Harappa civilization of ancient India, and the ancient Maya civilization of Central America that all thrived with dense forestation and rich water resources in a good natural environment, but all declined due to damaged ecological balance. In *Dialectics of Nature*, Engels wrote that "The people who, in Mesopotamia, Greece, Asia Minor and elsewhere, destroyed the forests to obtain cultivated land, never dreamed that by removing along with the forests the collecting centres and reservoirs of moisture they were laying the basis for the present forlorn state of those countries." "Let us not, however flatter ourselves overmuch on account of our human victories over nature. For each such victory nature takes its revenge on us."

The natural environment that human beings live in is the basis and precondition for the incubation, formation and development of human society. Throughout history, mankind has been living in the nature's grace, which provides abundant raw materials and living materials for human activities in much the same way that a loving mother raises her children, which is called 'the virtue of nature'. In the ancient times, people stood in awe of nature and searched for basic living necessities under the sky. Nature nurtures living beings and human beings, and enables mankind to make it to the top of the biological chain, like the most brilliant pearl on the earth. Since the Industrial Civilization, the belief that 'Mankind is the master of the world' has alienated the relationship between human and nature, and human beings have harbored an unprecedented passion for transforming and exploiting nature as if launching a greedy and relentless war against it. As productivity advances in an unparalleled manner, it at the same time changes the ecosystem and the environment at an unprecedented speed and to an unimaginable extent. In consequence, the damaged eco-environment has brought about catastrophic influence on human being themselves and their life. Many countries repeat the practice of, 'pollute first and remedy later'. During this process, water and soil are contaminated, and they are still beyond remedy to the present day. Among the countries, Britain took a lead in industrialization and London had long been the infamous 'City of Fog'. At the end of 19th century, the photochemical smog in London resulted in thousands of death in a short period of time. Then in the 1930s, the shocking Smog Incident in Meuse Valley broke out in Belgium. Later in the 1940s, the photochemical smog caused by exhaust gas emitted by millions of vehicles in Los Angles, U.S. led to numerous illness and death.

In China, over thirty years' rapid development, the accumulated ecological and environmental problems have surfaced more frequently and have reached a peak. The relationship between economic development and environmental protection is not addressed properly in some places and regions where, in wild pursuit of treasure, people fail to suppress their heated passion to demand foods from mountains, lakes and prairies by relentlessly exploiting various natural resources, deforesting to reclaim lands, cultivating grasslands abusively, and enclosing lakes for croplands. Soil fertility degrades greatly because of desertification from abusive cultivation of grasslands. Sandstorms can be constantly seen in cities, screening the sky, blocking the sun, and floating overhead like ghosts. Among the 74 cities monitored according to the new air quality measurements, only 4.1% of them stood up to the standard. Across the country, extensive and longstanding haze comes about frequently. Land-reclamation from lakes continuously shrinks water storage area, weakens the lakes' natural capacity to hold or regulate flood, and degrades the ecosystem around the lakes. The problem of scarcity of water resources is hanging over about two-thirds of small and medium-sized cities in China. The pollution of rivers and ground water has become quite severe. The area of arable land nationwide has dwindled close to the red bottom line of 1.8 billion *mu*, among which 150 million *mu* have been polluted, more than 40% have degraded, and moreover some of them are seriously contaminated with heavy metals. Deforestation and reclamation for croplands have greatly reduced forest coverage and accelerate global warming. Forests that used to be the lungs of the earth are weakening day by day. Large-scale water and soil erosion has caused more and more natural disasters such as floods and mud slides, swallowing our homes up...... In one event after another, ecological tragedy comes around us repeatedly. According to some statistics, it is estimated that the damage resulting from environmental pollution all over the country, including diseases caused by air pollution and loss from deforestation, may amount to 5% to 6% of our GDP in total. The degraded eco-environment is breeding a variety of diseases such as asthma, tracheitis, hypertension, and cancer that are on the rise, seriously threatening human health and making mankind more vulnerable. Human beings are trying their utmost to develop the so-called industrial civilization, while at the same time they have triggered divorcing of man from nature.

Human civilization and the eco-environment are interdependent and interrelated as an integral whole. Harmonious coexistence and mutual development with a dynamic ecosystem is not only the necessity for man's life and spirit, but also the cornerstone for the continuation of human civilization. In December 2014, Xi Jinping reiterated at the Standing Committee Conference of the Political Bureau of the Central Committee, "We must put the problem in the perspective of historical development of the Chinese nation. We should leave to our future generations a beautiful homeland. The pen of history will keep a record of the positive power of the contemporary Chinese people. "

The picture above is the Bauhinia scenic spot in Jinchang City, a live example for a unique urban construction of 'a city amidst sceneries' and 'sceneries all over a city', demonstrating the Jinchang Municipality's idea of an integral ecosystem of mountains, waters, woods, fields and lakes.

II. Clean Waters and Green Mountains Are Golden and Silver Mountains

In September 2013, Xi Jinping pointed out that "we shall never sacrifice eco-environment for temporary economic development." While he was answering questions from students at Nazarbayev University in Kazakhstan, he also said, "We want both clean waters and green mountains as well as golden and silver mountains. And if we have to choose between the two, we would rather choose the former over the latter. In essence, clean waters and green mountains are golden and silver mountains."

General Secretary Xi Jinping has reiterated the notion of 'Two Mountains' on a couple of occasions when he either took part in a Political Bureau group study, or had a discussion with NPC representatives, or conducted researches deep into grassroots and countryside, or even had state visits abroad, since the 18th CPC National Congress, vividly illustrating the dialectical relationship between economic development and eco-environmental protection and firmly interpreting and disseminating this governance ideology. Xi Jinping has made an in-depth analysis of the 'Two Mountains', and he said, "We have been through three phases in understanding the relationship between clean waters and green mountains, and golden and silver mountains. At first, we exchanged the former for the latter, while seldom or even never considered the sustainability of the environment and only took blindly from nature various resources. During the second phase, we want both a mountain of material treasure and a sound natural system with clear water and green mountains, when the conflict between economic development and scarce resources along with deteriorating natural environment becomes more conspicuous and people come to realize that a good natural environment is fundament for our survival and development. Metaphorically, at least by keeping a green mountain, we can get plenty of firewood for living. When we enter the third phase, we come to understand that lucid waters and lush mountains can bring to us mountains after mountains of material treasure like gold and silver, they themselves are indeed the material treasure and they can yield to us even more treasures continuously. We can turn the ecological advantage into the economic advantage and integrate them into an organic one in harmonious existence, which is the highest phase among the three." General Secretary Xi Jinping's strategic idea that, "To protect the ecological environment is to protect productive forces, and to promote ecological progress is to advance productivity," profoundly reveals the inner relationship of eco-environment and productivity. We should develop productivity while promoting ecological progress and protecting the environment, and vice versa, to realize a synchronized and coordinated advancement of both productivity and ecological progress.

General Secretary Xi Jinping's knowledge about the relationship between the Two Mountains does not arise on a whim, but has been acquired and accumulated from more than ten years' experience. In 1999, Xi Jinping conducted research in Changting, Fujian. Later, the water and soil erosion problem in Changting was enlisted as one of the 'Serving the People' programs by Fujian province and lasted for ten years. As an important habitation for the Hakka, Changting used to boast picturesque sceneries with clear waters, green mountains, dense forests and fertile lands where people lived and worked in peace and with contentment. However, in modern times, it has been experiencing deforestation which was worsened to the extent that that Changqing became one of the regions in China suffering the most from water and soil erosion. In 1985, the area of water and soil erosion in Changting reached 1.462 million *mu*, accounting for 31.5% of the whole county, which rendered a scene of 'bare mountains, muddy waters, infertile lands and impoverished residents'. Without a sound natural system with clear waters and green mountains, where can we find a mountain of material treasure with gold and silver? When he worked in Fujian province, Xi Jinping exerted himself to resolve water and soil erosion in Changting. He went to the county five times, visited farmers, explored real situations and endeavored to seek solutions. With more than ten years' continuous efforts, Changting has treated the problem land of 1.628 million *mu*, saved 988 thousand *mu* from the water and soil erosion problem, and also increased forest coverage from 59.8% in 1986 to 79.4% at the present, realizing a historic transformation from a desertified mountainous area to an oasis and then to an ecologically pleasant homeland. The example of Changting reflects Xi Jinping's acute understanding on ecosystem. In August, 2005, Xi Jinping, who worked then as General Secretary of Zhejiang province, visited Anji county for research, initiated the important statement that "clean waters and green mountains are golden and silver mountains". He proposed that "If we could transform these eco-environmental advantages into eco-economic advantages in eco-agriculture, eco-industry and eco-tourism, we are transforming the natural resources into a mountain of material treasures." On March 3, 2006, comrade Xi Jinping elaborated on the dialectical unification of these Two Mountains again in his article *A View of Two Mountains on Ecology and Environment* published in the column of '*Zhijiang Xinyu*' in *Zhejiang Daily* newspaper.

As time passes, the idea that 'clean waters and green mountains are golden and silver mountains' has been brought into effect as a general approach in Zhejiang province, and transformed into a vivid picture in the real world. Everywhere in Zhejiang, people make full use of their beautiful mountains and rivers, and at the same enjoy the economic development and its corresponding dividends yielded by virtue of the landscapes and natural resources.

The Yu village in Anji county, once inspected by General Secretary Xi Jinping, taking the opportunity of an overall planning exercise by the Tianhuang Ping Tourist Center, has developed its own plans in three areas, namely eco-tourism, eco-inhabitancy and eco-industry, and set a reasonable lay-out for the space of villagers' life, production and development.

Pan Chunlin, a villager who used to be a tractor driver in a quarry, said, "As I can tell, since 2005, the village officials have been guiding us to learn from the outside, and encouraging us to develop a leisure activity economy such as farm tourism." In expectation of a better life, Pan Chunlin invested all his belongings into this business and built up his 'Chunlin Villa' for farm stays. With 10 years' efforts, he has grown the villa to be the biggest one in Yu village and won the titles of honor as 'Hundred Excellent Enterprises in Municipal Services' and 'Beautiful Farm Tourism Model' in Anji county.

The change of Pan Chunlin is a miniature of the transformative development of Yu village. From 'selling stones' to 'selling sceneries', villagers in Yu have put an end to the simple and extensive production mode. Though both means of living are dependent on the mountains around them, the villagers now gain pleasure from their harmonious co-existence with nature, and at the same time get a keen awareness of the value of nature, which is quite different from the past.

Sheng Xiaomei, another villager in Yu, set up Yesheng Bamboo and Wooden Crafts in the planned eco-friendly industrial area in the village. Here are 32 enterprises among which 25 produce bamboo crafts. They all draw on the local resources of bamboos yielded by 6000 *mu* mountains, and enjoy the benefits to the full. Also a villager in Yu, Hu Jiaxing took the advantage of the increasingly lucid river, and started his own business by organizing tourists to appreciate lotus while drifting along the river. It is very popular in summer, attracting numerous tourists. Seeing more and more tourists coming, villager Yu Jinbao decided to set up an eco-friendly fruit planting and picking garden instead of making a living away from his hometown… By 2014, the per capita disposable personal income of Yu villagers reached to Rmb27667 almost five times their income at the end of 2004.

The green mountains and clear rivers attract more and more investors. Now, The Lotus Mountain scenic area, with funding by investors from other areas, receives nearly 100,000 visitors every year; The 'JinXi Hall Holiday Inn', invested in by Shanghai travelling merchants, is under construction… Up to the end of 2014, Yu village has established 3 tourism scenic spots and 14 hotels for farm stays with 410 beds.

The villagers changed the environment, and the environment changed these villagers' life in return. 64-year-old villager Hong Yuexian witnessed and keenly experienced the changes, and then said, "Now, there are no quarrels among neighbors any more, and no need to bother at all. We are all busy. You see, soon after a visitor litters a cigarette stub, one of us will pick it up and throw it into a dustbin……." The picturesque Yu village with old ginkgo trees and peacefully gurgling rivers around is a vivid illustration of the scientific argument of 'Two Mountains'.

In March 2015, the Political Bureau of the CPC Central Committee first proposed the concept of 'greenization' in its meeting, adding another item to 'New Four Modernizations' proposed by the 18th CPC Central Committee - 'New Industrialization, Urbanization, Informatization and Agriculture Modernization'. It is a natural result of the economic and social development of China and an outcome from the high level of attention paid by central government leaders, providing a practical path and theoretical spur to ecological progress. Then, what is 'greenization'? In terms of the economy, it is a way of production, namely 'an industrial structure and production model featuring high technology, low resource consumption and little pollution'. It is also a style of life, 'A transition of living and consuming mode from extravagance, waste and unreasonable consumption to a thrifty, green, low-carbon, civilized and healthy lifestyle, far distant from extravagance and unreasonable consumption.' Meanwhile, 'greenization' is also an outlook on value. We should integrate ecological progress into core socialist values, and cultivate a new social atmosphere in which everyone values ecological progress at all times and in all matters. We should highlight 'greenization' of production, lifestyles and values, and make the Two Mountains of natural resources and material assets bring forth the best from each other.

Nowadays, we have reached a consensus on the development theory of 'Two Mountains'–'clean waters and green mountains are golden and silver mountains'. In May 2015, there was issued *Opinions of the Central Committee of the CPC and the State Council on Accelerating the Promotion of Ecological Progress*. China is marching towards a new era with ecological progress under the important guidance of the notion of 'Two Mountains'.

III. The Ecological Red Line

On May 24th, 2013, General Secretary of the CPC Central Committee Xi Jinping stressed one more time that we should delimit and enforce the ecological red line and fully understand its importance when he presided over the sixth group study session of the Political Bureau of the CPC Central Committee. Any violations regarding environmental protection will be punished. The third plenary session of the 18th CPC Central Committee made setting ecological red lines a prime task and set as a top priority, reforming the regulation system for ecological progress and environmental protection and promoting the institutional construction of ecological civilization.

In recent years, the current situation on resource and environment is becoming grimmer with the fast development of industrialization and urbanization. In spite of increasing efforts in environmental protection and construction, in general, the pressure for scarce resources that curbs development is still on the rise, and the problem of environmental pollution is going from bad to worse. Deterioration of the eco-system is still severe, the ecological problem is becomiing more complicated, and the worsened situation has not been reversed. Problems also exit in spatial planning, such as overlapping of protection zones, unreasonable layouts, inefficiency in ecological protection, lack of holistic awareness and loosened control. Up to this time, a spatial framework has not yet been formulated for national and regional ecological security and for coordinated economic and social development.

Against this backdrop, to make more efforts in ecological conservation, the State Council issued *Suggestions of the State Council on Strengthening Major Activities of Environmental Protection* (Number 35 [2011]), and stipulated that the environmental protection authority should draw red lines for ecological conservation in regions with key ecological functions, and in terrestrial and marine eco-sensitive and fragile regions. For the first time, the concept of 'the red line for ecological conservation' was encoded in the State Council document, with specified tasks. This strategy is meant to construct and reinforce a national structure for ecological security, to curb the deterioration of ecosystem and environment, maintain a balance between population and resources, and coordinate economic and social benefits and ecological benefits. Setting red lines for permanent protection of the ecosystem reflects our scientific regulation to standardize ecological protection zones, and demonstrates policy orientation and our resolution to enforce the construction of national ecological security.

So, what is the ecological red line? What are the important connotations of the notion? The red line for ecological reservation refers to the minimal space in need of strict protection and the maximum or the minimum parameters of such space that functions to maintain national and regional ecological security and the sustainability of economic and social development; to safeguard people's health, to enhance ecological function and to improve environmental quality. Specifically, it includes the basic line for ecological function, the bottom line for environmental quality and security and the upper line for natural resource utilization in terms of efficiency. They are simplified as red lines of ecological function, environmental quality and resource efficiency. Among them, the red line of ecological function refers to the minimal space for ecological conservation in key ecological function zones, and eco-sensitive and fragile regions, and it is crucial to maintain the natural ecological system and safeguard national and regional ecological security. The red line of environmental quality refers to the minimal degree of environmental regulation that must be strictly implemented to ensure the basic needs of the living environment and people's health. The red line of resource efficiency is the highest or the lowest standard in safe and efficient use of resources in terms of energy, water and soil to promote resource and energy conservation.

Hereby, we need to illustrate the notions of ecosystem, resources, and environment, and the inter-relationship among them. Ecologically, the word 'ecosystem', short for the term 'natural ecological system', refers to the integral whole of all living creatures and their interaction with the environment through energy flow and material circulation in a certain time and space. The main body of an ecological system is the creatures, including plants, animals and microorganisms. That which surrounds the creatures in an ecosystem, namely the conditions the creatures are dependent on for survival, is called 'environment' in ecology. The resources that we often talk about refer to the things in the environment consumed by creatures, such as food, light, nutriment (for plants) and important space. We can conclude that creatures and environment are constituent elements for an ecosystem, while resource is part of the environment, so none of them can include or represent the whole ecosystem. Hence, when we mention 'resource conservation' or 'environmental protection', we cannot use either to cover the complete notion of 'ecological conservation'. Because the ecosystem, as an organic integration, consists of creatures, environment and resources, when we talk about 'ecological conservation', we have to consider 'resource conservation', 'environmental protection' and 'animal protection' at the same time. This is the reason why the '*Decision*' makes it clear that we have to delimit a red line for ecological conservation instead of for 'resource conservation' or 'environmental protection'.

Up until the present, we have set red lines with strict constraints in two basic national policies, one at a time, regarding family planning and resource conservation (protection of croplands, water and energy). In fact, these red lines represent the top-level design for ecological progress and sustainable development. China should establish a red line regulation system based on three basic national policies concerning 'population-resources-environment', with the ecological red line as one part of the system. The nature of setting up ecological red lines is fostering bottom-line thinking.

Within only a couple of decades, China has completed industrialization and urbanization which took developed countries hundreds of years, so the corresponding environmental problems that gradually surfaced in developed countries during past two hundred years emerged in a short period of time in our country, in the form of problematic structures, concentrated in style and with complicated features. Rome was not built in one day, and likewise we should not expect immediate success. To reverse the difficult environmental situation is to fight a protracted war that calls for our long and arduous efforts. Therefore, we must adapt ourselves to the new norm by strictly observing ecological red lines by way of bottom-line thinking. Institutionally, we should strictly observe the red lines to gradually restore the overdrawn resources, to enlarge the green ecological areas of forests, lakes and wetlands and to improve water conservation and environmental capacity. In practice, to set ecological red lines is hard, but to strictly implement them is even harder. To rehabilitate the eco-environment with real effects, the red line should be set as a 'high-voltage line' to guarantee not only that it can be set up, but also that it can be can be strictly carried out as a hard restriction and a task of necessity; these being the red lines of population, croplands and water resources in operation.

To consolidate the concept of the ecological red line, we should strengthen publicity of, and education on, ecological civilization. In particular, we should integrate them into the contents of official education and training to help officials at all levels cultivate awareness of the ecological red line, usher in the concept of ecological conservation during their decision making process, implement it in every sector of work concerning oversight of environmental influence, and play a leading role and set a good example in green development, clean production and low-carbon living. Meanwhile, we should strengthen public awareness of thrifty life, environmental protection and ecological conservation, and nurture a good atmosphere in which people know the existence of the red line, take part in its establishment, supervise its implementation and secure its function.

In addition, we should adjust the performance evaluation system scientifically. We should improve the economic and social development evaluation system by integrating into it all indicators such as resource consumption, environmental damage and ecological benefits, and make it a prime guidance and a strict regulation to promote ecological progress. Moreover, in different functional zones, we should implement different evaluation systems and follow different guidance. In areas under the ecological red line, we should place the emphasis of performance evaluation on the delivery of green GDP, integral enhancement of environmental capacity and improvement of the ecological environment. At the same time, we should highlight ecological achievements in terms of the appointment or promotion of officials, and enable good officials to come not only from areas with high productivity but also from places where ecological progress is well achieved.

IV. 'A Major Political Issue: Eco-Environmental Protection'

General Secretary Xi Jinping addressed the 18th Standing Committee Conference of the Political Bureau of the Central Committee, thus; "If we still follow the extensive approach to development, even if the GDP doubles, how serious the pollution would be then? I am afraid that the resource environment can hardly bear it at that time. What will it become if the people feel unhappy and have strong negative reaction even although the economy is improved? In conclusion, the construction of ecological civilization, protection of ecological environment and promotion of green and low-carbon lifestyle are not only economic issues but also political ones."

While actively promoting economic development, we have to realize that environment is both an important resource and a public product. Hence the air, water and soil in cities can be regarded as public products with political features, so, the question of how to explore and make use of the environment and resources also concerns fairness and justice. In recent years environmental pollution in big cities is escalating due to the high density of population and high intensity of economic activities, leading to numerous economic losses and detriment to people's health. It is becoming an important factor triggering social crises. May 5, 2015, saw publication of *Opinions on Accelerating the Promotion of Ecological Progress* that was previously deliberated and approved by the CPC Central Committee and the State Council. The *Opinions* highlights that group events caused by environmental pollution and the 'NIMBY' (not in my back yard) tendency due to project site selection problems have appeared frequently on the Internet and newspapers in recent years, arousing a great deal of attention from the masses and leading to a strong reaction in society. In the past few years, there have been many such cases centred on environmental pollution. Beginning in 2007, we can find the following group events, drawing much more public attention than usual: in June 2007, a large number of locals in Xiamen City, Fujian province, rallied against a PX project by walking together in a large group which resulted in the project's relocation; in 2008, citizens of Shanghai also demonstrated by walking together against the construction of Maglev; in November 2009, a massive group protest was staged against the construction of waste incineration plant in Fanyu, Guangdong province; in August 2011, there was another massive protest against a PX project in Dalian, Liaoning province; in April 2012, severe pollution by a PC project led to another group rally in Tianjin; there was an incident in Shifang and one in Qidong respectively at the beginning and the end of July, 2012; in May 2014, another group protest occurred against the construction of waste incineration plant in Yuhang, Hangzhou province; in April 2015, a large group of people gathered to protest against a coal coking plant because of the leaking of condensed gas in WeiRmb, Sichuan province.

Through analyzing these cases, we may find that these group events are usually caused by environmental pollution and are based on people's collective appeal for public attention. In contrast to other group events, these involved a very large number of people (according to the '*Report on the Rule of Law*' released by Chinese Academy of Social Sciences: environmental pollution is a major cause for big events involving more than ten thousand people), and usually led to a protest that had a significant influence, in which the government showed a lack of capability to respond and properly control the event. Invariably and ultimately, they were concluded by the local government's announcing the cancellation of projects soon after the event, resulting in an awkward situation where 'one place's event attracts massive attention from its neighboring areas and even involves criticisms nationwide'. These problems urge us to reflect on the following questions: How serious could the pollution be, caused by one of these projects? Did the local government prioritize economic development but neglect environmental protection? Was the evaluation for the environmental influence of these projects complete? Was the decision of the government transparent? Why did the local governments seek solutions after the outbreak of protests instead of enabling the public to participate in these projects initially? Were these public behaviors all rational and legal? Why did such events always involve radical behaviors such as 'breaking, smashing and grabbing'? How should the government respond to such sudden incidents? Will the government lose its credibility if it stops every project after the occurrence of of such an event?

As a big developing country, China has entered a sensitive period confronting many environment problems, when the economy develops rapidly while the environment is severely polluted. Meanwhile, conflicts in society are accumulating, with people's greatly increased environmental awareness and stronger desire to protect their environmental rights, according to law. The rapid progress of urbanization and intensive accumulation of conflicts both urge the government to improve its efficiency in resolving problems. In addition, when addressing the problems, the government quite often finds itself unable to adapt to spontaneous situations, lacking precautions and preparations in terms of system, knowledge and practice. With a tradition of prioritizing the economy but ignoring the ecosystem, some local governments lower the threshold of environmental protection when inviting business and attracting investment, to enhance their performance in their official career, while burying hidden hazards affecting people's health. Once these hazards cross a psychological bottom line, group events are likely to occur. Moreover, an inadequate approach to dealing with the event after it has occurred, inadequate recognition of people's great desires to guard their environmental rights according to law, and insufficient communication by the governments with the mass are major factors which aggravate the situation and escalate conflicts.

The outbreak of group events on environmental pollution can be regarded as a release of social emotions accumulated for a long time against the backdrop of rapid urbanization. This release reflects multiple problems, ranging from shortcomings of institutions and mechanisms in addressing environmental problems, a lack of government credibility in people's minds, poor communications between the government and the people, local governments' dilemma of priority choice between GDP and living environment and that between efficiency and people's will, and the long-term institutional problems of multi-participation in scientific decision-making; and problems of evaluating social risks. If these problems cannot be resolved at source and the people's appeal cannot be responded to reasonably, large-scale group events will be likely to break out, leading to serious impacts on our stable social life and political ecosystem.

Protection and improvement of the eco-environment is related to the growth of a state's comprehensive national strength. Practice has proved that economic development without environmental protection is as bad as, 'getting all the fish while draining the pond', while environmental protection without economic advancement is as impossible as, 'seeking fish in a tree.' Economic development determines people's living standard, while the ecological environment determines people's living conditions. It is inadvisable either to give priority to productivity while neglecting environmental protection, or to put emphasis on environmental protection while ignoring economic development.

As an old saying goes, one prospers in worries and hardships, but perishes in ease and comfort. We must hold the environment in respect and place the environmental protection in an important position in social development. As water can either carry or sink a boat, we must keep in mind the relationship among the ecological environment, political stabilization and economic development, and give a priority to the environmental protection in social development. In practice, we can learn a lesson from our ancestors in a Chinese legend as Gun and Yu: Gun blocked the river to control flood, but failed, while his son Yu guided people to dredge channels of the river to combat floods, and succeeded. We should always stay conscientious about our duty as citizens of China to protect our environment and integrate that duty into our daily political life. Only when we make more efforts in ecological conservation and environmental protection, can we achieve the social and political stability, and in return, a stable social and political life will be more conducive to creating a more harmonious and beautiful ecological environment for us!

Chapter 8

Exercise Strict Self-Governance in Every Respect by the Party

The party should supervise its own conduct so as to run it well; it should operate under strict discipline so as to govern it well. To such a party with 85 million party members and governing a country with 1.3 billion population for a long time, the CPC cannot afford to relax its efforts, for even a second, in supervising and governing itself. If the party cannot supervise its own conduct and run itself with strict discipline, and if the pressing problems of major concern to the people cannot be resolved, our party will sooner or later lose its qualification to govern, and will unavoidably be consigned to history. This is no intimidation.

— Part of *The Speech at the National Conference on Organizational Work* (June 28, 2013)

We are confronted with a complex and volatile international situation and arduous domestic tasks of continuing reform and development in China. To fulfil the various goals and tasks set by the 18th CPC National Congress and carry out great undertakings with many new and historic features, the emphasis should be placed on our party and our officials. 'It takes good iron to make good products.' Therefore, Comrade Xi Jinping proposed a series of new thoughts, new ideas and new requirements as to how to exercise strict self-governance. He stressed that "it should be substantial rather than abstract, sincere rather than perfunctory, in disciplining the party strictly." All these important statements pin down the direction for the grand new mission of pushing ahead party building in an all-around way, at a new historical starting point.

I. The Party's Great Emphasis on Exercising Strict Self-Governance

In response to new situations and new tasks, exercising strict self-governance in every aspect is a major strategic plan and also a general requirement set by the CPC Central Committee to enhance and improve the party's leadership and to press ahead with the new task of party building. Promoting the exercise of strict self-govenance in every respect is of great significance to a great undertaking with many new historic features, and to the achievement of the great rejuvenation of the Chinese Dream.

1. Exercising strict self-governance is a good tradition and important experience of the party. Ever since its founding in 1921, the CPC has upheld the principles of strengthening party building, strictly observing the party's discipline, and operating under strict discipline. The *Constitution of the CPC*, confirmed by the 2nd National Congress of the CPC, deliberately set up the party discipline and listed nine conditions for nullifying one's party membership, for example, absence without reason for a meeting, twice in succession, non-payment of party membership dues for three months, or no service for the party for four successive weeks. The 2nd CPC National Congress stipulated seven requirements for party members, and pinned down the nature of the party; that it should be the most revolutionary party among the proletariat, and that it would organize the masses to fight for the interests of the proletariat. During the Agrarian Revolution, the party held a meeting in Gu Tian in December 1929 and brought forth the issue of theoretical building of the party for the first time. The meeting prescribed very specific standards for party members, such as holding no erroneous political views, keeping loyalty to the party, staying courageous enough to brave death, making no attempts to make a sudden fortune, not taking any opium or getting involved in gambling, and so on. During the War of Resistance against Japanese Aggression, at the Sixth Plenary Session of the 6th CPC Central Committee in 1938, Mao Zedong also required that Communist Party members should play an exemplary role in every sector of work; such as, fighting heroically, following commands, observing regulations, doing political work, maintaining internal unity, working hard but asking for little remuneration, seeking truth from facts, being visionary, and intensifying study. In October 1939, Mao Zedong summarized the experience and lessons of the Chinese revolution in *Introducing the Communist* (*The Communist* was an internal party Journal from 1939 to 1941) that, "our eighteen years of experience have taught us that the united front, armed struggle and party building are the Chinese Communist Party's three 'magic weapons'." From 1941 to 1944, our party carried out the Yan'an Rectification Movement and created an effective means of addressing major problems of the party collectively through rectification. Before the founding of the People's Republic China, Mao Zedong proposed the 'two musts' in the Report to the Second Plenary Session of the 7th CPC Central Committee, which state, "our comrades must remain modest and prudent, neither conceited nor rash, in our practices; and our comrades must remain hardworking despite difficulties in our working experiences". After the establishment of the People's Republic China, the CPC became the governing party in China, and then the situations, the tasks, the position and function of the party underwent fundamental changes. During the struggle against the 'Three Evils' in the early days of the People's Republic China, we executed Liu Qingshan and Zhang Zishan – two corrupt officials, which demonstrated the determination of our party to operate under strict discipline and to uproot all evils, and at the same time achieved good results in deterring the corrupt, upholding integrity and eliminating evils. After the 'Cultural Revolution', our party summarized its lessons and stated more clearly the means of exercising strict party discipline and self-governance. At the beginning of reform and opening up, some proposed to relax control over both enterprises and party discipline. Comrade Chen Yun made a clear instruction, "There is no such a thing as 'deregulation' in party principles and discipline. Without good party Conduct, reform and opening up would be impossible. No matter when the party operates as an underground party or as a governing party, the party members should always abide by party discipline." Exercising strict party discipline was formally put forward at the 13th CPC National Congress in 1987 as the basic guideline of strengthening party building in the new era. In 1992, under a requirement of the 14th CPC National Congress, 'practicing self-governance' was formally written, for the first time, into the General Program of Constitution of the CPC. Over the past 90 years, we have grown from a small and weak party into the largest governing party of socialist countries in the world, and we have successfully led the Chinese people in achieving one victory after another on the path of revolution, construction and reform, the key to which lies in the fact that the party practices self-governance and is strict with its members, and that it constantly enhances its creativity, cohesion and combat effectiveness, and maintains its progressive nature and integrity, providing a solid and fundamental foundation for the success of our socialist undertakings.

2. Exercising strict self-governance is a response to the objective requirements of new situations and new challenges. In the decisive stage of building a moderately prosperous society in all respects, our party shoulders a glorious and grand historical mission, and confronts various challenges and risks that arise from both home and abroad, but most fundamentally from the party. From an international perspective, we can see that the world is undergoing a period of great reform and major adjustments with complex and profound changes. On the one hand, peace and development remain the themes of our times. As the trends of global multi-polarity, economic globalization and IT application in society are deepening, and scientific and technological innovation continue to accomplish a great deal, interdependence among countries has reached an unprecedented level. On the other hand, the deep impact of the global financial crisis will be felt for a considerable time to come, growth in developed countries' economies is sluggish, protectionism is gaining ground, hegemony, power politics and neo-interventionism is on the rise, terrorist activities remain rampant, and regional turbulence occurs frequently. Judging from the relationship between China and the world, through many years of rapid development, China's comprehensive national strength and international status have been growing and our influence continues to expand. Hence, on the one hand, these accomplishments have strengthened China's capability of promoting world peace and development, but on the other hand, they also aroused some countries' suspicion and vigilance against our country, resulting in these countries' intensified efforts to constrain and deter our development. Even worse, some countries take a hostile stance against us. From a domestic perspective, we can find that after 30 years of reform and opening up, people's material and cultural living standards have been greatly improved and urban and rural areas have changed tremendously. However, the basic fact that China is still in the primary stage of socialism and will long remain so, has not been changed; nor has the fact that China is the world's largest developing country. Unbalanced, uncoordinated and unsustainable development remains a big problem, and the development gaps between urban and rural areas and between regions are still large, and so too are income disparities. In particular, China's reform is sailing in uncharted waters with tough challenges, and the barriers set up by old notions and interest groups seriously restrict the reform process. In the ideological field, the tendency of local pluralism, diversity and variation is becoming increasingly obvious. Mainstream ideology and diversified social trends of thought coexist and interact with each other. All these difficulties are posing severe challenges to our party. Viewing from the party itself, we are in a great undertaking with many new historical features, undergoing tests of the times. In view of the need to manage changes in domestic and international conditions, and to accomplish its historic mission, there is still considerable room for our party to improve its art of leadership, governing capacity and organization, and the quality, competence, and practices of its members and officials, and there are many pressing issues within the party that need to be addressed. A small number of party members and officials waver in respect of the party's ideals and convictions and are not fully aware of its purpose. Muddling along and accomplishing nothing at all, as well as extravagance and waste, among some party members are serious problems. Some community-level party organizations are weak and lax, and fail to play the role of a fighting fortress. Some party members have diminished vanguard consciousness and weakened sense of organizational discipline, and have failed to play an exemplary role. There are also other prominent problems of misconduct among some party members and officials, such as being divorced from the people, showing no concerns for problems encountered by the people, or even oppressing the people or infringing upon the people's interests. Formalism, bureaucratism, hedonism and extravagance are prevalent, especially the problem of extravagance and waste. Some sectors are often prone to corruption and other types of misconduct. Not only do some appalling incidents happen at times, but misconduct and corruption problems that directly affect the people's livelihood have also become more pronounced, with many examples. Why should there be such problems? As General Secretary Xi Jinping pointed out, over the years, some localities and departments are lax in discipline and poorly organized; unhealthy practices have advantages over righteousness; hidden rules in the party and society are prevailing; the political ecosystem and social environment are contaminated. All these problems are rooted in the fact that the party discipline is not strictly operated. Some places and units seem to supervise their own conduct and exercise party discipline, but they are not strict enough, or show the necessary capability. If the situation is allowed to run rampant, it will be a threat to our party. General Secretary Xi Jinping once pointed out that, "If the party cannot supervise its own conduct and run itself with strict discipline, and if the pressing problems of major concern to the people cannot be resolved, our party will sooner or later lose its qualification to govern, and will unavoidably be consigned to history. This is no intimidation." Hereby, the 'Two Centenary Goals' and the 'Chinese Dream' of the great rejuvenation of the Chinese nation will be out of the question. Therefore, to govern the country well we must first run the party well, and to run the party well we must run it strictly. We should also constantly improve our self-purification, self-improvement, self-innovation, and self-enhancement, and assemble invincible power - as the 'good iron' - to accomplish brilliant achievements of historical significance.

3. Exercising strict self-governance is an inevitable conclusion drawn from lessons of the Communist Party of the Soviet Union. In the late 1980s and early 1990s, some of the long-term governing parties in the socialist countries collapsed one by one. There are various reasons, but the most essential one lies in the lesson that the governing parties in those countries had ignored their own party building, turned lax in discipline, and succumbed to decay and degeneration, resulting in its disintegration. Take the Soviet Union as an example. The Communist Party of the Soviet Union did not submit while confronting aggression from 14 countries and the German Fascist attacks, but marched with songs of triumph, and had created a gigantic economic miracle. Why, however, did such an accomplished party collapse instantly like 'an edifice crashing down' without the stimulus of any invasion or internal violence? The causes are manifold, but without any doubt, one of the most important reasons lay in its failure in supervising its own conduct and exercising strict discipline. For example, under the disguise of 'democratization' and 'openness', starting from the Communist Party Central Plenary Session in February, 1990 through the 28th Congress of the Communist Party of the Soviet Union to the Plenary Session of the Central Committee in July, 1991, Gorbachev made fundamental changes to the guiding ideology of the party, surrendered the dominant position of Marxist doctrines, and recognized pluralism in the guiding ideology. These changes were responsible for great commotions among party members and officials, for the loss of the party's cohesiveness and professional capability. Soon after the '8.19' event, the Communist Party of the Soviet Union collapsed, resulting from the loss of the principal position of Marxism-Leninism as its guiding ideology, which in turn was an inevitable result of the fact that the Communist Party of the Soviet Union allowed the development of such ideological trends as anti-communism and anti-socialism. As to 'democratization of political life within the party', in practice it was Gorbachev's abandonment of the organizational principle of democratic centralism, leading to two immediate consequences, namely, factionalization and federalization of the Communist Party of the Soviet Union. For lack of effective rules and organizational discipline, there frequently occurred various conflicts among different branches of the party, which greatly affected the fighting capacity of the party and its unity, tearing the party apart. As for the separation between the party and government, the Communist Party of Soviet Union made undue emphases, jeopardized its own governance, and finally lost its leadership of the country. The 19th Congress of the Communist Party of the Soviet Union raised a proposal that, 'all powers belong to the Soviet Union, the country'. From that point the Soviet Congress had lost control and had become the platform for power struggles among different branches, and the country was devoid of power: there was a 'power vacuum'. Due to the loss of support from the communist party, the administration system of the Soviet Union soon descended into total chaos. All in all, as General Secretary Xi Jinping summarized, "Before the collapse of the Soviet Union, under the guise of the so-called 'openness' and 'democracy', the Soviet Communist Party deserted the principle of democratic centralism, allowed party members to publicize opinions different from the organization's decisions, and called for the implementation of autonomy within the party at all levels. Some of the Soviet Communist Party members, even some leading officials, turned to become the vanguard in negating the history of Communist Party of the Soviet Union and socialism, trumpeting to disseminate western ideology. Accordingly, the ideological confusions in the Soviet Communist Party transformed to organizational ones. In the end, such a big and veteran party with a long-standing history of more than 90 years and with its governance of the country for over 70 years, just collapsed violently and instantly." To draw lessons from the failure of governance of Soviet Communist Party and to avoid repeating its frustrations, we should exercise our strict party discipline in all respects. The following remarks made by Lenin bear particular significance for our party. He said, "No matter when it is in the past or at present, our strength lies in our sober analysis of the bitterest failure...... If the past experience cannot bring to light the errors of our old methods, then we will never learn new approaches to tackle our own tasks."

The sixth plenary session of the 18th CPC Central Committee was held from October 24 to 27, 2016 in Beijing (Xinhua News Agency)

II. The Party's Strictness in Exercising Self-Governance in Every Respect

To adhere to the principle of exercising strict self-governance in every respect, we must emphasize 'every respect' and 'strict'. We should implement it throughout the whole process of party building so as to bring into effect strict theoretical education, strict official management, strict party conduct, strict organization construction and strict system enforcement.

1. We should remain strict in theoretical education and have firm faith in communism.

As a Chinese saying goes, "For a tree to grow tall, a strong and solid root is essential; for a river to reach far, an unimpeded source is necessary." As for the party members and officials, theoretical degradation is the most serious problem. If their 'ultimate switch' is not tightened, they cannot properly handle the relationship between public and personal interests, and may not have healthy outlooks on right or wrong, on justice and benefit, and on power and career. Hence, a variety of misconducts as well as derailed and erroneous behaviors may surface as a natural consequence. "A slight degree of slackness in thought will result in desultoriness in action to a large extent." Therefore, we must give priority to theoretical party building, strengthen education on ideals and conviction, and lay a solid intellectual foundation for exercising strict party discipline.

Ideals and conviction are the spiritual banner for struggles and for the unity of the nation, ethnic groups and political parties. Since the 18th CPC National Congress, General Secretary Xi Jinping has paid great attention to ideals and conviction, and pointed out that it has always been the foundation for the lifeline and pursuit of all Communists, to have full confidence in ideals of, and firm faith in, communism. Belief in Marxism and faith in socialism and communism are the political soul of Communists, enabling them to withstand all tests. Put figuratively, the ideals and convictions of Communists are the marrow of their faith. Without, or with weak, ideals or convictions, they would be deprived of their marrow and suffer from 'lack of backbone.' At present, we must attach great importance to the absence of ideals and conviction; or to wavering in ideals and conviction among some party members and officials. For instance, some are skeptical about communism, considering it a fantasy that will never come true; some do not believe in Marxism-Leninism but in ghosts and gods, and seek spiritual solace in feudal superstitions, showing intense interest in fortune-telling, worship of Buddha and 'god's advice' for solving their problems; some have little sense of principle, justice, and right and wrong, and perform their duties in a muddle-headed manner; some even yearn for Western social systems and values, losing their confidence in the future of socialism; and others adopt an equivocal attitude towards political provocations against the leadership of the CPC, the path of socialism with Chinese characteristics and other matters of principle. They passively avoid relevant arguments without the courage to express their opinions, or even deliberately deliver ambiguous messages. Facts have repeatedly proved that the most dangerous moment is when one wavers in, or begins to show doubt about, one's ideals and convictions. This has been proven true by the cases of some party members and officials who acted improperly due to lack of ideals, and confused faith.

Comrade Xi Jinping pointed out that whether an official is qualified or not is judged primarily by whether he is firm in his ideals and convictions. No matter how competent an official is, he cannot be regarded as the sort of good official that we need, if he does not hold fast to his ideals and convictions, does not believe in Marxism, nor in socialism with Chinese characteristics. Xi Jinping stressed that a party member devoid of ideals lacks an essential quality – as does one who engages in empty talk about lofty ideals without doing anything. In other words, we should be both forward-looking and down-to-earth. If the communists lose sight of ambitious goals, we would lose direction and might become utilitarianists and pragmatists. Once we have firm ideals and convictions, we will stand high and see far, with a generous mind, and we can follow the correct political direction and uphold the communists' political integrity. However, when we intend to underscore the communists' and officials' ideals and conviction, we should not simply pay lip service by shouting out the communist slogans or 'rushing into the communist society', but instead, we should make unremitting and pragmatic efforts to fulfill the party's basic program at the present stage – build socialism with Chinese characteristics, and adopt a down-to earth attitude to fulfill our present duty.

In order to stay firm in ideals and convictions and to build 'diamond-hard bodies', we must equip ourselves with various scientific theories and master Marxism systematically. The ideals and conviction should be founded on the bases of correct understanding about, and scientific mastery over the truthfulness of, Marxism and the inevitability of socialism and communism. General Secretary Xi Jinping stressed that faced with complex domestic and international situations and shouldering a heavy governance mission, we cannot conquer risks or difficulties; or move forward continually, if we lack powerful support from theoretical thinking. Officials at all levels of the party should meticulously study and research into the classical Marxist works, and earnestly learn Marxist philosophy, especially historical materialism.

Communists and leading officials at large should learn the fundamental theories of Marxism, especially the theoretical system of socialism with Chinese characteristics, and enhance their ability to work more systematically and with greater foresight and creativity, so as to keep up with the times, follow the law of development, and be innovative in our leadership and policy-making. Marxism must be a required course in party schools, executive leadership academies, academies of social sciences, institutes of higher learning and groups for theoretical studies. These places should serve as the centers for studying, researching and disseminating Marxism. We should guide party members and officials to learn theories of Marxism to enhance their theoretical qualification and moral outlook and to make continuous progress in their ability to apply Marxism to resolving practical problems. In particular, party schools should have proper orientation in this regard. Learning at party schools, officials should put in first place cultivation of firm ideals and convictions as well as improving the level of ideology and politics. They should sincerely and diligently study Marxism-Leninism, Mao Zedong Thought, especially Deng Xiaoping Theory, the important thought of the Three Represents, the Scientific Outlook on Development, and a series of important speeches by Comerade Xi Jinping. New and young officials in particular should work hard to study Marxist theory, learn to observe and solve problems from the Marxist standpoint, viewpoint and method, become firm in their ideals and convictions, improve their ability in dialectical analysis, and act with sincerity and persistence as well as honesty and prudence. He emphasized that it is quite necessary for officials to study in party schools to broaden their vision and update their minds with more knowledge, but it would be improper for them to act as presumptuous guests rather than learners. At the same time, party schools should intensify their efforts in fostering an all-pervading atmosphere of theoretical learning.

2. We should remain strict in official management, and especially with the 'key few'.

General Secretary Xi Jinping stressed that to supervise its own conduct, the primary work of the party is to manage its officials well; and that running the party with strict discipline lies in strictly disciplining the officials. We should endeavor more to train and select good officials who are willing to serve the people wholeheartedly, and implement the principle of exercising strict discipline throughout the whole process of building a contingent of officials. We should remain strict in educating, managing and supervising officials and enable every one of them to understand thoroughly that to be an official, one needs to toil more and be more strict with oneself. Otherwise, if one does not possess such mental preparation or awareness, he or she is ineligible for the post.

The first issue of personnel management is the criterion for official selection. What is the criterion of good officials who are required by the party and the people in the new era? At the National Conference on Organizational Work, General Secretary Xi Jinping concisely summarized the criterion into twenty Chinese characters concerning five aspects– literally in Chinese, they are *xin nian jian ding, wei min fu wu, qin zheng wu shi, gan yu dan dang, qing zheng lian jie*. To put them into English, they mean: good officials must be firm in their ideals and conviction, willing to serve the people, diligent in work, ready to take on responsibilities, honest and upright. To select good officials, we must stick to four principles. First, we should stick to the principle that the party should supervise the performance of officials, ensure leadership over officials and respond to the question of 'for whom to select officials'; Second, we should stick to the principle that the party should appoint officials on their merits and select them from all over the country to put into practice the principle that the party is founded for the public good, and thus address the question of 'how to select officials'; Third, we should stick to the principles that the party should select officials on the basis of both moral integrity and professional competence with priority given to the former, and make sure that officials have firm political orientation and good conduct, and thus we address the question of 'whom to select'; Fourth, we should stick to the principle that the party should value officials' performance as well as the approval by the mass, and test them in practice, and thus we address the question of 'what standards to apply'. To realize these four principles, we must integrate the leadership of the party and the full play of democracy, and reinforce the leading and supervising roles of party committees. We should make right decisions on such key issues as adopting what democratic method from many, correctly analyzing and treating recommendation results and official appointments, instead of using votes and scores as the sole standard, so as to find in good time, and reasonably use, good officials. To do so, we can conduct the following practices. Firstly, we should take loyalty, integrity and responsibility as the key guidance and major standards, and select those who have firm ideals and conviction, care for the people, and are honest and upright. We should never appoint as officials those who are wavering in convictions, divorced from the people or deceiving the party; Secondly, we should select those who are upright, law-abiding, disciplined, and earnest in governance at work. We should never appoint those who violate the law and discipline, abuse their power for personal gains, and are morally corrupted; Thirdly, we should select officials who uphold principles, are responsible and have the moral fiber to denounce and rectify violations of party discipline. We should never appoint those who seek for personal interests through trickery, tackle their responsibilities in a perfunctory manner or struggle for merits but shift the blame on to others.

Good officials do not emerge spontaneously. To become a good official, both personal efforts and organizational training by the party are necessary. We must pay more attention to the education and training of millions of officials at all levels, especially those working in important and key positions. We should educate and guide party members and officials to stand firm in the ideals and conviction of the party, strengthen morality, regulate their behavior in the exercise of power, cultivate fine conduct, conscientiously fulfill their duties prescribed by the *Constitution of the CPC* and work in accordance with strict rules and regulations of the party. We also need to strengthen the training of officials in practical circumstances to facilitate their progress through expanding channels and seeking more platforms. We should guide officials to go to the grassroots to see real situations and communicate with the people, and thus help them make a solid foundation for their work. We should step up efforts of officials at all levels to communicate across different sectors, fields, and regions of work, and make them experience something difficult, urgent, important or complicated. We should systematically arrange for new and outstanding officials to work at the grassroots, in tough conditions. Moreover, we should improve institutions and policies to cultivate and select new outstanding officials, further broaden the sources, optimize structures and upgrade working methods so as to improve the quality of party officials.

In reality, some officials act improperly due to relaxed requirements on themselves, and this is also closely related to inadequate management and loopholes in our management system. Therefore, we should focus on officials' daily management and supervision, further improve relevant measures, and strengthen supervision by organizations, public opinion and the masses to make sure that officials are subject to restrictions either in or after working hours.

General Secretary Xi Jinping emphasized that the exercise of power without supervision will definitely lead to corruption. This is an axiomatic law. It is not an easy process to train officials, so measures should be adopted to better manage and supervise them and keep them on the alert 'as if they were treading on thin ice or standing on the edge of an abyss.' As to the emerging and potential problems among some officials, we should give them timely reminders rather than turn a blind eye or even please or protect them in an effort to prevent minor flaws from becoming serious menace. We should strengthen the supervision over officials concerning the following issues: their observance of rules, especially political rules, implementation of democratic centralism, improvement of their work style, fulfillment of their work requirements and resolution of their own problems. We must strengthen oversight of officials of a higher level over those of a lower level within party organizations and also intensify mutual oversight among leaders.

Since the 18th CPC National Congress, we have made a regulation on officials' taking a part-time job (or full-employment) at enterprises. In 2014, we had cleaned up 63,000 people who assumed leading positions, with part-time jobs at enterprises, including 229 provincial-level officials. We have laid down rules of administration for those officials whose spouse or children have emigrated to foreign countries, and stipulated that 'naked officials' should not hold important or key positions in party or government organs. Also in 2014, we deposed more than 3,200 'naked officials' at or above the deputy county or division level. We should improve the reporting system of leading officials on their personal matters. In the same year, we randomly inspected more than 60,000 officials' individual cases nationwide, and accordingly cancelled the promotion qualifications of those problematic officials and gave penalties to those involved in the worst cases. Since 2015, the ratio of random inspection has increased to 10%, and every newly appointed official above the county or division level has been inspected after their promotion. Moreover, we began to lay down regulations about officials' spouses, their children and their children's spouses on their conduct of doing business or running enterprises, and we arranged special programs to oversee the officials' policy implementation. The aim of these measures is to bring into effect the principle of strict official management and carry it throughout the regulation of institutions and all sectors of officials' work.

General Secretary Xi Jinping pointed out that to implement strict management well, it is crucial for the leading bodies and leading officials to take the lead. Only when they set good examples, can the those at lower levels keep up and do the same. Officials at all levels, especially leading officials, should act in line with the requirements of 'Three Stricts and Three Earnests', diligently learn and sincerely practice the spirit of Jiao Yulu (1922 -1964, party secretary of Lankao county, Henan Province, devoted all his life to the cause of the party), and work hard to behave like Jiao Yulu, our party's good official. Party organizations at all levels should clearly and firmly recognize the achievements of, and reward, those officials who achieved a lot at work; should educate and help those who fail to protect the people's interests; should support and encourage the officials who act for the public good, dedicate themselves to work and are ready to take on responsibilities. Those who incur serious damages to the cause of the party and the people due to dereliction of duty or malpractice, should be punished accordingly and severely.

3. We should remain strict in party conduct, and uphold integrity all through the party.

The new CPC Central Committee with Comerade Xi Jinping at its core put party conduct improvement as a starting point of, and a breakthrough in, work to exercise strict self-governance all through the party and in all respects. Since the 18th CPC National Congress, we have worked out 'Eight Codes of Conduct' to improve our work style and maintain close ties with the people, have carried out an extensive program throughout the party to heighten awareness of, and implement, the party's mass line with the focus on serving the people and staying pragmatic and honest, and have launched a special education program on 'Three Stricts and Three Earnests' among leading officials, at and above the county level. All these allowed the people to witness substantial results and changes in party conduct, and thus won extensive approval and sincere support from the people.

General Secretary Xi Jinping pointed out that the issue of working style is in no sense a small one. If misconduct is not corrected but allowed to run rampant, it will build an invisible wall between our party and the people. As a result, our party will lose its base, lifeblood and strength. 'Hedonism and extravagance lead to decline and demise.' The farther we stay away from misconduct, the closer the people will approach us. The party has always emphasized that party conduct is vital for the survival of the party. Through a thorough review of history in China and elsewhere, we can see many examples of loss of lives and bankruptcy of administration due to misconduct. Therefore, we must take those as great warning and set strictest standards and measures to crack down on misconduct. It is undeniable that under the backdrop of developing a socialist market economy, the rule of commodity exchange would have permeated into the inner-party life, which is outwith the people's will. Party members and officials are overwhelmed with various temptations in society. Just like the proverbial slow-boiled frog, some party members and officials are unconsciously seduced into the traps. Despite years' promotion of good party conduct, some problems have not been resolved but instead have become intensified. Tackling misconduct is like cutting chives: while you cut them off, they grow up later, batch after batch. The root of the problem is the underestimation of conduct recurring and persisting, and the failure to resolve problems with tenacity and patience as well as a lack of a feasible system that can control problems over a long period and that can consolidate the basis of this operation. Therefore, it is impossible to accomplish the whole task at one stroke, and we cannot promote party conduct in temporary phases, like a passing gust of wind. Our efforts in this regard must be constant, and we must have long-term plans and establish new and strict rules in improving conduct to achieve solid results and prevent them from rebounding.

At present, the 'four forms of decadence' represent the majority of conduct problems within the party. General Secretary Xi Jinping stated that formalism, bureaucratism, hedonism and extravagance are the problems that the public hates the most. They are of the most pressing concern to the people, and they are at the root of the greatest damage to the relations between the party and the people and between officials and the people. Once the 'four forms of decadence' are resolved, there will be a sounder base for treating other problems. He also stressed that to solve the 'four forms of decadence,' we must set an accurate focus, locate the 'acupoints,' and firmly grasp the vitals. In fighting formalism, we should focus on promoting down-to-earth work and improving officials' approach to theoretical study, meetings and official documents, and working practices. And officials must spare themselves no effort in promoting concrete measures, and in achieving solid results through a down-to-earth approach. In fighting bureaucratism, we should focus on solving the problems of isolation from the people and failure to protect their interests. We must be resolute in correcting problems such as perfunctory performance of duties, evading and shirking responsibilities, and infringing upon the people's interests. In fighting hedonism, we should focus on overcoming indulgence in pleasure and privileges, and guide them in keeping to the 'two musts,' in upholding political integrity, and in preserving a spirit of high principles and hard work. In fighting extravagance, we should focus on putting an end to unhealthy practices such as self-indulgence, luxury and dissipation. We should guide the party in leading a simple life, in being strict with their spending, and in doing everything in a no-frills manner.

The Program of Mass Line Education and Practice was launched in June 2013 and has been unfolded in two sessions from the top down, and ended in October 2014. In this program, the Political Bureau set an example, learning from the experience of the Yan'an Rectification Movement, with the current requirements for studying and practicing the party's mass line clearly defined as 'examine oneself in the mirror, straighten one's clothes and hat, take a bath, and treat one's disease.' The whole party from top down had launched full-scale examinations, overhauls and clean-ups to eliminate defects and misconduct from the party. These measures have effectively addressed the four prominent problems, namely: formalism, bureaucratism, hedonism and extravagance. In addition, the tendency of isolation from the people has been clearly reversed, and party conduct, government conduct and social conduct have been greatly improved.

Facts have proved that misconduct is apt to recur and persist, so it should be constantly addressed. It is impossible to accomplish the whole task at one stroke, and we cannot promote party conduct in temporary phases, like a passing gust of wind. The practice of combating 'four forms of decadence' has also proved that nothing can be accomplished unless we take a serious, pragmatic and strict approach. Currently, on the surface, the 'four forms of decadence' have been pushed back to some extent, but they are deep-rooted and difficult to eradicate. A single light stroke after the suppression may result in its quick rebound, so how to prevent it from happening is still an arduous mission. 'Promoting good party conduct is always high on our agenda and will never end.' We should promote good party conduct with strong determination, 'leave marks when we tread on stones or grasp iron,' work long and hard without letup till we achieve final success. We will fall short of our aims if this program tails off and we become lax in the later stages. We should improve and strictly implement all regulations concerning conduct, enhance oversight of enforcement, set the 'four forms of decadence' as a key point to check the discipline of the party, establish sound and effective institutions and mechanisms, and voluntarily accept public assessment and supervision by the whole of society.

As General Secretary Xi Jinping requires, leading officials at all levels should be strict in self-development, the exercise of power and self-governance; be earnest in making plans, opening up new undertakings and upholding personal integrity. 'Three Stricts and Three Earnests' is the cardinal practice, the key to success and basic ethical principle of party members and officials, especially leading officials at all levels. Moreover, it is a new requirement for party members and officials, and a new starting point to reinforce cultivation of good conduct. As an extended and deepened practice of Program of Mass Line Education and Practice, and as an important measure of reinforcing the party's theoretical and political education, the special program of 'Three Stricts and Three Earnests' plays a key role in eliminating vulgar interests and resisting unhealthy practices and evil influences, upholding integrity and honesty and achieving the greatest possible success in improving party conduct.

"If you fail to attend to trifling matters, your virtue will be affected." Officials at all levels need to start from themselves and with small matters, take the lead in keeping to the right way, uphold integrity and endeavor to foster a better environment for the government. We should keep a close watch on new changes and problems in the field of our work style and promptly follow up relevant countermeasures without being insensitive to emerging situations or procrastinate in addressing problems so as to resolve conflicts in time. Those who violate the law must be resolutely corrected and punished. We should develop our work further in addressing the 'four forms of decadence,' and make headway in improving our approaches to ideology, working practice, leadership and life style as well as to theoretical study, meetings and official documents. We should strengthen the work of addressing causes that deters, stops, and discourages officials from being infected with unhealthy practices and evil influences so as to uphold integrity all through the party.

4. We should remain strict in the construction of party organizations, and keep them robust all the time.

Lenin said, "In the struggle to seize power, the proletariat had no other weapon but the organization." General Secretary Xi Jinping emphasized, "We should strengthen party organization and carry out its work in places with more complex conditions or weaker foundations, ensuring large-scale coverage of the work and consolidating our social foundations to prevent 'Cask Effect'." Therefore, the enforcement of strict discipline must be practiced and reflected in party organizations.

Party members are organizational cells of the party. The demands of governing the party with strict discipline must be implemented in the management of party members. On January 28, 2003, General Secretary Xi Jinping presided over a meeting of the Political Bureau of the CPC Central Committee. He researched into and worked out arrangements for the development and management of party members under new conditions, and set up general requirements for "controlling quantity, optimizing structure, improving quality as well as performing duties". We need to control the quantity of the party members. We should strengthen overall guidance in the work of recruiting new party members, formulate and implement recruitment plans, and keep a moderate amount of party members. We must be strict in the recruitment work, set political standards as the priority of work, and never allow those with impure motives or those seeking profits by taking advantage of being a party member to join our party, so as to guarantee the quality of party members from the start of work. Also, we need to optimize the structure of party organizations. We should make more efforts to recruit party members from workers, continue to conduct the job among farmers and attach importance to recruiting party members from among young workers, farmers and intellectuals. We should strengthen daily education and routine work, and impose restrictions on organizational activities within the party. It is an ideal for us to see that our party members can usually conduct themselves in an exemplary fashion, act resolutely while undertaking crucial work and brave dangers in crisis, setting a good example for the people. We need to clear the outlet of the organization, treat problematic members of the party in a timely way and accordingly, we should expel unqualified ones from our organization, nullify ineffective ones and tackle corrupted ones and violators of party discipline or state laws in accordance with the law.

Community-level party organizations are the foundation for all the work of the party and its governance capability. To carry out the policy of governing the party with strict discipline, we must do solid work to develop community-level party organizations, lay a sound foundation, and improve their systems. Under the new circumstances, there emerged a new situation and a new problem that organizations at the upper level are sound and complete, while those at the lower level, the community level, are weak and in need of improvement. If we want to have a larger coverage over communities for the establishment of party organizations, we should place more stress on cooperation with farmers' cooperatives, rural-urban fringe zones, gathering places of migrating population, industrial parks and so on, so that we can work out a new pattern of urban-rural integration in community-level party building. We should tackle feeble and lax community-level party organizations as an urgent task. To substantially strengthen community-level party organizations, we should draw on experience of state-owned enterprises in the construction of party organizations and on opinions and methods of social organizations in party building, to amend the *Regulations on the CPC*

Rural Grassroots Organizations Work so as to further regulate and standardize duty orientation, work requirements and activity style of community-level or grassroots organizations. We must establish rigorous regulations for the work of community-level organizations and make efforts to make the practice of serving the mass and engaging in the mass' work more institutionalized, more regular and ever-lasting. We should shift the focus of party organizations' work to serving the national development, the peoples' happiness and wellbeing, the masses and the party members, and cater to the requirements of serving the mass in terms of its leadership, working approach and activity style. With both sincere concern and strict requirements, we should be giving more understanding, trust, attention and care to officials at community-level while intensifying their education and training and advocating exemplary models, with the hope that they will work diligently and happily with honor and the aspiration to serve the people even better. Officials at all levels should pay attention to community-level party organizations, care for them, support them, increase investments, enhance the competence of their leaders, and ensure that they can be more resourceful and capable to serve the mass.

Intra-party political activities function as the major platform for the party to educate and manage its members and to cultivate their party spirit. To exercise strict self-governance, we must take these activities seriously. However, under the impact of various factors, regulations on intra-party political activities have not been fully implemented in some localities, leading to a tendency of being vulgar, entertainment-oriented, professionalized and arbitrary. Meanwhile, decentralization, individualism and the 'nice guy' mentality prevail among party members, and some of them, with a blurred judgment of right or wrong, do not even know what intra-party political activities are actually for. The Program of Mass Line Education and Practice is in essence a healthy and serious activity conducted within our party, widely tempering and baptizing party members for their spiritual pursuit and sense of party awareness. If we want to promote it further, we should continue to improve and implement various regulations on our political activities, and to promote them sincerely and strictly throughout the party. How can we conduct intra-party political activities under strict discipline? General Secretary Xi Jinping stressed that we should adhere to and fully utilize the 'four crucial weapons' - democratic centralism, criticism and self-criticism among party members, strict enforcement of regulations on political activities and strengthening solidarity and unity of the party. First, democratic centralism must be faithfully implemented. We should carry forward democracy in our party, foster a better atmosphere for democratic discussions, and encourage party members to speak the truth, allowing the collision and arguments of different ideas while properly using centralism, instead of discussing without making any decisions or making decisions without implementing them. We must strictly follow procedures, regulations and collective will, resolutely oppose and prevent arbitrary will of individuals or of the minority. Second, we should make good use of the weapon of criticism and self-criticism. The quality of intra-party political activities largely depends on how well this weapon is applied. We should use it courageously, frequently, fully and effectively, make it a habit, a kind of awareness and a duty of party members, and make it more flexible and productive at work. Positive and healthy ideological activities need to be carried out in the party to help party members and officials to learn right from wrong, tell truth from falsehood, firmly uphold the truth, correct mistakes, unify the will and strengthen solidarity. We should take party branch meetings as a crucial platform to solve leading groups' own problems, with leaders taking the lead, and enable them to accept advice with wide-open posture, hold positive and healthy theoretical arguments and truly improve the quality of democratic meetings. Third, we must exercise intra-party organizational activities with strict discipline to enhance the political, principled and militant character of party members, and make sure that all such kinds of activity are oriented to addressing real problems. Fourth, we should value the genuine unity of the party based on principles and party awareness, but resolutely fight against or correct a false façade of all getting on well with others on the surface, while rivaling or erecting barriers against each other behind the scenes.

5. We should remain strict in system enforcement, and exercise strict self-governance through party laws and regulations.

Before assuming the post of General Secretary, Comrade Xi Jinping had clearly pointed out that to deal with the issue of exercising strict self-governance, "The fundamental approach is building systems by strictly conforming to the law that applies for developing a governing party. Hereby, we should continue to strengthen intra-party activities and development institutions in a more rigorous and scientific way. We should establish both tangible institutions and procedural regulations. We should explicitly prescribe not only how to act but also how to punish in case of violation of provisions, and reduce the discretion space in the implementation of regulations so as to promote party building in a more scientific, institutionalized and standardized way." Since the 18th CPC National Congress, in light of the Program of Mass Line

Education and Practice, improving party conduct, upholding integrity while combating corruption, General Secretary Xi Jinping delivered a series of speeches on supervising and governing the party via institutions, and revealed that this practice is vital for the survival of the party. He stressed that we should strengthen the construction of party rules and regulations, improve the systems and mechanisms for their formulation, and correspondingly create a complete system of institutions within the party. We should apply these rules and regulations to the full implementation of the principle that the party supervises its own conduct, exercise strict discipline, and encourage party members and officials to take the lead in acting in accordance with state laws and party regulations. He points out that, "We should integrate the requirements of the Central Committee, actual needs, and fresh experiences to develop new systems that are appropriate to the current situation, to upgrade the existing systems and to abolish those that are not." Xi Jinping believes that, "Any newly-developed or improved system must be easy to implement, be coherent with the established laws, and function within the existing legal framework. Attention must be given to formulating supporting measures to match the new systems. Besides, we should apply revolutionary spirit and law-based approach, integrate the requirements of the Central Committee, people's expectations, actual needs and fresh experiences in an effort to develop a complete system of institutions that provide for rigid institutional constraints and strict systematic execution. With these practices, we may make it possible that the party work style is standardized, normalized and persistent", and may prevent our institutions from becoming a façade - like a scarecrow.

General Secretary Xi Jinping emphasized that the vitality of laws and regulations rest with the implementation of them, which in turn depends on taking real actions and performing with strict discipline. Efforts should be made to promote the awareness of laws, regulations and disciplines among the party's members and officials by carrying out publicity and education in the party, so as to create a fine environment of respecting, observing and guarding the laws and regulations. We should ensure that all people are equal before the law and regulations, and the enforcement of such rules allows no privilege or exception. We should intensify our efforts in implementing regulations, making rigid systems and prohibitions exert power and authority, and ensuring they are fit to resolve real problems. We should strengthen the exercise of the supervision and inspection institutions, exerting pressure and pushing forward their implementation. We must discipline violators seriously, making no exceptions for the powerful, not indulging minor offenses and not letting violators go, even if they are legion. The CPC should guard against 'broken windows theory,' referring to the idea that petty crimes need to be stopped to prevent more serious crime. Since the 18th CPC National Congress, the 'cage' of the party laws and regulations has been woven more closely and tightly. The *Regulations of the CPC on Formulation of Party Laws* and the *Rules of the CPCon Archives of Party Laws and Documents* were newly issued as an important move in using laws to regulate power. We intensively dealt with the party regulations and regulatory documents formulated since 1978, 40% of which were abolished or publicized regarding their invalidity. More than 20 new regulations on clean government were introduced, ranging from major matters such as the selection and appointment of officials, official receptions and department conference expenditure, to small matters like banning cigarette smoking in public, sending greeting cards, and purchasing fireworks. We have achieved remarkable results through formulating and strictly enforcing regulations and systems.

III. The Party Members' and Officials' Exemplary Role in Observing Rules and Disciplines

General Secretary Xi Jinping has repeatedly stressed that party organizations at all levels, and all party members, especially the party's leading officials, must abide by party rules and act in accordance with party discipline. At the Fifth Plenary Session of the 18th CPC Central Committee, he focused on the major issue of strict party rules and discipline, and also emphasized one more time that we should reinforce regulation construction and put observing rules and discipline in a more prominent position. Since the 18th CPC National Congress, we placed observing strict rules as an important measure for exercising strict self-governance. The rigidness of rule constraints has been more pronounced through intensified discipline reinforcement and strict execution. Indeed, we should realize that these results are only temporary at a certain stage, so we must persevere in efforts of regulation formulation and compliance, and make it as a high-tension line of deterrence so as to foster a lively situation in which party members stay true to party rules and discipline.

The *Guidelines of the CPC on Integrity and Self-discipline* (*Guidelines,* in brief, for later reference) and *Regulations of the CPC on the Penalty for Rule Violation* (*Regulations,* in brief), newly approved by the Political Bureau of the CPC Central Committee, are important fruits of the practice of the guiding principles of the 18th CPC National Congress and the spirit of a series of important speeches delivered by General Secretary Xi Jinping. They are also important achievements in strengthening the construction of the party laws and regulations, as well as fundamental measures to strengthen party building and exercise strict party discipline. Party members, especially leading officials, should consciously pursue high standards of integrity and self-discipline, stay away from regulation red lines by strictly observing party discipline, serve an exemplary role, and take a lead in fostering a good environment for the party in which rule and disciplines are respected, observed and safeguarded.

1. To exercise strict self-governance of the party relies on strict rules and discipline.

No political party can run without discipline or rules, and they are a must for all parties. In Britain where the earliest modern political party in the world emerged, all parties have strict rules and discipline. For example, as early as in 1903 in Britain, the Labor Party made it clear that its party members should promote the interests of the party and should not to contradict the 'vows' they made to the party. Besides, many political parties in Europe and the United States have a parliamentary supervisor, the so-called 'party whip', whose main responsibility is to urge the party members to comply with the rules of the party and to take disciplinary measures against members who violate the rules. Historical experience has proved that there is no such a political party without discipline in the world, not to mention a Marxist party. With lax discipline or rules, any political party is doomed to decline and even to collapse. An important lesson from the failure of the Communist Party of the Soviet Union is that they abandoned the principle of democratic centralism and strict discipline of the party.

Our party is a Marxist party, the organization of which relies on revolutionary ideals and strict discipline. This has always been our party's fine tradition and unique advantage. Under the new historical circumstances, our party must depend on strict rules and discipline to unite and lead the people in realizing the 'Two Centenary Goals'. Certainly, the party's rules and discipline have not emerged only recently. But why have the CPC Central Committee and General Secretary Xi Jinping been highlighting this issue since the 18th CPC National Congress? Because for a period of time, we have not been strict enough in governing the party; some party members nurtured wrong understandings and misconceptions regarding party rules and discipline. They took them for granted, regarding them as a façade, and even worse, some of them recklessly breached party rules and discipline. If this tendency cannot be reversed in timely and effective fashion, a big problem will develop for our party. Therefore, General Secretary Xi Jinping stressed, "The party must supervise its own conduct and run itself with strict disciplines." Our party, with more than 88million members, should make it a higher priority that party members will strictly conform to party rules and disciplines, so that our party can maintain its status as a governing party in running a big developing country with a population of over 1.3 billion.

2. The priority of the party's self-governance is to stay true to strict political rules and discipline of the party.

The party has both written and unwritten rules and discipline. Some of the fine traditions and routines are formed during long term practice. Though some of them are not in a written form, they are still party discipline that must be followed by party members and officials. Among the written documents, there is the *Constitution of the CPC*, two Guidelines, more than twenty Regulations and many other rules, standards, measures and specifications. The CPC *Constitution* is the party's 'fundamental law' with general rules by which all comrades of the party must abide. The newly amended *Guidelines of the CPC on Integrity and Self-discipline* and *Regulations of the CPC on the Penalty for Rule Violation* are specified rules of the CPC *Constitution* and should also be observed by all party members. Among all types of rules of the party, the most important, fundamental and critical ones are political rules and discipline. The party's organizational discipline, regulations of work and mass line rules are reflections of the party's political discipline in different aspects and in different sectors of work. Any type of violation will undermine our governing foundation and sabotage our political discipline. On the contrary, if we can stay true to our political rules and discipline, sober in political awareness and firm in political conviction, we may avoid doing anything in violation of party rules and discipline. Therefore, to abide by the party's political rules and discipline is the important foundation for observing all other rules of the party.

The essence of observing the party's political discipline is to adhere to the party's leadership, basic theory, basic line, basic program, basic experience and basic requirements, keep in line with the party Central Committee, and conscientiously safeguard its authority. The party's political rules and discipline are not abstract but concrete, and to align with the CPC Central Committee is not an empty slogan but a major political principle. Oriented to outstanding problems of discipline violation at the present stage, the *Regulations of the CPC on the Penalty for Rule Violation* underscore political rules and discipline, and specify penalties over any opposition against the party's leadership, basic theory, basic line, basic program, basic experience and basic requirements. We should always put priority on strictly observing political rules and discipline, and sincerely abide by political rules of the *Regulations of the CPC on the Penalty for Rule Violation* in an effort to promote the strict enforcement of other rules or discipline.

3. To observe rules and discipline is a test of party spirit for members and officials of the party.

The party's rules and discipline are behavioral yardsticks for party organizations and members, while the national laws and regulations are basic rules for all Chinese citizens. The nature and purpose of the party have determined that the party's rules and discipline are supposed to be stricter than our national laws and regulations. Whoever breaches the national law must have already violated the party's regulations. Therefore, to help party members and officials avoid ending up as criminals, but consistently stay as good comrades, we should prioritize the enforcement of party rules and discipline, and tackle small problems as early as possible to stop them from developing into big disasters. The observance of discipline is an important test of party spirit and loyalty for party members and officials. Leading officials of party members should play an exemplary role in practicing honesty and self-discipline, and voluntarily maintain the authority of the discipline. Also, they should act as a sensible promoter, take the lead in learning, promoting, and elaborating the *Guidelines* and *Regulations* as well as various other rules of the party, raise the consciousness of observing these rules, and always bear them in mind. We should always be strict with ourselves, improve our own conduct, resolutely discard the idea of 'privileged party member', work and exercise authority under strict discipline, do what we ask others to do and never do what we ask others not to do, and subject ourselves to the supervision and restraint of party organizations and party members, playing a leading role in observing the party's rules and discipline. We should perform our duties with loyalty, operate under strict party discipline, take the lead in enforcing discipline and upholding integrity, and seriously tackle problems and the violations of rules and discipline, even in our own working units. We should not evade or shirk responsibilities, or behave only like 'nice guys', but instead we should perform as discipline guardians to ensure the strict exercise of all rules and laws of the party.

IV. Understanding regarding 'Make Party Building Our Biggest Achievement'

At the concluding conference of the Program of Mass Line Education and Practice held in October 2014, General Secretary Xi Jinping emphasized, "Party committees at all levels and in all departments should have a clear understanding of job performance, always examine situations from the perspective of a governing party and with a consideration of how to consolidate the ruling status of our party, and make party building our biggest achievement." He pointed out, "If our party is weakened, disintegrated or collapsed, what's the point of other achievements?" The succinct statement of "make party building our biggest achievement" reveals the important position of the work of party building in new situations, and brings to light its practical and far-reaching significance, receiving active responses from party members and officials. However, some comrades have some doubts in their mind, for example; 'Isn't it contradictory to our repeated principle that development is the top priority', or 'whether we should only attach importance to party building rather than development', and so on. The answer is definite: NO. Then, what is the relation between these two principles? How can we correctly understand and properly handle it?

1. The key to development lies in promoting party building, which is a sure requirement of the principle that 'development is the top priority'. The victory of the independence and liberation of the Chinese nation has been achieved under the leadership of the CPC; the success of settling the problem of food and clothing of over 1.3 billion Chinese people and essentially completing the building of a moderately prosperous society in all respects is also accomplished under the party's leadership. All the historical experiences in modern times have come to the basic conclusion that without the CPC, the birth of new China, the formation of socialism with Chinese characteristics, and the modernization of socialism would have been impossible. With the practice of contemporary China and the features of the times, the party is going to lead the people in carrying out the great undertaking with many new historical characteristics, withstand and overcome various risks and challenges. Among them, a primary and essential task is to advance party building, a basic prerequisite and fundamental guarantee for the attainment of the 'Two Centenary Goals'. If our party is weakened, disintegrated, or even collapsed, the great cause of socialism with Chinese characteristics will come to an end, and the accomplishments of national prosperity and rejuvenation as well as the people's happiness and wellbeing will be groundless. As Comrade

Deng Xiaoping pointed out, without leadership by the party, a big country like China would be torn by strife and incapable of accomplishing anything. And likewise, with degraded atmosphere, disintegrated teams and distracted minds, we may gain temporary achievements, but they are definitely not what we want. At the same time, leading officials at all levels should be aware that outstanding performance in a mis-directed development will not receive natural political recognition. If we do advance the economy greatly, but corruption grows worse, people may harbor an even stronger sense of deprivation against us. Deng Xiaoping, as early as in the 1980s, warned the whole party that, "If standards of social conduct are deteriorating, what's the use of achieving economic development? Worse, deteriorating social standards will in turn lead to a qualitative change in the economy, eventually producing a society in which embezzlement, theft and bribery run rampant." In this sense, it is essential to promote party building if we want further development, so party building will be the greatest achievement of development. Research by politics of development also shows that a powerful political party plays a crucial role for the stability and development of modern developing countries. The success of our modernization and the creation of 'Chinese miracles' are all achieved under the leadership of the CPC. It is a natural conclusion from the experiences of modern Chinese history that the key to resolving Chinese problems lies in the party. Therefore, party committees at all levels must have the following consciousness: it is our task to do a good job in party building, and if not, it will be our dereliction or malpractice of duty. We must concentrate on party building, take it as the greatest achievement of our party so as to provide a solid political guarantee for the realization of the 'Two Centenary Goals'.

2. Development is also a must to party building, for the requirement for development is an implication of the statement: 'make party building our greatest achievement'. The frustrating and humiliating experiences of China since modern times tell us that the weak is prone to be bullied, and that a nation can never stand firmer and stronger among the world's nations without self-improvement. Development is of primary importance to China as a key to addressing all of our problems. Thanks to our development strategy, it only took China a few decades to travel a journey that took developed countries several centuries to cover. Eventually, we should proceed with the journey of development to realize the 'Two Centenary Goals' and the Chinese dream of the great rejuvenation of the Chinese nation. At present, China as the largest developing country in the world, is still in the primary stage of socialism, and will remain so for a long time to come, so taking economic development as the central task is vital to national renewal, and development is still the most important matter for our party, to govern the country well and rejuvenate the nation. Only by promoting sustainable and sound economic development can we lay a solid material foundation for enhancing the country's prosperity and strength, improving the people's wellbeing and ensuring social harmony and stability. Party building has been long connected with its political lines, serving the historical mission of the party and its central task. At present, party building must be oriented to the realization of the 'Two Centenary Goals' as its fundamental direction, so we must focus our work closely on development, that is the most important thing for our party to govern the country well and rejuvenate the nation, and endeavor to transform the advantage and fruits of party building into the competitive edge and achievements of our national development, making party building more aligned to the requirements of socialist modernization. Only when party building is oriented to serving the overall situation of the party and the state, can we secure the foundation for, and ultimate attainment of, the great practice of socialism with Chinese characteristics, and thus broaden our stage for development and obtain the source of vitality. Hence, party committees at all levels and in all departments must take development as the most important thing for our party to govern the country well and rejuvenate the nation, and pursue development wholeheartedly so as to promote the coordinated, sustainable and overall development of economic, political, cultural, social and ecological progress, consolidating the foundation for party building and the governing status of the party.

We should organically integrate party building with development, truly concentrate on party building and pay full attention to development. Party building is the support and guarantee of development, while development is the foundation for and ultimate attainment of the advancement of party building. They complement each other and form an integral and organic whole. However, for a long time, some party committees, leading party members' groups and party officials have not been able to understand or handle their relationships well. In their view, development is a crucial and solid task, but party building is virtual and ignorable and does not require much attention. Currently, it is prevalent among them to believe that more importance is attached to development rather than party building, resulting in an unbalanced relationship between party building and development. Over time, the problem of 'four forms of decadence' tends to pile up, hidden rules prevail and the political ecosystem deteriorates. The root cause lies in the fact that party building has not yet been well conducted and the requirement of exercising strict discipline has not yet been sincerely implemented. Party committees at all levels should correctly understand the relationship between party building and development so that they would no longer judge the performance of officials merely by GDP growth rate, or conduct 'Party building solely for the sake of party building'. Instead, they should continue to plan, implement and assess party building along with the central work of development. They should adopt a concrete and profound approach to promoting party building in all types of work, in all areas and in all sectors, and make sure that equal emphasis and mutual reinforcement are put on them simultaneously.

Party committees at all levels must shoulder the responsibility of exercising strict discipline, and implement it throughout their work. In his speech to the concluding conference of the Program of Mass Line Education and Practice, General Secretary Xi Jinping expounded thoroughly on how to supervise our party's conduct and exercise strict discipline in all respects, and he also brought forth clear requirements in this regard. In this speech, he initiated the description of 'three NOs', corresponding to the lesson we draw from history and reality, and especially from this program. He said that if there is no clear prescription of duty, no genuine fulfillment of work and no accountability system for performance, it is impossible for us to govern the party strictly. Therefore, to exercise strict self-governance of the party, we must better understand the importance of the accountability system and heighten our awareness and sense of responsibility for this task. Soon after, General Secretary Xi Jinping raised 'three questions' with regard to the same issue, strict party self-governance. He pointed out that party committees at all levels, through years of efforts, have completed the construction of a system of institutions accountable for the responsibilities of party building. Under this system, a party committee supervises its secretary who in turn is responsible for the work of party building in his field, and this operation goes on hierarchically throughout all sectors of work in the party. "Nonetheless, have the party committees (leading party member's groups) at all levels and in all departments been dedicated to promoting party building? Have their secretaries been taking the lead in exercising strict discipline the party? Have the members of the party committees performed their duty in this regard at their work?" General Secretary Xi Jinping thought that some localities and departments might not have met those standards, and could not give satisfactory answers to the three questions mentioned above. These three thought provoking questions, hit the nail on the head – sharply locating "three misunderstandings" regarding responsibility for party discipline enforcement. First, some leading officials think that, compared with development, party building is more intangible and it is not easy for them to attain outstanding accomplishments. Second, they think they don't need to bother too much but just organize a couple of meetings every year. Third, some of them think that we are endeavoring to develop socialist market economy, so there exists a dilemma for exercising strict party discipline: on the one hand, if the discipline is not strict enough, some people will cross the 'red line' and lots of others will follow suit, making punishment impossible; on the other hand, if the discipline is too strict, officials may be fettered by stringent rules, weakening their vitality at work, making them fail to accomplish a lot and even affecting their votes. All these are misconceptions. Therefore, party committees (leading party members' groups) at all levels and in all departments should have a clear understanding of job performance, put consolidating the party's governing status first, and take supervising and governing the party as a significant political responsibility. In practice, party committees at all levels should assume and fulfill the responsibility for exercising strict party discipline. They should adhere to the principle of planning, implementing and assessing party building simultaneously with the central work of development. They should adopt a concrete approach to deepening party building in all types of work, in all areas and in all sectors, with equal emphasis on development so as to guard against 'a firm hand on one type of work, but a soft hand on the other'. Our performance appraisal of the head of party committees (leading party members' groups) at all levels and in all departments, especially party secretaries, is firstly targeted at the effectiveness of party building in order to encourage them to be strict with discipline enforcement. In addition, the performance appraisal system for other members and leading officials should include more assessment indicators in this regard, so as to boost their responsibility for exercising strict party discipline in their field and make it possible that our party can truly operate under strict discipline in all sectors of work.

Chapter Follow-up Questions and References

Chapter 1

Questions:

1. What is the new normal in economic development?
2. How do you understand supply-side structural reform?

References:

1. *Xi Jinping: The Governance of China*. Beijing: Foreign Languages Press. 2014.
2. Publicity Department of the CPC Central Committee: *A Series of Important Speeches by General Secretary Xi Jinping* (2016). Beijing: Xuexi Publishing House, People's Publishing House. 2016.
3. *Central Committee of the CPC: Recommendations for the 13th Five-Year Plan for Economic and Social Development. Xinhua News Agency.* November 3, 2015.
4. Liu Wei. *Six Points of View on the Relationship between Government and Market.* China Times. June 5, 2014.
5. *A Renewed Definition of Informationization with Internet+: A Research Report on 'Internet+' (Part A, Part B).* Guangming Daily. October 16, 2015.

Chapter 2

Questions:

1. Why does reform and opening up play a decisive role in determining the destiny of contemporary China?
2. What are your understandings on the targets and tasks of an all-around and deeper-level reform?

References:

1. *Xi Jinping: The Governance of China.* Beijing: Foreign Languages Press. 2014.
2. *Excerpts of Xi Jinping's Remarks on the Overall Deepening of Reform.* Beijing: Central Party Literature Press. 2014.

Chapter 3

Questions:

1. How do you interpret that the leadership of the CPC is the soul of rule of law for socialism with Chinese characteristics?
2. Why is the rule of law working as the basic means of governance in China?

References:

1. *Xi Jinping: The Governance of China.* Beijing: Foreign Languages Press. 2014.
2. *Guidance Book to 'Decision of the Central Committee of the CPC on Some Major Issues Concerning Comprehensively Promoting Rule of Law'.* Beijing: People's Publishing House. 2014.

Chapter 4

Questions:

1. What is the socialist deliberative democracy?
2. Why can't China implement a 'Multi-Party System'?

References:

1. Xi Jinping: *The Speech at the Conference to Celebrate the CPPCC's 65th Anniversary. People's Daily.* September 22, 2014.
2. Xi Jinping: *The Speech at the Conference to Celebrate the 60th Anniversary of the National People's Congress. China Daily.* September 6, 2014.
3. *Central Committee of the CPC: Recommendations for the 13th Five-Year Plan for Economic and Social Development.* Xinhua News Agency. November 3, 2015.

Chapter 5

Questions:

1. Why is ideological progress one of the Party's top priorities?
2. Why is building core socialist values functioning as a significant aspect of a nation's governing system and capacity?

References:

1. Xi Jinping. *A Speech at the Forum on Literature and Art Work (2014)*. *People's Daily*. October 15, 2015.
2. Central Commission for Discipline Inspection of the CPC, Party Literature Research Centre of the CPC Central Committee: *Excerpts of Xi Jinping's Exposition on the Construction of the Party Conduct and of an Honest and Clean Government and on the Struggle against Corruption*. Central Literature Publishing House, China Lianzheng Publishing House. 2015.

Chapter 6

Questions:

1. Why do the CPC and the Chinese Government pay special attention to people's livelihood?
2. How do you understand equity and justice during the process of reform?

References:

1. Party Literature Research Centre of the CPC Central Committee: *Excerpts of Important Speeches by General Secretary Xi Jinping*. Beijing: Party Building Books Publishing House, Central Literature Publishing House. 2016.
2. *Central Committee of the CPC: Recommendations for the 13th Five-Year Plan for Economic and Social Development*. Xinhua News Agency. November 3, 2015.
3. Luo Huide: *Experiences and Implications of Foreign Governing Parties on Solving Livelihood Problems. Journal of The Party School of Tianjin Committee of The CPC*. 2012 (1).

Chapter 7

Questions:

1. Why is it of great necessity to promote socialist ecological progress?
2. Why is setting ecological red lines reckoned as a prime task and a top priority to promote the institutional construction of ecological civilization?

References:

1. *Opinions of the Central Committee of the CPC and the State Council on Accelerating the Promotion of Ecological Progress.* Beijing: People's Publishing House. 2015.
2. *For the Ever-Growing of the Chinese Nation: Records on General Secretary Xi Jinping's Activites in Support of the Construction of Ecological Civilization.* Beijing: Xinhuanet. March 9, 2015.

Chapter 8

Questions:

1. Why does the CPC especially stress exercising strict self-governance in every respect?
2. What are the proofs of 'strictness' in exercising strict self-governance in every respect by the CPC?

References:

1. Publicity Department of the CPC Central Committee: *A Series of Important Speeches by General Secretary Xi Jinping* (2016). Beijing: Xuexi Publishing House, People's Publishing House. 2016.
2. Party Literature Research Centre of the CPC Central Committee: *Excerpts of Xi Jinping's Remarks on Exercising Strict Self-Governance in Every Respect.* Beijing: Central Party Literature Press. 2016.
3. Central Commission for Discipline Inspection of the CPC, Party Literature Research Centre of the CPC Central Committee: *Excerpts of Xi Jinping's Exposition on the Construction of the Party Conduct and of an Honest and Clean Government and on the Struggle against Corruption.* Central Literature Publishing House, China Lianzheng Publishing House. 2015.

Lightning Source UK Ltd.
Milton Keynes UK
UKOW01f1136020817
306527UK00001B/86/P